CLOUD DANCERS

CLOUD DANCERS

Portraits of North American Mountaineers

EDITED BY
JONATHAN WATERMAN

THE AAC PRESS

An AAC Press book published by
The American Alpine Club
710 Tenth Street
Golden, Colorado 80401
(303) 384-0110

This publication made possible through the support of W. L. Gore & Associates, Inc.,
manufacturers of Gore-Tex® fabric and WindStopper™ fabrics
and the Premier Sponsor of AAC Press.

Credits:
"Pioneers of Mountain Exploration: The Harvard Five" from © "Five Who Made it to the Top,"
reprinted with permission of the publisher from *Moments of Doubt and Other Mountaineering Writings*, by David Roberts, The Mountaineers, Seattle.

"A Direct Style: John Roskelley" from © "The Direct Style of John Roskelley," reprinted with permission of the publisher from *Moments of Doubt and Other Mountaineering Writings*, by David Roberts, The Mountaineers, Seattle.

"Expatriate Thugs: Aid and Al Burgess" from "Burgess Boys," *Eiger Dreams* by Jon Krakauer, courtesy of Lyons and Burford, copyright © 1990 by Jon Krakauer.

"Ascending: Yvon Chouinard" reprinted from *Mountain Passages*, by Jeremy Bernstein, by permission of the University of Nebraska Press. Copyright © 1977 by Jeremy Bernstein. Copyright © 1978 by the University of Nebraska Press.

Cover photograph by Jonathan Waterman
Text and cover design by Dianne J. Borneman, Shadow Canyon Graphics

First Edition
10 9 8 7 6 5 4 3 2 1
Printed in the United States of America
ISBN: 0-930410-54-8

Contents

Foreword
By Jed Williamson • 1

Introduction
By Jonathan Waterman • 3

A Man for All Mountains
FRITZ WIESSNER
By Ed Webster • 9

Pioneers of Mountain Exploration
THE HARVARD FIVE
By David Roberts • 23

Ascending
YVON CHOUINARD
By Jeremy Bernstein • 45

A Climber of Genius
LOU REICHARDT
By Geoffrey Tabin • 71

Boy George
GEORGE LOWE
By Alison Osius • 87

v

Expatriate Thugs
AID & AL BURGESS
By Jon Krakauer • 105

Captain Fun Hog
RICK RIDGEWAY
By Tim Cahill • 125

A Direct Style
JOHN ROSKELLEY
By David Roberts • 143

A Journey of the Spirit
MUGS STUMP
By Michael Kennedy • 163

A Mountain of Trouble
JEFF LOWE
By David Roberts • 185

A Thoughtful Approach to Mountaineering
ANNIE WHITEHOUSE
By Beth Wald • 211

Solving the Riddle
CARLOS BUHLER
By Jonathan Waterman • 227

The Survivor
ED WEBSTER
By Jonathan Waterman • 243

The Natural
GREG CHILD
By Jonathan Waterman • 263

The Wilford Case
MARK WILFORD
By John Sherman • 283

The Education of an Alpinist
KITTY CALHOUN
By Jonathan Waterman • 303

About the Writers • 315

*This book owes its construction to these generous people,
who contributed their writing, photographs, and editing:*

*Jeremy Bernstein, Tim Cahill, Ann B. Carter,
Greg Child, Chris Jones, Michael Kennedy,
Jon Krakauer, Peter Nichols, Alison Osius,
Rick Ridgeway, David Roberts, Steve Roper,
John Sherman, Geoffrey Tabin,
John Thackray, Beth Wald,
Bradford Washburn, Jonathan Waterman,
Ed Webster, Jed Williamson,
and Mark Wilford.*

Foreword

The effort and style behind *Cloud Dancers* is an inaugural event, representing the new direction of The American Alpine Club (AAC). After two decades of deliberation, the AAC has renewed its commitment toward serving the climbing community and the mountain environment by moving from our New York City headquarters of half a century to the mountains and the center of America. Here in Golden, Colorado – in a historic, renovated school purchased with the Colorado Mountain Club – we have tripled our space. Our new headquarters features the most extensive mountaineering library in North America, a mountaineering museum, and an auditorium with an ongoing lecture series. We have returned to our mountain roots.

Since its incorporation in 1902, the AAC has pursued its original Charter and Bylaws:

> The scientific exploration and study of high mountain elevations and of the regions lying within or about the Arctic and Antarctic Circles; the cultivation of mountain craft; the promotion and dissemination of knowledge regarding the regions above indicated; the promotion of good fellowship among climbers; and the preservation of mountain and arctic regions.

The founding members also stated:

> It shall for its primary work undertake the study of the high mountains of the world, gathering in the facts and observing phenomena pertaining to them, and shall (produce) a series of illustrated publications . . . for the purpose of presenting a complete description of the alpine mountains of the world.

The scope of these concepts has changed dramatically. Some of our senior members have determined elevations first by lugging monster-sized theodolites up glaciers, and more recently, by having speedy alpinists placing small prisms on summits, for surveyors miles below. Our pioneering members (some are profiled in *Cloud Dancers*) have been on early expeditions with hundreds in support, and have now adjusted to the modern style of climbing with only a few friends. They started dressed in wool and now they wear synthetics. They have camped under canvas droptents and on nylon portaledges, they have seen multi-day climbs reduced to several hour ascents, and some of them have been seen practicing on artificial climbing walls.

The mountains are still there, still beckoning. However, the methods of engagement have changed, and balancing the critical issues of preservation and access have taken over the forefront of the Club's work. The AAC Press books to follow will reflect these changing times in an environment and a sport still mostly mysterious and misunderstood by the general public.

Our special appreciation goes to Jonathan Waterman, who is guiding the AAC Press as Publications Director. As a result of his initial efforts, we can also thank W. L. Gore and Associates, who will act as our Premier Sponsor for five years. We would also like to acknowledge our late President and his wife, Henry and Lydia Hall, whose legacies have provided us with a Publications Endowment Fund.

We welcome all readers to join us in celebrating the mountaineering pioneers and history within these pages. Armed with the kind of knowledge presented here, we can all look forwad to the prospect of continuing the pursuit and spirit of mountain exploration.

– Jed Williamson
AAC President, 1993

Introduction

Mention one of North America's best mountaineers to a sports fan and the name will not register. Indeed, most of the twenty-one subjects within this anthology have realized that if they were Europeans, they would probably sign film contracts, write autobiographies, endorse products, appear on television and in sports pages, and be household names. Here in the United States, outside of the insular mountaineering community, these accomplished alpinists languish in relative obscurity.

Nonetheless, these men and women have been internationally acclaimed for advancing the art of mountaineering to new heights. Most of these mountaineers have played crucial roles in the evolution of Himalayan mountaineering — usually considered the ultimate frontier by any climber who wears double boots.

By selecting the most influential mountaineers, as well as some of the finest climbing writers, this collection shows the evolution of North American mountaineering. Herein is the hall of fame. Collectively, the achievements of our subjects include: new routes and oxygen-mask free ascents of 8,000-meter peaks; the most difficult route up Everest; first female ascent of Makalu; a new route and second ascent of Gasherbrum IV; big wall climbs on Himalayan peaks; the first ascent of a 7,000-meter peak. Most of our subjects have also imprinted their ice axes on the mountains of Europe, Alaska, South America, and the lower 48.

Charlie Houston and Brad Washburn put K2 and Alaska on the map in the 1930s and 1940s, then Rick Ridgeway and George Lowe closed the circle on these same mountains forty years later. Yvon Chouinard constructed the craft of Yosemite wall climbing in the 1960s; then Mark Wilford took it to the limits on Nameless Tower thirty years later. Ad Carter tackled Nanda Devi in 1936; and, forty years later, John Roskelly finished business there.

Undoubtably, if you are not interested in climbing, you might replace this book on its shelf because, to be true to mountaineering and its practitioners, there is no mainstream interpretation of the craft here — no appendices to explain that "Friends" are vital pieces of "pro," or that "cerebral edema" is not a clever method to induce swelling. Here, nouns are shamelessly pumped into verbs, aberrant conjugations and colloquialisms hold fast, and the language is frozen tight to the gritty gestalt of mountaineering.

This anthology of mountaineers is unique because it has been written for climbers and by climbers. Within the substrata of climbing literature, profiles represent the heart and soul of a sympathetic reader, if only because holding a magnifying glass up to a fellow seeker sheds light on ourselves.

There were also several fine portraits (and crucial influences upon the North American mountaineering scene) that could not be included because of upcoming anthologies and conflicting rights. It is a good time to be a climber writing about the craft you love.

Choosing the proper potpourri of North American mountaineers means, in part, selecting those players who have changed the course of history and ventured up into untrodden heights. It is also about finding writers committed to prose, their ears tuned to the nuances of climbing, and doubting their subjects rather than adoring them. Many of these writers in this collection are equally renowned, if not for their own climbing achievements, then for writing frequently about climbing. The expected profile form for athletes (an imprecise genus for mountaineers) is to be kind because they have little effect upon the world outside of their sport. Nonetheless, these climbers have been prodded into confessing their infidelities, their recklessness behind the wheel, or that they've courted what little fame can be milked from their achievements — read, in this country, crazed mountain climbing.

So, with radar detectors on high alert, our profilers have pressed Ridgeway, Bates, Chouinard, the Burgesses, the Lowes,

INTRODUCTION

Child, Houston, Stump, Webster, Carter, Buhler, Moore, Reichardt, Calhoun, Washburn, Roskelly, Whitehouse, Wilford, and Wiessner. *Tell us,* they asked, *were you scared shitless? Did you regret your partner's death? Do you mind if I poke around your house? Could I talk to your wife/husband, in private?*

Greg Child's profiler clocked eight rewrites over a year and a half, with twenty-nine hours of formal interview time (not counting the beer and Chianti blowouts while trailing Child to his lectures from Denver to Boston to Banff to Florence) and more than 250 hours of actual writing time. Conversely, at least one of the writers in this collection can lay claim to sharing a long day climb with his or her subjects and penning a polished profile within a mere week.

Dave Roberts followed Jeff Lowe to the Eiger and acted as his basecamp manager while struggling (successfully) to maintain objectivity over a subject of whom he grew increasingly fond. The motion-sick prone Alison Osius let George Lowe fly her in a small plane to a desert spire and show her how epics are really concocted. Ed Webster interviewed Fritz Wiessner on his death bed. Two decades earlier, Webster hauled me (an unknowing profiler to-be) — with a broken leg and dislocated shoulder — down from Mount Washington in January. Jeremy Bernstein shivered near a frozen waterfall in a Sierra gale as Yvon Chouinard soloed the ice above. Geoff Tabin climbed to the top of Everest via the unclimbed East Face with Lou Reichardt. John Sherman let Mark Wilford sandbag him on difficult boulder problems. And Michael Kennedy intuited Mugs Stump's dreams during their bold climbs in India and Pakistan.

Although idolatrous prose is not a motif here, even the best journalists must tenuously juggle respect for their subjects with objective skepticism. For instance, allowing any media-conscious subject to review his or her own profile manuscript before publication is a technique not practiced by the journalists herein. Why risk having to delete unflattering quotes or hard-won anecdotes that the subject would rather not reveal? As Dave Roberts wrote in his anthology, *Moments of Doubt* (after his subject balked at

Robert's portrait): "A writer must not become too dependent on the approval of his subjects."

Some subjects are terribly difficult to fathom. At least one mountaineer from the following pages would clam up and smile vacantly when motives were queried. Others have done so many climbs and shared so many partners that the correct names and dates, if not deliberately suppressed, may well have been erased by the brain-debilitating ennui of high altitude. Any copy editor would call these stories fact-checking nightmares. If you happen to aspire to write about climbing, stick to first-person narratives, news stories, anything but the laborious art of portraiture. Writing about mountaineers is as perversely arduous as mountaineering itself.

While mountaineers labor anonymously beyond the public eye, Wall Street and the mainstream have meanwhile latched onto the more accessible and equally talented sport climbers. So, if readers show interest in this collective laundering of mountaineers, expect a sequel.

Certainly this book would not have been possible without the eleven writers generously donating his or her work to this anthology. Because of this generosity, royalties from *Cloud Dancers* will infuse prize money for the winner of each year's American Alpine Club literary award.

The sixteen stories in this book were mostly published in *Climbing*, with one or two stories from the *Mens Journal, Outside, The New Yorker, Rolling Stone,* and *Harvard*; pieces were also culled from the book-length anthologies: *Moments of Doubt, Eiger Dreams,* and *Mountain Passages.* All have been edited for space and consistency. Two decades stretch between the original publication of these stories, so to preserve the context of the moment, as well as the flow of history, ages and dates have not been changed.

An entire essay could rise upon the merit of our subjects as heroes. After all, aren't they somewhat famous? Or at least efficacious in achieving their goals? If any adjective were to apply to our subjects, "dreamlike" is a lot more appropriate than "godlike." Indeed, our society is built, in part, upon modeling ourselves after the mythic components of our heroes. It is alluring sport to fantasize of those parts within ourselves that might equal or transcend the greatness of our so-called legends; hopefully in *Cloud Dancers,* the reader can identify rather than simply fantasize.

So the unsung icons of the following pages are mountaineers — a term errantly used by urbanites to denigrate country bumpkins. Without these people, modern-day mountaineering wouldn't be where it is today. Nonetheless, our subjects are unlikely to initiate world peace, end starvation, cure AIDs, reduce population growth, or impact global politics. These mountaineers are interesting because they climb mountains; they are fascinating because they hold up a mirror to ourselves. While the world howls and twists in its chaos below, we too would like to be dancing above the clouds.

— Jonathan Waterman

Fritz Wiessner. *Photo by Steve Roper*

A Man for All Mountains

FRITZ WIESSNER

By Ed Webster

[From CLIMBING , December 1988]

No less a figure than Reinhold Messner once called Fritz Wiessner the most pivotal mountaineer of the twentieth century. Wiessner had a profound impact on each of the different schools of the sport, from rock climbing to Himalayan mountaineering. He is probably best known for his tragic, but nearly successful, expedition to K2, which he has called "the hardest struggle, the highest hope, and the greatest disappointment of my climbing life."

A German climber transplanted to the United States, Wiessner had a long life marked by controversy, achievement, disaster, a contented family and business life, and an insatiable appetite for climbing. After advancing free-climbing ethics and standards early in the century in Europe, he introduced new codes to America in the 1930s. Wiessner also applied high standards to the mountains — in the Alps, the Tetons, and in Canada and the Himalaya.

There were few climbing areas and mountain ranges Wiessner did not visit, as numerous Wiessner Routes and Wiessner Cracks attest. His many partners were equally prominent: Willo Welzenbach, Lionel Terray, Bill House, Hans Krause, and Henry Barber, among others.

His boldness and creativity had their cost. Wiessner was blamed for the death of Dudley Wolfe and three Sherpas during the closing days of the 1939 K2 expedition. In the resulting dispute, Wiessner resigned from the American Alpine Club, although he was unanimously voted an Honorary Member in 1966. Nevertheless, the K2 tragedy always haunted him — a troubled undercurrent to an otherwise contented old age. "The mountains have given me my greatest joys and most profound sorrows," Wiessner once said, "but always it was men who failed me."

Wiessner was set in his ways from an early age, an original thinker unaffected by the boundaries imposed by others. He was a stern person; but, learning of another's accomplishments, he became increasingly accepting and generous in his respect. Having made a personal connection, he was very gracious. That rapport, however, might be a year or two in coming. In the mountains or on the rocks — in his element — Wiessner was overwhelmingly self-assured, at times vital, even jaunty.

In his last three decades, he took a patriarchal interest in younger climbers. He loved to reminisce to them, telling stories of color and character. He spoke of Terray and other ropemates as if he'd seen them the day before. Wiessner often said that younger climbers respected him and his climbs and knew him to be a good man.

* * *

Born on February 26, 1900, in Dresden, Germany, Wiessner taught himself to climb at the age of seventeen. His playground was the Elbsteingebirge, the vertical sandstone towers south of Dresden. In the mid-1920s, Wiessner helped pioneer the controversial concepts of free climbing — avoiding the use of pitons or the rope for progress. "I felt very strongly on this subject and climbed without aid whenever possible," he wrote. In the Tirol region he made the first ascent of the Southeast Face of the Fleischbank in 1925 — then proclaimed as the hardest rock climb ever done. Other "last great problems" in the Dolomites of Italy soon followed, including the first ascent of the North Face of the Grosse Furchetta. These two climbs sealed Wiessner's reputation as the best rock climber of the decade.

Professionally, Wiessner began managing a pharmaceutical business in 1923. In 1929, he immigrated to New York City, studied chemistry, and landed a good job. He became a U.S. citizen ten years later. "European climbers had no conception what American climbers were like during the 1920s, because what American climbers were there?" Wiessner asked rhetorically. "Robert Underhill was the only exception." Meeting in 1928 after separate ascents of Mont Blanc's Peuterey Ridge, Underhill and Wiessner became best friends.

In 1932, Wiessner joined the German-American Nanga Parbat Expedition. While team members reached several subsidiary summits of the Rakhiot Face, the main summit eluded them. Willy Bechtold, Willy Merkl, and Wiessner established Camp VII at 7,000 meters on the East Ridge, but storms ended further progress. Still, Wiessner was a convert to the world of Himalayan climbing.

During difficult business times in the early 1930s, Wiessner stayed close to home in New York, climbing with friends such as Percy Olton, Jr. and Robert and Miriam Underhill. Their favorite destinations were New Hampshire's White Mountains and the Hudson Highlands. But the highlight of the period came in 1935 with Wiessner's discovery of the Shawangunks, whose sharp flanks he spied from the Hudson River on a day when a thunderstorm had left the air intensely clear. Overwhelmed, Wiessner had no idea where to begin. He drove straight to Millbrook, one of the area's steepest walls, and climbed Old Route (5.5), the Shawangunks' first climb. In many respects, the times that followed — Wiessner's Shawangunk explorations — were his happiest.

There were new ropemates and, even better, acres of unclimbed routes.

In 1940, Wiessner met Hans Kraus, an Austrian native also yearning for local climbing. Wiessner's relationship with Kraus was competitive, but theirs was a great partnership as well. In 1941, the pair made the first ascent of High Exposure (5.6), a radically steep and bold line Kraus had picked out.

Additionally, two of Wiessner's best-known firsts were Mount Waddington in Canada's Coast Range and Devil's Tower in Wyoming. The two were thoroughly different in character: success on Waddington proved Wiessner's mountaineering skills, while his 1937 free ascent of Devil's Tower demonstrated he was America's best rock climber. In 1936, Waddington (13,260 feet) was regarded as the foremost problem in North America. Thirteen attempts on it had failed. As Wiessner, Bill House, Betty Woolsey, and Allanson Wilcox prepared for the climb, so did two other parties. Led by William Dobson and Bestor Robinson, they included some of the best climbers from British Columbia and the Sierra; and since some of them had been on previous attempts, Wiessner's group agreed to wait at basecamp while the others made their attempts. Then, when three separate efforts failed, Bill House and Wiessner got the green light. Woolsey and Wilcox provided support as the climbers attempted to ascend a couloir, only to be turned back by rotten rock. The next day, they climbed directly up the sheer South Face. Toward the end of the thirteen-hour push, the keyed-up Wiessner changed into rope-soled shoes and gave his boots, ice axe, and a 300-foot rappel rope to House. A chimney led to the summit ridge, then he continued through three overhanging, highly technical pitches to the mountain's highest point, which he later described as "covered with two feet of icy, windblown snow crystals — a spot just large enough so that one man could stand upon it."

Devil's Tower was an altogether different proposition. Partnered by House and Lawrence Coveney in 1937, on the first attempt Wiessner lost a contest between his face and a gooseberry bush. The next day, armed with a sickle, the trio progressed smoothly until confronted by a formidable eighty-foot crack. Tense but determined, Wiessner organized several thick, knotted slings and a few pitons for protection. He led on a double manila rope. Wiessner climbed with his usual rhythmic, flawless technique, although his breathing sounded like a locomotive. Soon Coveney's and House's intense silence gave way to spontaneous, but soft-spoken, words of admiration. "We knew that we were watching an exhibition of leading such as few climbers ever see," Coveney later wrote. Wiessner disappeared over the top of the crack, then a garbled shout blew back. House had heard that shout before, on Waddington. "It means we are going to the top," he said.

After Devil's Tower, Wiessner turned to loftier summits. Vittorio Sella's superb photographs of K2 strengthened Wiessner's wish to climb the giant peak. The American Alpine Club sponsored an expedition under Wiessner's leadership, which finally obtained a permit in the fall of 1937. Unfortunately, by that date, Wiessner could not afford to take the necessary amount of time away from his small chemical company. As a result, in 1938, Charles Houston led the first American K2 expedition. After much difficult climbing up the Abruzzi Ridge, including House's lead of the now-infamous House's Chimney, Houston and Paul Petzoldt reached a high point of 7,925 meters.

Wiessner tried hard to convince House and Petzoldt to return to K2 with him in 1939 but with no success. "Now it was up to me," wrote Wiessner. His 1939 team consisted of Chappel Cramer, Eaton Cromwell, Jack Durrance (one of America's best skiers and climbers), G.S.C. Trench, George Sheldon, and Dudley Wolfe. Wiessner, then thirty-nine years old, was leader. The thirteen Sherpas would include Pasang Kikuli (the Sirdar, or Sherpa leader), Pasang Kitar, Pinsoo, Dawa, Tendrup, Pasang Lama, and Tsering. Chandra Pandit, an Indian schoolteacher, came as interpreter. "Will this be the crowning achievement of my climbing career?" Wiessner wrote in his diary upon his first sight of K2.

"Everything that I have learned in my long years in the mountains; whatever degree of strength, energy, endurance, and instinct that they have given me, is dedicated to this effort — cool and deliberate, but with a warm heart!"

On the mountain, progress initially went well. Then Cranmer suffered a near-fatal illness, probably pulmonary edema. Durrance, the expedition doctor, tended him devotedly. As the team gained a foothold on the Abruzzi Ridge, two storms moved in. During the second, Wiessner and several Sherpas gained some ground, climbing to about 7,400 meters by July 5. On July 8, the weather cleared, but no support came from below. Wiessner descended to Camp II to investigate. Cromwell, Durrance, Trench, and two Sherpas remained tentbound; Sheldon had descended to basecamp with frostbitten toes.

"I gave them hell," said Wiessner. "I just couldn't conceive that they hadn't come up to bring the supplies." The team then divided into three groups: Durrance, Wolfe, and Wiessner up high; Cromwell and Trench at Camp IV or lower; Sheldon and Cranmer, injured, at basecamp.

On July 13 and 14, Wiessner, Wolfe, and Lama climbed to Camp VII at 7,525 meters, and Camp VIII at about 7,711 meters. Durrance became ill and turned back just above Camp VI, but the group decided that, health permitting, he should return to oversee the camps or even to join in the summit bid. In any case, he was to send the Sherpas and their loads up to resupply Camp VII. But Durrance did not recover at Camp VI and descended, insisting that Pasang Kikuli and Dawa accompany him. Making matters worse, Cromwell and Trench also left their supporting role at IV. Unknown to the three summit climbers, eventually there would be neither sirdar nor sahib above basecamp to oversee the Sherpa load-carrying.

Wiessner and his teammates had built up a series of fully stocked camps: tents, sleeping bags, and provisions stood ready at camps II, IV, VI, and VII. Wolfe settled in at Camp VIII with additional supplies. Heading for Camp IX (7,940 meters) with Pasang Lama, Wiessner felt all bases were well covered. "We would be safe even if communication (was) completely severed," he wrote.

On July 19, in surprisingly warm temperatures, Lama and Wiessner left Camp IX at about 9 A.M. for a summit push. Unable to determine if the prominent ice cliff before him was avalanche-prone, Wiessner chose a gully to its left. The steep, icy couloir ended in an overhang; he climbed the 5.6 rock in bare hands. From his new vantage point, he could see that the right-hand alternative would have been safe as well as easier to climb, a recent avalanche having scoured its upper slopes clean. He and Lama had perhaps 800 feet more to go along a fairly straightforward snow ridge to reach the summit. Foretelling a future trend in Himalayan mountaineering, Wiessner intended to climb all through the night. He speculated that they could descend in sunshine the next morning. But as the afternoon waned, the situation had become increasingly tense, with Pasang Lama murmuring and praying constantly. Now he held the rope tightly and said, smilingly, "No, Sahib. Tomorrow!" With a heavy heart, Wiessner gave in. "Pasang could not grasp that it would be easier to go to the summit than to risk rappelling in the dark," he observed heavily later.

The descent was hellish. Night fell as the two rappelled past an overhang. Suddenly the ropes caught in the crampons tied to Lama's pack. In freeing the rope, he knocked off his crampons, losing them into the void below. At 2:30 A.M., the pair reached Camp IX.

The next day warm sunshine revitalized them, and Wiessner sunbathed nude. On the following morning the snow was rock-hard; the two could have made good time upward on the right-hand ice gully but without crampons would now have to cut hundreds of steps. There was no choice but to descend. As Wiessner and Lama approached Camp VIII, Wolfe greeted them. "Those bastards! They never came!" said Wolfe of Durrance and the Sherpas. "I'll give it to them when we get home."

Descending to resupply at Camp VII, the trio was crossing an icy slope when Wolfe stepped on a coil of rope, pulling Wiessner off. Seconds later, all three men plummeted down the slope. "I thought to myself, Goddamn it! Here I have this thing in the palm of my hand," Wiessner recalled. "I knew what was below us — a 6,000-foot drop." He gouged in his ice axe, dug in his nailed boots — and stopped. Wolfe and Lama fell the full rope length, halting sixty feet above the dropoff. "How did you do that?" an incredulous Wolfe exclaimed to Wiessner. Lama looked up at him as if he was some sort of a god, and even Wiessner, who always said he was "not a very religious man," admitted to himself that it was a miracle the three had stopped.

No one was hurt, so they headed for Camp VII, where they found "the disappointment of our lives," as Wiessner wrote. "When I first saw the tents at Camp VII, I could hardly speak. We almost knew that we had been sabotaged. "Our food reserves and, critically, the extra sleeping bags which we ourselves carried up with great effort, had completely disappeared." With only one sleeping bag between them, the three talked all night to stay warm. They speculated that Durrance had not recovered and that something had gone very wrong with the Sherpas. The next morning, Wolfe decided to remain at Camp VII. "In retrospect, certainly (Dudley) should have descended then," said Wiessner. "He would have lived, because I would have brought him down even if he had been weak — which he wasn't at that time." Wiessner and Wolfe planned another summit bid for July 17, but, "I never saw Dudley Wolfe again," wrote Wiessner. "As we turned away, neither of us for a moment thought this would be our last sight of each other."

Wiessner and Lama descended to Camp VI and found it also empty. As Wolfe had kept the sleeping bag, descent became their only option. Camp V was supposed to be a depot, but here again — nothing. Wiessner and Lama continued to IV. Again, empty! Camp II, the low headquarters, was intended to have supplies and bags — but except for two tents, it too was deserted.

"With our last ounce of strength, we took the empty tent down and used it as our cover for the night," Wiessner wrote. "To describe in words the horrible feelings and thoughts I had during this day would be futile."

On July 24, after crawling for several kilometers along the glacier, the pair staggered into basecamp. They met Cromwell and three Sherpas, who had been searching for their bodies beneath the Abruzzi.

What had happened? Why had the camps been evacuated?

Chandra Pandit, the interpreter, wrote that from basecamp on July 18, he saw Durrance, Kikuli, and Dawa coming down the mountain. "I ran to see what the matter was, and was shocked to find that they had brought down eleven sleeping bags — all the reserves from Camps II and IV," he wrote. "I told them that they should return all the equipment to the sites, and that they had made a terrible mistake."

According to Pandit, two days later the unsupervised Tendrup and other Sherpas witnessed what they said was a "fatal" avalanche above them, and cleaned the mountain of the sleeping bags at Camp VI and Camp VII. Pandit further wrote that he, Kikuli, and the cook were alarmed at Tendrup's arrival with the gear and begged the Americans to send it and the Sherpas back up. But Cromwell, Durrance, and Trench forbade all further discussion. The Americans, wrote Pandit, were sure an accident had taken place. Had they returned the bags, Pandit added, "I am sure that the catastrophe would not have taken place. It was because of this mistake that the expedition failed to reach the summit."

After Wiessner's arrival, Durrance, Pinsoo, Kitar, and Dawa left basecamp on July 25 to rescue Wolfe. At that time, Wiessner wrote, "Jack, who is feeling well, may go on another summit attempt with me." That afternoon Durrance again became too weak to continue and returned to basecamp. Pinsoo and Kitar refused to go past Camp VI alone.

In an astounding effort on July 28, Pasang Kikuli and Tsering climbed 6,800 feet from basecamp to Camp VI, joining the two Sherpas there. Next morning the Sherpas found Wolfe in his tent at Camp VII. Apathetic, he had not eaten recently or been outside. He refused to descend, saying he would be ready the next day. The Sherpas descended to Camp VI, intending to return in the morning. Instead, bad weather pinned them down. Two days later in better weather, Kikuli, Pinsoo, and Kitar set off again, leaving Tsering at VI. If Wolfe again refused to descend, they intended to drag him. Failing that, Kikuli would demand Wolfe write a note to Wiessner, saying the Sherpas had done everything they possibly could. Tsering's friends never returned. For two solitary nights he waited. Finally he descended alone.

From August 3-7, Wiessner, Dawa, and Tsering made a final rescue attempt. When a raging storm dropped over two feet of snow, they had to retreat. Two days later, the remainder of the party left for Askole. There was now no chance that those above could still be alive. Of his lost teammates, Wiessner was to write, "They have, as their monument, a more beautiful structure than any man will ever erect — K2."

Then and afterwards, Wiessner did not doubt his own actions, but the events remained incomprehensible to him. Meanwhile, all of the factors in the tragedy were hotly debated. Cromwell and Trench, in particular, held Wiessner accountable. Three months later, Wiessner found a piece of the puzzle — a note. Durrance had left the message at Camp II, congratulating the summit team on conquering K2. The note went on to say that the day before, he had ordered Kikuli and Dawa to remove all the sleeping bags at Camp IV, and then the bags from Camp II. Durrance assumed Wiessner, Lama, and Wolfe would bring their own bags down. Unfortunately, when he wrote the note, Durrance could not know that Tendrup and the Sherpas with him would follow his example and clean out Camps VI and VII.

Back in the United States, the American Alpine Club appointed an investigating committee, comprised of J. Ellis Fisher, Bill House, Terris Moore, Bestor Robinson, and Walter A. Wood. The committee worked into 1940. Beyond the immediate facts, many other elements were part of the context in which the tragedy was viewed. One was World War II. "Here was this bastard from Germany who took away these climbs from the American climbing community," as Wiessner put it, looking back. "I was a bad man — and that was the feeling amongst that small group in the club which still exists today. These sentiments all go back to Hitler and the Nazis. I don't even like to think about that time, it was so terrible." However, it is unlikely that his immediate investigators were affected by such sentiments.

A more important factor was the reigning sense among American climbers then that one did *not* get killed in the mountains. Death was not considered an acceptable part of mountaineering. Furthermore, at that time returning home from a country like Pakistan took up to a month. Erroneous reports had long preceded Wiessner's arrival home, including rumors that he had abandoned a sick teammate, leaving him with insufficient food and fuel. In fact, Wolfe had six days' worth of provisions. Finally, some peers felt that Wiessner was so bold, so flat-out, as to be dangerous. It may have been that Wiessner was so far ahead of his time that others thought he put summits and success above camaraderie and the feelings of others. In any case, the fact that Wiessner was a central player in the K2 accident hardly helped the way in which it was perceived.

Many questions lingered. "I have no definite proof about Durrance," Wiessner would later say. "What can I say about him? What I feel inside me, I must keep to myself. He was a good man otherwise, and dutifully took care of me on the march home. When we talked about these matters, as we did on the way home, Durrance would say: 'Fritz! Fritz! Stop it! Stop it! Stop it! I don't know!' He was almost crying when he spoke." Another central question was why the bags were not immediately returned to the camps once it appeared a mistake might have been made. Only Cromwell, Durrance, and Trench remained at basecamp; due to declining health, Sheldon and Cranmer had left for Askole on July 18. According to Wiessner, the climbers at basecamp "were too lazy to check out the word of one Sherpa, Tendrup," who had witnessed the supposedly disastrous avalanche.

In the hospital suffering from frostbite and exhaustion, Wiessner answered the investigating committee's questions and gave them his expedition papers, including Durrance's congratulatory note — which subsequently vanished. Cromwell and Durrance were also questioned. Finally, the AAC Board of Directors stated in a letter that the exhaustive K2 report would not be published. Wiessner, who had made thirteen question marks on his copy of the report, felt the whole affair had been whitewashed. On December 26, 1940, in a brief letter to AAC President Henry Hall, Wiessner resigned from the club.

Wolfe's decision to remain at Camp VII has remained controversial for nearly fifty years. In *The American Alpine Journal* in 1985, referring directly to the K2 incident, Charles Houston wrote, "After a bold bid for a very high summit a climber found his companion sick and unable to descend. With their only Sherpa, he went down to the next camp for help, but finding no one there or at any of the lower camps, the two were slowly drawn down the mountain, reaching basecamp exhausted."

Yet Wiessner says Wolfe was not sick. Only several days later, after Wiessner and Lama were forced into their harrowing descent, did Wolfe become weak. Lama confirmed to Pandit that Wolfe was healthy when last seen, saying, "Because we had been sure to win the mountain, Mr. Wolfe had been standing outside of his tent when we descended, and he waved to us." Wiessner says the pair did not descend "for help" either, but to resupply and to locate Durrance and the Sherpas.

It becomes a poignant footnote that, had Wiessner and Lama made the top, the event would have changed the course of Himalayan mountaineering. Not only would K2 have been the first 8,000-meter mountain climbed, it is the hardest of those in that category. In fact, no 8,000-meter peak would be climbed for another decade, until the ascent of Annapurna in 1950. Finally, Wiessner and Lama would have made their ascent in admirable style, carrying no oxygen. Indeed, for them to have reached such a high point is extraordinary.

Wiessner never really got over K2, which would remain an inflammatory subject his whole life; but climbing was, conversely, his best solace. He never returned to the high mountains, perhaps because he could not trust a partner again to the degree necessary there. Still, he certainly never lost his zest for rock climbing, nor for hard alpine climbs. He climbed frequently in the Gunks and in Mexico, England, France, Italy, and, of course, Dresden. He made ski-mountaineering ascents and in 1960 completed his ascents of all 4,000-meter peaks in the Alps. Soloing hundreds of 5.3s in the Gunks, which he was to continue into his seventies, was another Wiessner trademark. "I like to be alone in the peace of nature. The joy of nature," he said.

In 1945, he married Muriel Schoonmaker, with whom he had two children. In 1952, the family moved to Vermont.

At eighty-six, Wiessner climbed several 5.6s in the Gunks and in Eldorado, although arthritis in his knees made reaching footholds a struggle. The tenacious Wiessner had always said, "You've got to fight it," and, truly, he did. In 1987, Wiessner suffered a series of crippling strokes that partially paralyzed him and would eventually take his life.

On a cold February day, Wiessner sat in his wheelchair beneath Vittorio Sella's black-and-white prints of K2. Dusty mountaineering books lined the shelves of his study. Outside, above the drawn shutters, birds fluttered in the treetops. Watching them, Wiessner's eyes darted back and forth in silent admiration. He was the embodiment of the mountaineer Elizabeth Knowlton described in *The Naked Mountain*. "To those men who are born for mountains, the struggle can never end, until their lives end," she had written. "To them, (mountaineering) holds the very quintessence of living — the fiery core, after the lesser parts have been burned away."

"I think a lot about climbing still," Wiessner said, "but not during the daytime. I think about it mostly at night, and on special occasions. I think about climbing when I am fed up with life in general. When I wish I could go over to the rocks or the trees. I enjoy my dreams about climbing."

Above, left to right: Charles Houston, Bradford Washburn, Adams Carter, and Bob Bates.
Photo by Ann B. Carter

Terris Moore.
Photo by Bradford Washburn

Pioneers of Mountain Exploration

THE HARVARD FIVE

By David Roberts

[From "Five Who Made It To The Top," HARVARD MAGAZINE, January 1981]

During the 1930s , a small group of Harvard students reached the forefront of American mountaineering and managed, over the course of that decade, to carry out most of its finest expeditionary accomplishments. Never before or since have the members of a single university club so dominated the national climbing scene. Among the dozens of brilliant projects they initiated, three stand out today as hallmarks in the history of mountaineering: the first ascent, in 1932, of Minya Konka, the storied Chinese mountain rumored to be higher than Everest; the first ascent, in 1936, of Nanda Devi, in India, which remained for fourteen years thereafter the highest mountain ever climbed; and the gallant attempt on K2, the world's second-highest mountain, in 1938. In 1953, the two men who had organized the 1938 expedition returned to the still-unclimbed mountain with high hopes but were thwarted by an improbable tragedy.

Within the active and ambitious Harvard Mountaineering Club (HMC) of those years, five men in particular stood out as central figures. All of them are still alive. As different from one another temperamentally as can be, these five are still close friends and get together frequently. Their lives since Harvard have borne striking similarities. Despite highly successful, even distinguished, professional careers, each has kept up a physically adventurous life well into his sixties. Each of them has integrated, in one way or another, both work and family life with mountaineering. All five men today are remarkably fit, and you cannot escape the impression, if you spend time in their presence, that they look back on their years as having been deeply fulfilling—with mountains, as one of them puts it, the "backbone" of life's enterprise.

Their lasting gift to American mountaineering was the perfection of a lightweight, mobile expeditionary style in the great ranges of the world. Almost single-handedly, they reopened Alaska as a field for mountaineering endeavor, after nearly twenty years of neglect that followed the ascent of Mount McKinley in 1913. On snow and ice they were virtuosos, pushing standards higher than they had been anywhere outside the Alps. They ranked with the great early Himalayan travelers as pioneers of mountain exploration, and they managed to take some of the last blank spots off the map of North America.

Yet in two important senses, the HMC group was reactionary, a throwback to earlier ideas in the face of mountaineering trends that would turn out to be the mainstream of the 1950s and 1960s. Contemporary with them was a group of Western climbers, centered in the Tetons, who were developing rock-climbing techniques that had filtered over from the Alps. The Harvard group had little interest in rock climbing and tended to see it only as a means to an end. Even within HMC circles, their view diverged from that of key figures from five or six years before, men who had been instrumental in advancing standards on rock in the United States. More than forty years later, the tensions produced by that split can still be felt in the mountaineering community.

24

All five men live today in New England. Bradford Washburn, at seventy-one, recently retired as director of Boston's Museum of Science; he is still the world's foremost aerial mountain photographer. Terris Moore, seventy-three, lives in retirement in Cambridge, having been, among numerous other things, the second president of the University of Alaska and one of the country's pioneering wilderness pilots, a three-time breaker of the North American altitude record for airplane landings. Charles Houston, sixty-eight, retired two years ago as a professor of community medicine at the University of Vermont. One of the world's leading experts on high-altitude illness, he was also a trailblazer in heart-transplant research and for two and a half years was director of the Peace Corps in India. Robert Bates, now seventy, lives in retirement in Exeter, New Hampshire, where he taught English at Phillips Exeter Academy for thirty-six years. A past president of the American Alpine Club, he directed the Peace Corps in Nepal when it was first established in the early 1960s. Adams Carter, the youngster of the group at sixty-seven, has edited *The American Alpine Journal* for twenty years, turning it into the outstanding publication of its kind in the world. He recently retired from Milton Academy, where he had taught French, German, and Spanish since 1946.

In 1932, Terris Moore, at age twenty-four, graduated from Harvard Business School. Three years earlier, as a senior at Williams, he had accompanied his scientist father on an expedition to Ecuador and made the first ascent of the active volcano Sangay; the following two summers had seen him pull off deft first ascents in Alaska. Now, with his nearly unprecedented string of first ascents behind him, Moore was ready to hatch a bold scheme. It would grow to maturity in the first of the three Asian expeditions that were the glory of the HMC in the thirties.

The idea really began with Moore's desire to go to Everest. He went so far as to get Hiram Bingham, a U. S. senator and the discoverer of Machu Picchu, to try to use his influence within the exploration bureaucracy. But the British had the traditional India-Sikkim approach to Everest pretty well sewn up and were not eager to take an American along on one of their expeditions. In the meantime, Moore had joined the Explorers Club and met Gene Lamb, who made the startling suggestion of approaching Everest from Peking via a long traverse of China and Tibet. In 1921-22, a British general, Pereira, had walked with a small party from Peking to Lhasa. Why, then, Lamb reasoned, couldn't a small American climbing party do the same on the way to Everest?

Moore's interest was further aroused by a perusal of Kermit and Theodore Roosevelt's recent *Trailing the Giant Panda,* in which he found reference to a "Mount Koonka, 30,000 feet?," in the unknown border region of western China and eastern Tibet. Moreover, an issue of *National Geographic* had just suggested that the Amne Machin Range, also in the border area, was believed to reach 28,000 feet and possibly considerably more.

Thus the idea of a Chinese approach to Everest fused in Moore's thoughts with the allure of a search for a mountain higher than Everest. When Lamb determined to visit Tibet to make sound recordings of the wild cries of the Ngolok tribe, Moore joined him. The Lamb Expedition to Northern Tibet left New York City by steamer in November 1931.

Moore and Lamb had each recruited various team members, and the personnel shifted in and out over the ensuing months. The party of four that emerged consisted of Richard Burdsall, Jack Young, Arthur Emmons, and Moore. Burdsall had little mountain experience and was originally recruited as a cartographer. Young, a native Chinese who was attending New York University, had been the Roosevelts' hunting guide. Emmons was a junior at Harvard concentrating in engineering. A strong member of the Mountaineering Club, he had already climbed in the Alps and the Canadian Rockies and had been on Bradford Washburn's 1930 Fairweather expedition in Alaska.

Little did Moore realize as he embarked that he would be gone fifteen months and would spend a year to the day in China. So many unexpected incidents interrupted the party's plans that it's a wonder the expedition ever got west of Peking. The party had been in Shanghai only a week when, lunching at their hotel, they heard a huge, booming sound and looked up to see their balcony doors blown inward. A powder barge on the Hwang Pu had been blown up; Japan had attacked China. Within hours, the Americans had reported to the tiny U.S. Marine headquarters in the international settlement and had "volunteered" their way into military duty. Armed with rifles and bayonets, wearing armbands in lieu of uniforms, the men were separated from each other during the next five days while they apprehensively patrolled the settlement perimeter. Moore, at one point, found himself behind a machine gun he didn't know how to operate. Young, who had been through the 1927 revolution on the side of Chiang K'ai-shek, had immediately left to fight with his people.

The Shanghai alarm blew over—at least for those in the international settlement—and eventually Lamb got the party to Peking by steamer. But the war continued for months, and there seemed to be no chance of seeing Minya Konka. Undaunted, the group of four bided its time, taking classes in conversational Mandarin (only about twice as difficult as Spanish, according to Moore). A letter from home indicated that economic conditions in the United States made living in China look rather comfortable. At last, in early summer, after several months of peace, the group got permission to travel to Tibet. Everest was out of the question by now, but Minya Konka remained to be reconnoitered and, if at all possible, attempted.

There followed an epic journey of more than 1,500 miles by boat up the Yangtze River, across Szechwan by bus, and through the labyrinth of foothills by porter, yak, horse, and even cow. The voyage was conducted in swashbuckling style, cheerfully overcoming all obstacles. One time, a group of soldiers stole one of the party's horses in the night. Young and Moore caught up with the thieves, and Young questioned them in Chinese while Moore held a pistol trained on them.

Finally the group penetrated the great mountain's defenses and arrived at basecamp. Young went off to collect scientific specimens for the Chinese government, leaving the other three to come to grips with the mountain. After considerable reconnoitering, they settled on the northwest ridge for their attempt. The mountain, it turned out, was 24,900 feet high—not 30,000—but it had the size and grandeur of a Himalayan giant. By early October, the trio had established a third camp at 20,700 feet, and on the sixteenth an attempt by Moore and Emmons reached 23,400. Storms intervened, and Burdsall was feeling rather sick, but by establishing a fourth camp at 22,000 feet, the men had put themselves in a strong position for a final attempt on the summit when the weather improved.

Then occurred one of those apparently trivial incidents whose reverberations echo through the rest of a man's life. It was October 26. Moore and Emmons had decided to use the next day to scout a route while Burdsall gathered his strength; the first clear day thereafter, the three would go for the summit. As Emmons told it in *Men against the Clouds*:

> Scarcely had this plan of action been evolved when I attempted to slice a frozen biscuit with my pocket knife. The biscuit was tough, and its frozen exterior yielded but little to my efforts. Suddenly it gave way and the knife broke through, cutting a deep gash in the palm of my left hand nearly two inches long. The wound was so deep that a number of the sensory nerves in the two little fingers were severed.
>
> I sat and watched the thick drops of blood ooze out and drip slowly onto my sleeping bag. Suddenly the significance of what had happened penetrated my altitude-benumbed consciousness. . . .

To his great dismay, Emmons could not join in the summit attempt. His hand sterilized and bandaged, he waited in camp on October 28 while Burdsall and Moore went for the summit. It was an anxious day for Emmons, full of foreboding; he tried to read a book of Kipling's ballads to while away the time and keep his mind off the cold. In the last moments of daylight, he heard the other two returning. They had reached the summit—the highest point Americans had yet attained. But the day's wait in camp, combined with the loss of blood, had put Emmons in a bad plight. During the descent, he felt himself seriously weakened, and his feet lost all feeling. The others had to go ahead to reclaim their camps while he hobbled desperately along in the rear. With a gutsy effort, the three men reached basecamp and sent ahead for help. It was clear now that Emmons's frostbite was grave; by the time they reached the town of Tatsienlu, thirty miles from the mountain, gangrene was about to set in. There was no doctor in town, and, to make matters worse, civil war had broken out in Szechwan, blocking all roads to the coast.

After excruciating delays, Emmons finally reached a hospital. Later he devoted one stoic sentence to the aftermath: "Yachow was destined to be my home for seven months while my feet underwent renovation and my toes were removed."

Costly though it was, the triumph on Minya Konka represented one of the most brilliant pieces of exploratory mountaineering in history—all the more remarkable in view of the paucity of technical climbing experience shared by the three men. Almost fifty years later, Washburn appraises the climb: "Both of them [Moore and Emmons], when they got onto Minya Konka, were up to their necks in something they had never gotten into before at all. God, I think it was just incredible what they did.'"

For Moore the climb was a watershed. He got married the following June and then, for want of time and money, "I pretty much put mountaineering behind me." He took up flying, however, and threw into his new avocation all the verve and skill he had cultivated as a climber.

By 1936, Adams Carter, then a Harvard senior, had done significant climbs in the Alps and the Tetons. In addition, he had stood with Washburn on top of Alaska's Mount Crillon in 1934 and the next year had played a crucial role in Washburn's epic winter traverse of the Saint Elias Range in the Yukon and Alaska—the biggest blank spot on the North American map at the time.

Charlie Houston had come to Harvard in 1931, fresh from a precocious teenage career in the Alps. He had teamed with Carter and Washburn on an attempt on Crillon in 1933 and the following summer had led the successful first ascent of Mount Foraker, which is second in height only to McKinley in the rugged Alaska Range.

Now Carter and Houston felt they were ready for a major challenge — in particular, a Himalayan first ascent. Implicated in the scheme from the start was a third HMC figure, a classmate of Carter's whose mountaineering career at Harvard would be nothing less than meteoric. William Farnsworth (Farney) Loomis would climb for only two or three years, yet would be a prime mover in one of the finest expeditions of the century. The fourth member of the party, incredibly enough, was Arthur Emmons—who, despite losing all his toes after Minya Konka, had subsequently gone back to the Alps, determined not to give up climbing. In the Himalaya, the chance of further frostbite was too great to take; still, Emmons wanted to go so badly that he volunteered to act as base-camp manager. That he could even walk was remarkable. The New Hampshire shoemaker Peter Limmer had made Emmons a special pair of toeless boots. "He was limited pretty much," Bob Bates recalls, "because his feet were cut off about there" (Bates draws a line midway up the laces on his own shoe). "So he had to walk on his heels all the time. Since he had no toes, this meant coming down a mountain was especially hard on him, because it would be bang-bang-bang, instead of easing himself down with his toes."

The party's original plan was to try the Bavarian ridge of Kangchenjunga in Nepal and Sikkim, the world's third-highest mountain. Loomis went to England to talk to the top British climbers and get official permission. As Houston reconstructs it, "in a very pleasant and tactful way they suggested that Kangchenjunga was a bit much for a group of neophytes in the Himalaya, and some of them suggested that we go to Nanda Devi instead."

At 25,645 feet, Nanda Devi, though one of the most striking mountains in British India, was 2,500 feet lower than Kangchenjunga (which, in fact, would not be climbed until 1955). One of the Englishmen who suggested scaling Nanda Devi was Bill Tilman, who, with Eric Shipton and only three Sherpas, had made a daring reconnaissance of the mountain in 1934 and solved the puzzle of the intricate approach to the inner basin, called the Sanctuary, that was the key to any attempt on the mountain. Shipton and Tilman—who today occupy places as revered as those of A. F. Mummery and George Mallory in the pantheon of British climbing heroes—were then the world's outstanding practitioners of lightweight Himalayan mountaineering, their expeditions involving from two to four climbers and a handful of porters. Temperamentally, therefore, Tilman was attuned to the Harvard group's style. On learning that the Britishers had suggested Nanda Devi, Houston cabled Loomis and urged him to invite Tilman and Shipton along.

Thus the first Anglo-American Himalayan expedition was born. Over the years, despite the supremacy of the British, a number of climbing links and friendships with the Harvard undergraduates had developed. The Everest veteran Noel Odell (the last man to see Mallory and Andrew Irvine as they disappeared into the mists in 1924) had taught briefly at Harvard and had climbed with the students. And T. Graham Brown, whom Houston had approached with trepidation when he recognized him in Montenvers in 1934, was now a fast friend from the Foraker expedition. In 1935, Emmons and Houston had dinner with Brown in the Monte Rosa Hotel, in the Italian Alps, with "lots of wine." The two college students decided to make the veteran of fifty-four an honorary member of the HMC. Houston remembers:

We blindfolded him and told him he had to be initiated. We roped him up and made him cut steps up the paths of the hotel gardens. Then we made him climb the stairs to the second story of the annex and rappel

out the window blindfolded. Then we made him climb
a small boulder in the garden and belay while we tried
to pull him off. We ended up by having him bivouac on
a chair tied to one of the trees on the main street. We
tied him in snugly and took off his blindfold. I don't
think I'11 ever forget his look of astonishment and hor-
ror when he looked around at the considerable crowd—
fifty or a hundred people—who were watching all this,
and realized that some of the leading lights of the
Alpine Club were there.

Despite such ordeals, Brown agreed to join the Nanda Devi
expedition, as did Tilman and Odell. Because Shipton was headed
for Everest, the party was rounded out by Peter Lloyd, a fine
British rock climber. Houston's father, who had been on the
Foraker expedition, wanted to walk in to basecamp with the
group. "But the consensus of the Britishers was that he was too
old, and it fell to Odell to break this sad news to him," Houston
recalls. "My father was pretty disappointed."

Because much of the planning was last-minute, the party assembled in India in bits and pieces, and the advance group was
well on its way in to the mountain before the last climbers arrived
in the country. This potentially divisive situation seems not to
have marred the expedition's extraordinary harmony at all. Carter,
the last to arrive, was in Shanghai when he got word that the others were on their way in. He was thus consigned to hiking in with
an Indian who spoke almost no English. But this didn't trouble
him. "I think in some ways it was good luck. For a week, as we
walked together, I was getting a complete Hindi lesson. Then he
left, and the last week into basecamp I was with the three porters
who were carrying my food. I either didn't speak or I spoke
Hindi."

Following the 1934 route, the party found its way up the
awesome gorge of the Rishi Ganga and into the Sanctuary. Crossing the Rhamani River, easy in 1934, was a desperate proposition,

one that terrified the porters. The British and Americans got along handsomely from the very start and even climbed in "mixed" pairs. To such a strong party, the defenses of the formidable mountain succumbed one by one. It began to seem likely that the summit could be reached, even though no mountain as high as Nanda Devi had ever been climbed. But it also was becoming apparent that only a pair of climbers could make the final assault. So far it had been, according to Houston, "a completely harmonious, happy, together group." But Brown, who was severely affected by the altitude, began to have the delusion that he was the strongest of the party. "And so we did an unusual thing," says Houston. "We had a secret ballot to elect a leader." Tilman won, and he selected Odell and Houston for the summit pair.

The two men were established in a camp at 23,000 feet, in good position to go for the top. The others were camped below. One morning on a possible "summit day," the lower men suddenly heard Odell shouting. Carter, who had the loudest voice, went out of the tent to communicate. "I heard coming down from above, 'Charlie — is — killed.' " Immediately Lloyd and Tilman started up to the higher camp, with Brown and Carter close behind carrying medical supplies. "We figured if Charlie was killed, Noel must be in bad shape. Probably they had had a slip or something." Tilman and Lloyd arrived, gasping for breath, to have Odell, sitting in the tent door, greet them with, "Hullo, you blokes, have some tea."

The emergency message had been "Charlie is *ill*." (To Carter, a person got sick, not ill.) The night before, Odell and Houston had eaten some bully beef from a can that had been previously punctured. They had cut away the portion of meat that was obviously spoiled, but Houston had come down with severe food poisoning; Odell for some reason was unaffected. For Houston, the illness meant not only the dashing of his hopes for the summit, but a grim and enervating descent.

Tilman replaced Houston, which was fitting, for he was perhaps the expedition's strongest member. Carter reminisces: "He was tough. He didn't need any of the amenities, like real food. He called it 'bloody muck.' " A few days later, on August 29, he and Odell stood together on the summit. Tilman later wrote: "I believe we so far forgot ourselves as to shake hands. . . ."

Nanda Devi remained the highest mountain climbed in the world for fourteen years, until the French conquered Annapurna in 1950. Houston recovered sufficiently to make "one of the more exciting and difficult efforts" of his life—a ten-day hike-out with Tilman to Ranikhet via the previously untraversed Longstaff's Col, averaging twenty to thirty miles a day. Loomis never climbed seriously again; tragically, after a brilliant career in medical research, he committed suicide in his mid-fifties. For Emmons, too, there would be little more mountaineering, but he would rise to distinction in the U.S. State Department, be interned in Tokyo during World War II, and come home on the famous voyage of the *Gripsholm*. Tilman and Shipton both continued the expedition life well into their sixties and became pioneers in combining sailing with climbing in the remote ranges. Tilman, in fact, was lost in the Antarctic Sea in November 1977, in his eightieth year. Houston adds: "It's been reported to me that Shipton said later in life that one of his greatest regrets was going to Everest instead of going to Nanda Devi with us."

The climb made the British climbers even more famous, and Tilman's book, *The Ascent of Nanda Devi*, was a great success in England. But when the Americans tried to sell the story to *Life*, the magazine showed not the slightest interest. Their main chance at notoriety, Carter recalls, came from the makers of Camel cigarettes, who had celebrities like baseball player Rogers Hornsby endorsing their product. The company's agent seemed dumfounded when none of the four men responded to his entreaties. "He said, 'Aren't you even going to ask how much we're going to pay you?' I said 'no.' "

The following year, in 1937, Bradford Washburn returned to Alaska for his seventh campaign. Already an innovator in the use of the airplane to support expeditions, and a pioneer in aerial photography, Washburn found a pilot bold enough to force his latest idea—a remote glacier landing to short-cut weeks of packing in supplies. His goal was Mount Lucania, at 17,150 feet now the highest unclimbed mountain in North America. The already legendary Bob Reeve had recently put a new wrinkle into bush flying. "He'd made his money," Bob Bates remembers, "by taking an old cocktail bar and making a pair of stainless-steel skis out of it, then flying to a mine that was owned by some Chinese fellow who couldn't operate it in the summer because there was no way to get in." For his "field" Reeve used the mud flats at Valdez. "He had a tide table, which he always carried with him. He could only land when the tide was right. So he had to think pretty carefully where he was before he took off."

Washburn persuaded Reeve to try to fly his party of four into the 8,500-foot level on the gigantic Walsh Glacier, at the base of Lucania. Washburn and Bates accompanied the pilot on the first flight. On the landing, one ski sagged into a crevasse. It took a day to dig it out, and by then the snow was so soft that Reeve could not get up enough speed to take off. Suddenly the three men faced the very real possibility that they were marooned in the heart of the Saint Elias Range.

They spent the next two and a half days stomping down a runway that bent, of necessity, in a gradual curve as it threaded its way between a field of crevasses on the one side and a steep slope down to a glacial lake on the other. Each time Reeve gunned the plane down the runway, he failed to gain enough speed to get airborne and had to give up and taxi back to the head of the makeshift snow-ramp. Finally he decided to give it all the plane he had. Bates recalls:

> He had taken his ball-peen hammer and changed the pitch of the propeller to get more bite, and he'd stripped the plane, taken everything he could out of it. This time he went bouncing down the runway. He hit a great big block of snow, and it bounced him off the left

35

side, where the slope went down quite steeply toward the lake. Quick as he could, he turned the nose of the plane right for the lake, gave it everything he could, and by the time he got to the lake he had enough speed so he got off, just missing the water. He kept going right toward the cliff on the side of the glacier, turned that, and went on out. We just sat down. We were absolutely stunned, it was so close.

Their relief was short-lived. A freakishly warm rainstorm descended on the region, turning the already soft snow into a soggy cushion. It became obvious not only that Reeve would never get the other two men in, but that Washburn and Bates would have to get themselves out. The nearest "civilization" was a trading outpost at Burwash Landing on Kluane Lake, far to the northeast, on the other side of Lucania. Mount Steele, the 16,644-foot neighbor of Lucania, had been climbed by Walter Wood's party the year before, and the two men knew Wood had left caches of food at the base of that mountain. With a boldness born of many mountain adventures, Washburn and Bates decided to hike out by traversing over both Lucania and Steele. It was, in fact, the shortest way out, and they reasoned that if Wood could get up Mount Steele, they could follow his route down it.

Traveling with astonishing speed, thanks to their superb fitness, the two men carried out the double ascent and traverse without a hitch. Surely never before had a party bent on escaping from a range made a major first ascent along the way! To shed weight, they threw away all expendable gear and some of their food and even cut the floor out of their tent. At the base of Steele, however, they found that one of Wood's caches had been swallowed up in a glacial surge, the other ransacked by bears. "We only found this one little can of Peter Rabbit peanut butter," says Bates wistfully.

Carrying sixty pounds each, they made fast time down the Wolf Creek Glacier and out to the lowlands. And then the first serious blow fell. They reached the Donjek River, which they had to cross, and found it a swollen torrent. Bates put some rocks in his pack to hold him down and tried the crossing three times but couldn't make it. They had no axe with which to cut wood to build a raft. Only one option remained: they would have to walk back upstream all the way to where the Donjek emerged from the glacier that fed it, cross the glacier's snout, and emerge on the other side.

Weary and famished, and apprehensive that they might come to an uncrossable tributary of the Donjek and thus be boxed in, the two men trudged upstream. When the glacier came into view, they received another shock: instead of issuing from the glacier's snout, the Donjek flowed parallel to the glacier for what looked like miles. Washburn and Bates grimly started up the bank of the river. "Finally we reached one place where it looked as if we couldn't go on. We were stopped cold. But Brad cut a big bollard of ice, and we roped off. We figured we wouldn't be going back anyway."

After several hours they found a place where the river spread out, and they tried to cross. A kind of quicksand nearly defeated them, but they persisted.

> We got, I'd say, two-thirds of the way across the river with our packs and duffel bags before the current was so strong it knocked us off our feet, and then we swam the last part. You would touch bottom, then sort of spring up and take a couple of strokes. We were so cold on the other side . . . I don't know if I've ever been so cold. We got out a sleeping bag and got in it, and just shivered and shivered for a long time.

Now it was only a matter of plodding ahead; but the two men were already weak from hunger and fatigue.

> We had this old revolver that shot high and to the left. The first thing we had a chance to shoot was a squirrel. He was chattering at us from up in a spruce tree. I shot—missed. Brad groaned. I went around, shot from

the other side, and missed. Brad groaned. The third try, I shot the branch right out from under the squirrel, and he fell down and hit his head. I ran up and grabbed him and finished him, and Brad said, "Gee, that was a good shot. " (I didn't dare tell him until much later.)

So we had him, and we had quarts of mushrooms that we'd found. Brad said, "What do you know about mushrooms?" I said, "Not very much. I know if there's a death cup you certainly shouldn't eat them. What do you know?" He said, "They say if you cook 'em with a quarter and the silver turns black, they're poisonous. Do you have a quarter?" "No," I said. And then he said, "Well, Jim Huscroft said there's nothing poisonous in Alaska or the Yukon." So anyway, we cooked them up as a kind of soup, with the squirrel. As we walked along afterwards, I remember looking back at Brad and seeing him turning and looking at me. . . ."

Despite their desperate state, Bates claims the two men never got depressed. "I think we always thought we were going to get out. We were dubious about the next stage often, but we never gave in." At last they chanced upon a French Canadian hunter with two Indian guides and a small packtrain, and they rode the last thirty miles in style into Jean Jacquot's store on Kluane Lake on bare pack-saddles—a ride Washburn later described as one of the worst agonies of his life. "We were kind of bony," Bates explains.

Houston and Bates organized the first American attempt on K2, the world's second-highest mountain, in 1938. Though originally intended as a reconnaissance, the expedition made a gallant dash up the southeast ridge and reached 26,000 feet—only a little more than 2,000 feet below the summit—before running out of supplies. By the early 1950s, K2 was still unclimbed. Houston, his interest reawakened by an exploratory trek into newly opened Nepal to the foot of Everest, started negotiating for permission to return to K2, and approval came through in 1952. Bates, of course, had been in on the idea all along. Thus began perhaps the most monumental—and most harrowing—of all the expeditionary deeds of the five Harvard men who had met in the 1930s.

It would have seemed selfish for Bates and Houston simply to fill out the expedition with friends. By 1953, an attack on K2 was felt to be a genuinely national effort, and there were many more outstanding climbers in the United States than there had been fifteen years earlier. Yet the two organizers knew that compatibility was more important than sheer talent. They set up an interviewing operation in Exeter and tried to screen all the serious candidates. Houston recalls, "My children looked at them, the dogs looked at them, we looked at them." Gradually a strong team of eight was assembled.

At forty-two and forty, respectively, Bates and Houston were the oldest men in the expedition—older, in fact, than most of the active climbers in the country. But as the trip to Pakistan approached, there was a feeling of high optimism. Wartime improvements in gear had made certain advances in climbing possible. And with the French triumph on Annapurna, a major psychological barrier seemed to have been removed. The time was at last ripe for climbing the highest mountains in the world. (Indeed, virtually all the 26,000-foot peaks would succumb between 1950 and 1960.) Bates and Houston were particularly sanguine. After all, they had found the route in 1938, they knew that it would go from their high point of 26,000 feet to the summit, and this time they would not have to waste weeks in reconnaissance.

Everything went smoothly to the foot of the Abruzzi Ridge, and on June 26, in perfect weather, the team began the actual climb. At the limestone cliff that was bisected by House's Chimney, Houston almost sheepishly asked his partners, "Would you fellows mind too much if I tried to lead this?" As in 1938, they had trouble finding decent tent sites, and some fierce weather slowed progress, but by August 6, a Camp VIII had been established at 25,200 feet. All eight men were together there, waiting out a storm, with supplies ready to stock a two-man camp above, from which a pair of climbers would go for the summit. The party elected the summit team by secret ballot.

Then, on August 7, an unforeseeable calamity struck. Crawling between the tents during a lull in the storm, one of the strongest men, Art Gilkey, collapsed, unconscious. As he came to, he apologized, "It's just my leg, that's all. I've had this charley horse for a couple of days now." Houston examined him immediately and knew within moments that it was no charley horse. Gilkey had thrombophlebitis—blood clots—in the left calf. Today Houston reflects:

> From that very moment it was my feeling that he was doomed, and perhaps we were all doomed. I couldn't conceive then that he'd be well enough to walk down. From the very first I was sure Art was going to die on the mountain. But I shielded the others from this knowledge, because I think that's part of a doctor's responsibility. I tried to keep everything optimistic. Not very successfully.

Gilkey took his disability with great courage. But he soon was unable to walk, and then began a nightmarish effort to evacuate him from high on K2 in bad weather. On August 8, the men made a cocoon out of a smashed tent, a rucksack, and some ropes and tried to haul and lower their teammate over the awkward terrain; but they had to turn back because their ascent route had become an avalanche trap. Two days later, Gilkey's condition was much worse. He had a dry, hacking cough and a pulse rate of 140, and Houston found that some clots had migrated to his lungs. And the storm had returned in full fury.

Bates wrote later: "We all knew now that some of us might never get down the mountain alive. . . . We had told one another that 'if somebody broke a leg, you never could get him down the mountain.'" Yet the men had to try.

On August 10, after eight hours in constant storm, the men were making a complicated maneuver to lower Gilkey sideways across a steep ice slope that plunged off into the void. Pairs of climbers roped together were scattered in various places about the slope. All the men were in a state of anxious exhaustion from the cold, the altitude, and lack of sleep. For some reason, one man slipped. His partner, unprepared, was pulled off the rope, and the two men hurtled down the slope. Their rope crossed and got tangled with the rope between Houston and Bates, and with the weight of two falling men suddenly coming on their own rope, first Houston, then Bates, were plucked out of their steps. At this point, Gilkey's cradle was being belayed by two different ropes, with a man on each end; the four falling climbers fell across the rope between Gilkey and the lower anchor man, and he too was pulled violently off his feet.

Seven of the eight members of the expedition seemed about to die in a monstrously long fall down the mountain. At the top end of the other rope securing Gilkey, Pete Schoening saw the fall. He had previously thrust the shaft of his ice axe into deep snow behind a small boulder. Now, instinctively, he did the only thing he could—put all his weight on the head of his axe and hope that it would not be jerked loose.

The impact came, fortunately, not all at once but in a series of shocks. Schoening held on, and miraculously the belay worked. All five falling climbers were brought to a halt by one man, in a truly extraordinary demonstration of belaying skill.

The situation remained desperate, however. Several of the men had badly frostbitten hands, and Houston had a concussion. When Bates got to him, he said groggily, "Where are we? What are we doing here?" Bates could not get him to move, or even to comprehend his words. Finally, with the utmost intensity, looking straight into his eyes, Bates said, "Charlie, if you ever want to see Dorcas and Penny [his wife and daughter] again, climb up there right now." The words managed to penetrate, and within moments Houston was swarming up the slope.

Those less seriously injured worked feverishly in the rushing wind and blowing snow to scratch out a narrow ledge and put up the tents, though the slope was too steep to pitch them well.

Gilkey had been left, tied off to two ice axes, until the party could go back for the difficult task of moving him across to the bivouac. As they worked they thought they heard him calling out weakly. After half an hour or perhaps longer, Bates and two others went back to start the shift. Bates remembers:

> What we saw there I shall never forget. The whole slope was bare of life. Art Gilkey was gone! . . .
>
> Even the two ice axes used to anchor him safely had been torn loose. The white, wind-swept ice against which he had been resting showed no sign that anyone had been there. It was as if the hand of God had swept him away.

The avalanche that took Gilkey's life must be seen as a blessing in disguise. Today Bates reflected: "It wasn't until after it happened that we realized that there was something we had been unwilling to recognize. After it had all been taken out of our hands, suddenly we recognized this feeling of relief." Houston calls Gilkey's death "a miraculous deliverance from an intolerable and fatal situation."

For even without Gilkey, the party was in a grim situation. Houston was delirious all through the night and repeated "Where are we?" without cease. Yet his sense of responsibility made him inquire constantly about the others. "How's Pete?" he would ask anxiously; then, moments after Schoening reassured him, "Bob . . . how's Bob?" Constriction in his chest convinced him that there was not enough oxygen in the tent, and he had to be restrained from cutting his way out with a knife. "I know about these things," he would say. "I've studied them. We'll all be dead in three minutes if you don't let me cut a hole in the tent."

It took the weakened party four agonizing days to complete the retreat to base. During much of the first day after the fall, they climbed down over rocks spattered with Gilkey's blood and rags of his sleeping bag and tent; no one mentioned this, not for many years. Houston was confused, often irrational, but the others felt he climbed perfectly. He insisted on being the last down House's Chimney, an obstacle that had worried all of them. Alone in the dark at the top, he had a moment of panic when he realized he could not distinguish the new, safe fixed rope from the rotten leftovers of 1938.

Even at basecamp the party's problems were not over, for the frostbite incurred during the accident was serious enough that one of the men had to be carried out by the Hunza porters. An expedition that had begun full of health and confidence limped and hobbled back to civilization, less one of the team.

Houston today remembers vividly all the details up to the fall but has only the haziest recollection of the rest of the descent.

> Not until recently have I been able to think or talk much about it. I suspect that for a long time I had a rather profound blank. I suppose I felt some sort of guilt. . . . It was the first fatality I'd had on any of my climbing expeditions. I think I took it very hard. The blood on the rocks was a very upsetting experience for all of us.

It was an experience that, all the members agree, welded the team tightly together for life. Three years ago, on the twenty-fifth anniversary of the expedition, the seven met in the Wind River Range in Wyoming for a week of climbing and reminiscence. Among the memories Charlie Houston shared with his friends on that occasion were the feelings he had during the journey back from Pakistan in 1953:

> I remember thinking that after that experience nothing would ever upset me again, I would be a different person, that I had been miraculously saved for some purpose I didn't understand. But it didn't take very long before I was back in the real world, a real person, and nothing much had changed.

Yvon Chouinard. *Photo by Rick Ridgeway, Adventure Photo*

Ascending

YVON CHOUINARD

By Jeremy Bernstein

[From "Chouinard, Ascending," THE NEW YORKER, January 31, 1977]

Devotees of mountain climbing say that Yvon Chouinard, a fifty-one-year-old climber who lives in Ventura, California, cannot get his hands on a piece of mountaineering equipment without instantly trying to think of ways to improve it. Chouinard has been climbing as often as possible, wherever possible, since he was sixteen-years old, and today he is regarded as one of the greatest active mountain climbers in the world.

He has done extreme climbing — often first ascents — in Canada, the United States, and Mexico, and as far south as Patagonia. He has made innumerable climbing trips to Britain and the Continent. He has climbed in New Zealand, on Mount Kenya (where some of the guides used the metal climbing loops known as carabiners for earrings), and in the Himalayas of Pakistan.

A list of Chouinard's first ascents would be almost endless, but one of the most notable was made in October 1964 with Thomas Frost, Royal Robbins, and Chuck Pratt, all well-known California climbers. This was the ascent of the North America Wall of El Capitan, in Yosemite National Park, an area so called because in the middle of the wall is a large section of black diorite whose shape is roughly like that of the North American continent. The climbers spent ten days on the wall, with nine hanging bivouacs — nine nights in hammocks suspended horizontally from the rock face, and with only down jackets for warmth. Harder climbs have subsequently been made in Yosemite, but when Chouinard and his friends climbed the North America Wall it was regarded as the hardest rock climb ever done anywhere in the world. The four men managed to haul 200 pounds of food and 60 quarts of water along with them up a rock face that is 3,000 feet high and absolutely vertical.

Quite apart from his extraordinary record as a climber, Chouinard has the reputation of being a virtuoso in the design of equipment. Alone or in collaboration with Frost, who was his business partner from 1966 until 1975 and then retired, Chouinard has systematically redesigned almost every piece of equipment used in climbing. His company, the Great Pacific Iron Works, in Ventura, has become one of the largest manufacturers of climbing equipment in the world, and this year Chouinard expects more than two million dollars in gross sales of climbing gear — both hardware (nuts, ropes, ice axes, crampons, carabiners, pitons of all sorts) and software (climbing pants, shirts, sweaters, packs). His spin-off company, Patagonia, now sets the standard in the sale and manufacture of outdoor wear.

The improvements made by Chouinard and Frost in the design of climbing tools over the years have always had their start in some difficulty that the two men encountered in adapting existing equipment to their own climbing. The number and variety of their innovations are as dazzling as the list of their climbs; among their designs are the Chouinard-Frost ice axe and the RURP (Realized Ultimate Reality Piton).

The design of the ice axe grew out of an attempt by Chouinard in 1968 to learn the French technique of ice climbing. Essential to ice climbing are crampons — downward-pointing metal claws that are strapped to the soles of climbing boots. In 1908, a British climber named Oscar Eckenstein developed a ten-point design that became widely accepted, and in 1931 an Italian guide and blacksmith named Laurent Grivel modified this design by adding to it two prongs pointing forward from the toe. The change enabled the climber to mount steep ice by driving the two forward prongs into the ice with hard kicks and climbing the ice as one would climb stairs. This technique, which came to be known as the German method, is especially suitable for the eastern Alps, where the climber encounters what is known as water ice.

Water ice is frozen water that has been running such as a frozen stream or a waterfall. It is brittle and extremely hard. In the western Alps, the ice that is encountered is glacier ice, which is compacted snow, and it is much softer and more porous. With the French technique, the climber on steep glacier ice ascends sideways, the feet placed firmly parallel to each other and at right angles to the inclination, making as much use as possible of the ten bottom points of the crampon. To maintain his balance, a climber using the French technique drives his ice axe in point first, like an anchor, above his head — a position that the French call *piolet ancre*. Chouinard, who was climbing in Europe when he tried to learn this technique, found that unless the ice axe was placed perfectly, it tended to come out of the ice as soon as one began to climb.

In 1968, he wrote an article on ice climbing, with photographs by Frost, for the Sierra Club journal *Ascent*. He noted:

> The designs of most of the modern ice axes have evolved into all sorts of grotesque forms with weird handles, serrated and cupped adzes, ice-pick spikes, and other abnormalities that make them more suitable for assassinations than for climbing ice. I could write an entire treatise on the subtle forms and lines of the correctly made piolet. Try and use the average axe in the piolet ancre position and you will find that as you start putting weight on it, the pick will probably pop out

and hit you in the eye. I had to forge my own axe before I realized that the French technique was not impossible to learn.

Indeed, after almost being hit in the eye a few times, Chouinard borrowed every kind of ice axe that was then being used and went out on the Bossons glacier, in the Chamonix Valley of France, to see which axes worked best and why. He then designed his own model, and Frost, who has a bachelor's degree in aircraft engineering from Stanford and is an excellent draftsman, drew up the design. In the Chouinard-Frost model, the pick is replaced by a curved blade with deep serrations. The curve is designed so that it is consistent with the arc made by the arm when the axe is swung. This axe sticks into ice of any hardness and requires some effort to remove, yet it also works well for cutting steps, the purpose for which ice axes were originally designed.

In any event, since 1972, when the first substantial company catalog appeared (the company was then known as Chouinard Equipment and changed its name when it incorporated in 1973; it was recently sold and renamed Black Diamond), Chouinard has done everything possible to discourage the use of pitons altogether in favor of the climbing implements known as chocks. Unlike most pitons, they are easily removable. In 1971, Chouinard became an apostle of "the clean-climbing ethic," and if he had his way, there would be few circumstances in which a rock climber would be allowed to hammer a piton into a rock and leave it there.

According to Doug Scott, a British climber and the author of *Big Wall Climbing*, the use of the chock began in 1926, on a climb of Clogwyn du'r Arddu, a rock face in Wales. The climbers carried chock stones — small rocks — which they wedged into cracks in the wall.

By the 1940s, it was common practice for British climbers to stuff their pockets with pebbles from local streams before heading for the crags. There is a railroad in Wales that runs close to Clogwyn du'r Arddu, and climbers would trudge along the tracks before making an ascent. From time to time, a large nut would detach itself from the railway tracks, and in the early 1950s, climbers began picking up these nuts and making use of them. The nuts were better than the chock stones, for a rope could be fitted through the hole, and the metal would stick solidly to the rock. In the early 1960s, a British blacksmith named John Brailsford began machining metal wedges of various sizes that were even better than the railway nuts. By 1967, these wedges were fitted with wire loops. The modern version does not differ from them greatly in basic design.

Chouinard began using chocks (his first ones were made from aluminum aircraft nuts) in 1959 and 1960 while he was climbing in the Tetons, but it was more than a decade later when he became a really strong advocate of them. Scott quotes a response to a letter that he wrote Chouinard in 1970 asking him about the attitude of Yosemite climbers toward this technology Chouinard replied, "I've found nuts very useful on artificial climbing [climbs that require the use of pitons or other aids for progress or rest] when the rock is very poor. . . . But I would never substitute a nut for a piton in a normal situation. I've climbed with nut fanatics like Robbins, who insist on using them. . . . I can assure you he spends twice as much time . . . placing them [as] if he just nailed it."

Not long after making that comment, however, Chouinard discovered that pitons in Yosemite were ruining the rock. Pitons can destroy delicate cracks in rock, and some climbs, where it is customary to remove pitons, have been ruined by piton scars. The cracks become perforated, like the edges of a postage stamp. Chouinard said, "I always thought of rock climbing as a completely harmless sport — one that did not hurt anyone. But I came to realize that it could do great harm to the rocks." Small cracks that could once take only small pitons now needed large pitons, and soon new cracks developed every few feet. The rock was simply being beaten to pieces.

When Chouinard and Frost changed their technique, they began to manufacture a wide variety of chocks. For a time, some of the younger climbers accused Chouinard of a certain hypocrisy, claiming that he had used pitons on all his hard routes but was now recommending to them strange and perhaps unproven practices. As an answer, in 1973 Chouinard and a Washington climber named Bruce Carson (who died during an ascent in India in 1975) climbed the Nose route on El Capitan taking along only chocks — not pitons. This is one of the hardest rock climbs in Yosemite, and the two men completed it with no serious hitches — a feat that quieted the skeptics.

The 1972 Chouinard catalog is regarded by climbers as something of a collector's item. It sold for a dollar, and 10,000 copies were printed. Not a single copy is left in the Chouinard office. On the cover is a sixteenth-century Chinese scroll painting, Landscape in the Spirit of Verses by Tu Fu, by Wen Chia, and among the contents are quotations from a variety of notable intellects. Page one has a magnificent photograph of the east face of the Moose's Tooth, a mountain in Alaska, over which is printed a sentence from Albert Einstein: "A perfection of means and confusion of aims seems to be our main problem."

To prevent any confusion of aims, there is an excellent fourteen-page instructional section written by the well-known Sierra guide and alpinist Doug Robinson on how clean-climbing equipment is to be used. Using chocks requires a more intimate relationship with the rock than does hammering in a piton.

The whole catalog so much resembles a small book that it has been reviewed as one. Writing in the 1973 edition of the *The American Alpine Journal,* climber and photographer Galen Rowell asked, "What is a commercial catalog doing in the book-review section?" He answered, "It contains more information on the ethics and style of modern climbing than any other publication in our language."

* * *

I decided not long ago to go to California to meet Chouinard. When I called him to arrange the visit, he said that he would pick me up at the Ventura County Airport and added, "Stay at the house. We have visitors all the time and live on the beach. It's not bad."

When I arrived, I was greeted by a short, rugged-looking man in blue jeans and a wool shirt. Like many of the world's best mountain climbers, Chouinard is short — perhaps five feet five. Like every first-rate climber, Chouinard has very powerful hands and fingers that, for a man of his size, are unusually large. He has a broad, open, tanned face.

We got into a well-worn car and after a drive of twenty minutes arrived at a white wooden cottage whose back door was only thirty-five feet from the ocean. Chouinard's wife, Malinda, whom he met some years ago when both were mountain climbing (they have been married for nineteen years), has had to put up a small wooden gate on the back porch to keep their son Fletcher from following his father out to sea.

The beach on which the Chouinards live is known in Southern California as one of the best beaches for surfing, and each morning at sunrise Chouinard gets up to examine the quality of the waves. If the waves look good, he dons a black wet suit and selects one of two translucent surfboards he has stored on the ceiling beams of his living room.

When I was there, gray whales were migrating south to Baja and could be seen spouting behind the congregating surfboard riders. From time to time, the phone rang in the living room, and Malinda gave out information to surfing friends who were not in a position to inspect the waves.

Probably because Chouinard has spent so much time on expeditions, he does a good deal of cooking. He was at the time of my visit learning Japanese cookery, and soon after I arrived he began to study a cookbook to find out how to prepare a substantial fish in Oriental style. After dinner, which featured the fish (and was excellent), I asked Chouinard if he would tell me something about his life and about how he had discovered the mountains.

I was born in Lewiston, Maine, on November 9, 1938, of French-Canadian parents. We lived in Lisbon, Maine, a town that was almost evenly divided between French-Canadians and Yankees. Until I was seven, I went to a parochial school, where everyone spoke French. In fact, until I was eight I couldn't speak English at all. When I was seven, my father, who was a plumber, moved the family — I have two older sisters and an older brother — to Burbank, near Los Angeles. They put me in public school — an English-speaking school and I couldn't speak English. It was traumatic. I can understand how Puerto Ricans and Chicanos feel about going to an English-speaking school. After about a week, they took me out and put me in a parochial school, where I got along a little better. The teachers spent more time trying to get me to talk. But I became sort of a loner — a wise kid.

All through that period, I was spending my time out of school outdoors in the hills — the Hollywood Hills and the like. Before the other kids were even allowed to cross the street, I was taking my bike and riding for miles to sneak in to private lakes to go fishing. My big dream was to become a trapper — my French-Canadian background — and I read every book about trapping I could get my hands on. I spent all my time either outdoors or reading about the outdoors.

I couldn't adapt to high school at all. I had a few friends. All the geeks. Couldn't dance, scared to death of girls. We joined a club — the California Falconry Club — and spent our time looking for hawks' nests and trapping hawks and banding them for the government. There were some adults in the club, who taught us things and kept an eye on us — particularly Robert Klimes, who was a schoolteacher. But it was a man named Don Prentice, another member of the club who first taught us something about climbing. We had been climbing hand over hand on ropes down to these falcon aeries on the ledges of cliffs. But he taught us how to rappel — to wrap the rope around one's body and slide down on it. We just went crazy over that. We thought that rappelling was the greatest thing in the world. I'd go out and practice rappelling for hours. We'd take a 100-foot cliff and instead of rappelling down it in twenty hops, we'd see how few hops we could do it in. We developed all-leather outfits, huge leather pads and everything, so that we could do these hot, burning rappels — just smokers — in one or two hops.

I went out in the desert with a friend — Ken Weeks, with whom I did a lot of climbing later — to a prairie falcon's aerie. There was this tremendous overhanging cliff, more than 400 feet high, and I tied three ropes together. The hanging rope was so heavy I could hardly pull it up with my arms to feed it through to rappel. Weeks grabbed the rope and wrapped it around his body and stuffed himself behind some boulders so that he could hold me. I had some rope slings around my neck, and when I hit the first knot it wouldn't go through the slings. My arms were so tired from lifting the rope that I couldn't pass the knot through. I just hung there in midair with the rope wrapped around my body. I finally reached the point where I couldn't hang there anymore. I was going to count to ten and then let go. I started to count and got to eight and the knot came through — popped through. I slid down to the ground and went into convulsions, because my body had been so tense. Weeks, who hadn't known what was happening, found me, and said I had been hanging on the rope for three and a half hours. It was one of the closest calls I have ever had. That was the end of the rappelling.

Don Prentice showed us a little about climbing — how to use ropes, and so on — and we began to climb up to falcon aeries instead of rappelling down into them.

I asked Chouinard if there had been many climbers in California at that time — in the first half of the 1950s.

No. There were just a handful. Those were the days of wearing tennis shoes for rock climbing — there were no climbing boots, or anything like that. In fact, even five years later, if you were hiking along in a mountain area and you saw the footprint of a cleated sole, that meant a climber, and if you caught up with him you probably knew him or you both knew the same people. I got in with the rock-climbing section of the Sierra Club in Los Angeles, along with people like Royal Robbins, Bob Kamps, Mark Powell, and T. M. Herbert. Another strong climbing group was in San Francisco. They had Al Steck, one of the best American climbers, and Chuck Pratt and Warren Harding, and people who had climbed in Europe and had kept up with what was going on. In Los Angeles, we were cut off from that group. They were doing their climbing in Yosemite, and we were doing a lot of ours at Tahquitz Rock — a big rock near Palm Springs, about a thousand feet high. But it was a good area and produced some fine climbers. We got to climb all the time.

At this point, the conversation was interrupted by the appearance of Fletcher, who was learning to walk. He was attempting a delicate traverse along a living-room couch. He misjudged a maneuver between two cushions and sat down on the floor, look-ing puzzled. "Fletcher, you are a turkey," Chouinard said. Fletcher stood up shakily and continued. Chouinard went on:

When I was in high school . . . I drove out to the Wind River Range, in Wyoming to meet Don Prentice and a few others. We were going to do Gannett Peak, which is the highest mountain in Wyoming — my first real climb. Well, there were no guidebooks, and we didn't even know which peak was which. Then when we found Gannett Peak, which was nearly 14,000 feet, we couldn't decide what route to take. I thought we should go up a face, and they wanted to keep in the gullies and go off in another direction. So we split up, and I soloed the face. I never dreamed that mountains were that big. I couldn't believe it. Everything looked so short, but it went on for hours and hours. As far as I know, that was a new route on Gannett Peak, but, God, I don't know where it is — somewhere on the west side. I remember doing some hairy things, not knowing what I was doing. I had some Sears, Roebuck boots on, with no cleats, and I got up onto the snowfields near the summit — these big snowfields that drop off for thou-sands of feet. A thunderstorm was coming on. I was really psyched out, but somehow I got out of there.

I was sixteen, but all I had been doing for nearly sixteen years was climbing trees and hiking. Climbing was just natural to me. In fact, I went from the Wind Rivers directly to the Tetons, also in Wyoming, for my second climb.

I had no experience, and the climbers there didn't want to fool with me at all. Finally, I got in with a cou-ple of guys from Harvard or Dartmouth or somewhere. They were going to do a climb known as Templeton Crack, on Symmetry Spire. The crux pitch is a chimney crack — a three-sided slot where you wedge your body in and inch your way up. It is a very disagreeable climb. The crack is covered with slime, and early in the season — late June — it was about the worst thing they could have picked. Anyway, we were climbing along, and I was making believe that I knew what I was doing. They roped me up in the middle. We got up to the crux pitch, and the lead guy went up and came down, went up and came down — he really didn't want to do it. Then the other guy went up and tried it, and he couldn't do it. So they looked over at me and said, "It looks like you're going to have to do it." They roped me up first and said, "Here are the pitons." I didn't even know what pitons were. So I just faked it all and went up there and did the thing — my second climb. Pretty lucky there. You can make a lot of mistakes. And so in the next few years I went into the Tetons for three solid months every summer.

After leaving high school, Chouinard attended a junior college in the San Fernando Valley, where he studied geography for two years. He extended his climbing activities to the Canadian Rockies, where he went with Ken Weeks. "All during those years after high school, I was very, very poor, and so were the people I climbed with," Chouinard said. "We rarely got a square meal. The Alpine Club of Canada had a big basecamp, and we knew that when the climbers abandoned the camp they would leave a lot of food behind. So we waited, and carted the food back to where we were, fifteen miles away — loads and loads of potatoes, carrots, and flour. We ate ground squirrels and porcupines and wild grouse. In the Tetons once, we cleaned out some old incinerators — huge concrete incinerators — and lived inside them for the summer."

Eventually, Chouinard borrowed $825.35 in cash from his parents to pay for a forging die of a type sold by Alcoa in Los

Angeles, which he planned to use in the manufacture of carabiners. "There was this big, fancy building in Los Angeles, and this eighteen-year-old kid — me — walked in with cash to pay for a machine. They didn't know what to do with cash — how to process it. Anyway, I got it. I had a drill press and a grinder, and I did everything by myself, just about by hand. You see, up to that time all the climbing equipment here was imported from Europe, but I thought I could make better stuff." The Chouinard carabiner, made of aluminum, went through five design changes.

Next, Chouinard turned his attention to the manufacture of pitons. Until the 1940s, climbing pitons were made of malleable iron so that they could be more easily wedged into irregular cracks. These pitons were not meant to be used over and over, and on long climbs dozens of them had to be carried. Then, in 1946, John Salathé, a blacksmith living in Palo Alto, California, worked a radical change in the design of pitons. Salathé, who was born in 1901 in Switzerland, had taken up climbing in California in his mid-forties after experiencing a series of mystic visions.

Although Salathé had made pitons for his own use, they were so good that they revolutionized the construction of the climbing piton. The reason was that these pitons were just the opposite of the classic European piton — they were *not* malleable. This meant that they could be used again and again. More important, they were much safer than the malleable ones.

Chouinard continued:

> In 1957, when I started my equipment business, Salathé had almost quit climbing, and his pitons were not available anyway. Almost no one in the country was making pitons. So I bought myself a little hand forge — a coal forge — and an anvil and some hammers and some tongs. I got some books and learned blacksmithing,and started making pitons out of chromemolybdenum steel. [Now most pitons, including European ones, are made of a tough steel alloy.] All my

machinery was portable, so I just loaded it all in my car and made the stuff wherever I was. I'd sell it directly to climbers.

About the same time, I took up surfing, so I'd travel up and down the California coast from Big Sur to San Diego, staying in a place for a day or two and hammering out pitons before I moved on to another place to work some more. The same with the carabiners. They were almost handmade, and I had portable vises. I'd hold the carabiners in a vise and file on them or hand-drill them.

By that time, there were enough climbers. I'd sell the pitons and the carabiners in climbing areas in the summer, and in the winter, when there wasn't anybody climbing, I'd stockpile them to sell the next summer. I'd move from one climbing area to another, just climbing and selling my gear. I could make two pitons an hour. For years, I used to sit at the forge sometimes eight hours a day making pitons. That was hard work. I sold my pitons for a dollar and a half. At first, there was a lot of resistance to paying that much for them. The European pitons were selling for something like thirty cents. It took quite a few years before people realized how good mine were and that they were worth it.

I did not think I would make it my life's work. I never knew what I wanted to do, really. I enjoyed traveling, but I never dreamed that I was going to make a business out of selling climbing equipment, although I did know that someday climbing would become popular. I had seen some sports, like skin diving, grow from just a few freaks to an incredibly technological sport, with millions being made in the business of selling equipment for it. I knew that climbing would be the same someday, even though climbing tends to be a little

different from a lot of other sports. It attracts the intro-
verts — the real oddballs. They are the people who stay
in climbing. They get into it and stay in it for quite a
while. But in the last few years climbing has become an
"in" thing. A lot of college kids take it up, through their
outdoor clubs, and just the guy off the street wants to
get into it. But they go into it and they get out of it fast,
because they soon realize that it's not as glamorous as
they thought it was. It's not like athletics, where you get
good and do your thing in front of an audience. There
are a great many athletes who need an audience to perform to, or need at least one other person — like a partner or an opponent — watching them. In climbing, at
the end of the rope there, you're pretty much by yourself, and that burns a lot of people out.

Chouinard might have continued to wander in and out of the
mountains and up and down the California coast for years, but in
the winter of 1962 the army called him. He was in the army for
two years, including thirteen months in Korea. The previous summer, he had been climbing in Wyoming and Canada, and in the
autumn he had continued in the Shawangunks, a celebrated rock-
climbing area near New Paltz, New York.

"I had a load of hardware with me to sell, and I sold about
$300 worth," he said. "It was a lot of money for me — a lot of
money — and I was going to head back to California with it." He
got a "drive-away car" — a car to be driven across the country for
someone else. The car kept breaking down before it could be
delivered to its owner in New Mexico. As instructed, Chouinard
got it repaired each time and saved the bills. In Boulder, Colorado, he ran into Chuck Pratt, and the two of them continued.
By the time they reached New Mexico, they had fifteen cents
between them, which they used to buy three candy bars. When
they delivered the car, the owner accused them of wrecking it and
refused to pay and even called the police, who gave the two of

them five minutes to get out of town. "I had lost all my money," Chouinard recalled. "And I just sat down on the curb there and bawled."

They managed to hitchhike as far as Grants, New Mexico, where they and the driver of the car with whom they were riding were thrown into jail for three days, because the police thought that the car looked suspicious. By then, it was midwinter. They went on to Gallup, New Mexico, and there they were stranded. "We could not get a ride out of Gallup," Chouinard told me. "It was unbelievable. We were desperate. All the Santa Fe freights keep the doors of the empty railway cars locked, to keep hoboes out." So they found a Santa Fe train that was carrying automobiles.

> We checked all the automobiles and found one that had its doors open — a station wagon. We got inside — got on the floor and went to sleep. We got as far as Winslow, Arizona, where we were awakened by a flashlight. A railroad bull. He had seen that the windows of the car we were in were foggy, meaning that there had to be someone inside. We were hauled up in front of a judge and told that if we pleaded not guilty to vagrancy we'd go to trial in a month or two but that if we pleaded guilty they'd just check us out and let us go. Well, we pleaded guilty, and they locked us up for eighteen days. They gave us one slice of Wonder bread in the morning and a bowl of oatmeal and a bowl of pinto beans at night with a slice of Wonder bread. Pratt was allergic to oatmeal, so he gave me his oatmeal and I gave him my Wonder bread. He came out of jail weighing 115 pounds; he had lost twenty-five pounds. After a while, they had me working on a garbage truck with some Indians, collecting garbage. That was some trip. To top it all off, when we got home, we both were drafted.

Chouinard was sent to Fort Ord, in California, for basic training, and then to Huntsville, Alabama, where he studied guided-missile mechanics before being sent to Korea. At Fort Ord, he was told that he would be issued a three-day pass if he got the highest score in his company, made up of some 200 soldiers, in a physical-training test — grenade throwing, push-ups, and the like. Such was his dislike of the army that he did get the highest score. It turned out that some of the climbers he knew — Ken Weeks, T. M. Herbert — had also won such competitions in the army. "It was not because we were physically superior," Chouinard said. "It was just because we had to have those three days."

Before leaving for Korea, he encountered a Korean who said that his brother was the best climber in Korea and that Chouinard should be sure to look him up. This turned out to be nearly impossible. The army was not liberal in giving weekend passes in Korea, and the men hardly ever got off the base — in theory, at least.

> To get free time to go climbing, I had to cause a lot of trouble. So I went on hunger strikes — a couple of quite long hunger strikes — and I refused to follow orders. I purposely acted eccentric — half crazy — until they finally let me alone. The company commander put me in with some civilians who were working on missiles. All I had to do was to turn some generator on in the morning and then turn it off at night. The rest of the time, I went climbing.
>
> There is some great climbing near Seoul — big domes and pinnacles, beautiful granite. Once I got in touch with the Korean climbers, they kept a set of civilian clothes for me at their house. I had my climbing gear sent over from the States. The climbing routes that existed in Korea then had been established by the Japanese during their occupation. The Koreans learned to climb from the Japanese. All that the Koreans wanted to do was to repeat the old Japanese routes.

There were such a lot of new routes to be done, and finally we just went out and did them. Once we started, the Koreans really got behind the idea. We did some high-quality climbing, even bivouac climbs, and everyone in the mountains got to know me. It was almost like not being in the army. So it turned out that Korea, in the end, was a pretty good experience.

When Chouinard was shipped back to the States, the army sent him to the Presidio, in San Francisco, where he was assigned to maintain a baseball diamond. A climbing friend, Douglas Tompkins, had started a climbing shop not far away, and each morning he would arrive at the base on a motorcycle. He would call up Chouinard's sergeant and shout over the phone, "This is Major So-and-So! Where the hell is that goddamn Chouinard? I want him here at the library in ten minutes. Ten minutes! Do you hear me?" The sergeant would say, "Chouinard, get over to the library on the double. Major So-and-So wants to see you." Chouinard and Tompkins would then go off on the motorcycle for a day's outing.

Chouinard was separated from the army in July 1964, and headed directly for Yosemite, where, with Chuck Pratt and Warren Harding, he participated in a first ascent of the south face of Mount Watkins.

That fall, Chouinard went back to making climbing equipment. "I came out with my first mail-order catalog," he told me. "It was a one-sheet mimeographed price list. At the bottom of the list, it said, 'Don't expect speedy delivery in the months of May, June, July, August, and September.' " That was climbing season.

Until 1965, Chouinard's shop was in the backyard of his parents' house in Burbank. Then he rented some old tin shacks, also in Burbank, for a total of sixty dollars a month. But he was spending so much time driving back and forth to the beach to surf that, in 1965, he decided to move to Ventura, and, in 1966, he set up a small shop near a railroad siding there, next to an abandoned slaughterhouse. Now Chouinard's company, the Great Pacific Iron Works, has taken over the site of both the siding and the slaughterhouse. It was at the time of the move to Ventura that Chouinard went into partnership with Frost, who was from Orange County, and with whom Chouinard had climbed in Yosemite. "Making hardware was getting a little more complex," Chouinard said. "The demand was such that I couldn't make things fast enough by hand anymore. I had to go into making things by machine — designing sophisticated dies, and so on. That's where Frost came in especially handy. He had been an aeronautical engineer, and it was really valuable to have engineering experience."

Chouinard and Frost began with two or three employees, and there were thirty-two at the time of my visit. In the early days, the workers were usually itinerant climbers. "They wanted to work for a while, then they'd take off and go climbing," Chouinard said. "Often, we'd hire British climbers who needed a few bucks. It was a very loose organization, and in some ways it still is."

Perhaps the most extraordinary of the British climbers who worked for them was the late Donald Whillans. Books have been written about Whillans. He was born in Salford, England, in 1933, and got into climbing after the war. In the past, British climbing had been the province of a relatively upper-class segment of society. After the war, however, a number of working men discovered climbing as an escape from a life of drudgery, and they became known as "the hard men." Whillans, a plumber by trade, was the quintessential hard man. He was about five feet three and was constructed like a small tank.

Chouinard told me a Whillans story that I hadn't heard before. One afternoon in the 1960s, he and Whillans found themselves in a small cafe in the Alps. On the terrace were two substantially constructed Continental climbers with two pretty women. To pass the time, the climbers had taken the parasols out of two heavy concrete umbrella stands and stuck the stands together to make a barbell. They succeeded in lifting it a couple of times, to the admiring glances of the women. At the bar, Whillans had been drinking his pint and watching this performance with growing distaste. Finally, he put down his glass and said, "Right." He strode out onto the terrace and began lifting the barbell up and down, up and down, indefinitely. Chouinard thought that Whillans might continue for the rest of the afternoon, but in time he lost interest and went back inside to finish his drink. The Continental climbers and the women went off in search of another cafe.

At the end of his career, Whillans turned to lecturing, mainly to workmen's clubs in Britain. Chouinard sells something called the Whillans Sit Harness, a device made of nylon webbing that a climber wears like a parachute harness. The climbing rope is tied to the harness so that a climber who falls will not be cut in two by the rope around his waist. Most climbers now wear harnesses of some sort, and these have all but eliminated the kind of accident in which a climber falls, is suspended in midair at the end of the rope, and suffocates within a few moments.

After several months during which Whillans tried his hand at various sorts of shopwork, Chouinard found that his services could be dispensed with. Whillans retaliated for this affront in his autobiography, *Portrait of a Mountaineer,* by neglecting to mention Chouinard at all, even though he and Chouinard had done quite a bit of climbing together.

In any event, Chouinard's Ventura business began with a few thousand dollars in sales in 1966 and doubled its sales each year thereafter for five years in a row. Chouinard decided that he had better look elsewhere for his work force. In 1971, he brought in the first of what eventually became half a dozen Koreans. At the time of my visit, there were five, along with an Argentine toolmaker and several Mexican craftsmen. Malinda Chouinard also works at the Iron Works, and so does Vincent Stanley, Chouinard's nephew and sales manager. Stanley is responsible for one of my favorite lines in the 1976 catalog, of which 35,000 copies were distributed. In writing of Mountain Spectacles, goggles that filter ultraviolet light, he notes, "The round shape is tasteful and makes you look like a large fly."

The atmosphere of the Great Pacific Iron Works is rather like that of a large family. Many of the employees live on the beach, close to the Chouinards. When I visited Ventura, the newest employee was Kenneth Deprez, a thirty-three-year-old business graduate of Stanford, who had been at the Iron Works for a couple of weeks. Before that, Deprez had been general manager of Camp 7, a company near Boulder, Colorado, that is noted for its sleeping bags and down jackets. Deprez had the task of introducing modern accounting and business methods into what had been, and still is, largely an informal company. To handle several million dollars in annual sales and all the inventory problems that such a sales volume poses, Deprez has installed a computer and has reorganized things, and he feels that everything will now run by itself. While I was there, a Ventura banker dropped in and was taken for a tour of the premises. It was his first visit, and he appeared to be rather astonished by the extent of it.

For someone with a fondness for climbing equipment, a tour through the Iron Works can be an incredibly satisfying experience. There is a retail shop, in which all the Chouinard-Frost products are displayed and sold. It includes a small climbing library and a little piton museum in which there are some original Salathe' pitons, some of the early, hand-forged Chouinard pitons, and a primitive RURP. There are row upon row of bright-colored down jackets, tents suspended from the ceiling, sleeping bags hanging from the walls, climbing shoes, ropes, and display cases full of chocks and pitons.

Chouinard, who once designed a rock shoe (the Shoenard) for a bootmaker, once remarked that the best boot he knew about for rock climbing was a mountain goat's hoof. It has a hard perimeter, with a soft interior for adhesion. If he could figure out how to duplicate this in rubber, leather, or the like, he said, he might go into the shoe business.

After visiting the retail shop, I wandered into the factory

behind it. Chouinard's old portable forge is there, but idle. The machining is done now with stamp dies and presses. A block of metal goes in, a piton comes out. Workers were busy adjusting carabiner gates and ice-ax handles. In one corner stood a wooden board several feet long to which Chouinard had attached a large number of irregularly shaped wooden blocks, to make it resemble a rock face. It was rigged up so that he could place chocks in the fissures in all sorts of combinations and was designed to illustrate how clean-climbing equipment works. When I saw it, it was full of chocks with bright-colored rope loops through them.

While I was wandering around, I asked Chouinard about the economics of the climbing and backpacking industry.

> It's a funny business. It started traditionally with very, very low retail markups — 20 or 30 percent. Now the markup is 40 — which is still low — and it has taken a long time to reach that. If a carabiner, for example, were an item for yachting, it would cost $15.00. But it's an item for climbing, so it costs $3.65. I don't make any money selling hardware. The best I have ever done in twenty years of business is a net profit of two and a half percent one year. That's pretty bad. I generally end up with one and a half percent from the hardware.
>
> It's the clothing [now sold through Patagonia] that subsidizes the hardware. The dies that we use to make pitons, and so on, cost thousands of dollars, and often I don't get my money back for five to ten years. We want to manufacture old-fashioned hiking and climbing clothes — the kind that never wear out. [I had just bought a pair of thick corduroy hiking shorts in the retail shop.] Take that pair of climbing shorts you bought. They are made in England. There is one machine in an old mill in Lancashire — a mill that goes back to the Industrial Revolution and used to run on water power — that turns out that kind of corduroy.

Workmen's clothes were made out of it before denim was used. Well, only a handful of old men know how to make the stuff on that machine. Whenever we need some corduroy, seven of them come out of retirement and crank up the machine to run some off for us. You can't wear those shorts out. They'll last forever. That's the kind of stuff we want to make. It will cost more initially, but it will last. The climbing and backpacking business is not like the ski business, which is incredible. A pair of plastic ski boots that costs fourteen or fifteen dollars to make sells for a one hundred dollars or more. The backpacking and climbing business is very ethical — very, very clean — and people are really getting their money's worth out of it. I make a comfortable living. I don't have any money in the bank, but I have a living, and that's all I want out of it.

While I was in Ventura, Chouinard decided one day to go up into the High Sierra near June Lake, not far from Yosemite, to test a new pair of crampons that he had designed, and also a pair of ultralight plastic ski bindings. He asked if I would like to come along.

Eight hours later, after a beautiful drive up the eastern slopes of the Sierra range, we reached June Lake, a small mountain town. We were joined by Doug Robinson, the professional guide and writer of articles for the Chouinard catalogs. Robinson, who is in his fifties and is about the same height as Chouinard, lives in the Mammoth Lakes area, not far from Bishop, California. He and Chouinard, between them, have accounted for most of the difficult ice climbs in the Sierra.

The next morning was extremely cold, with the temperature about ten degrees and gusts of icy wind blowing plumes of snow off the tops of the nearby mountains. After breakfast, we headed for the pass. There was limited room in the cab, so Doug Robinson, who was heavily equipped for winter climbing, volunteered to sit outside, in the truckbed. He bundled up in his down jacket, and off we went. We stopped near the top of the pass, at about 10,000 feet. The wind was unbelievable; Chouinard and Robinson estimated that there were gusts of sixty- and seventy-mile-per-hour. I am not capable of vertical ice climbing in a sixty-mile-per-hour wind, so after they started out I stationed myself a bit down the road, where I could get a view.

The climbers descended into a canyon. From the bottom of the canyon, a tiny ribbon of vertical ice led back up to the top. Chouinard, who was the first to tackle it, had an ice axe and a small ice hammer. He hit the ice above his head with the hammer until it stuck. After that, he kicked the front points of one crampon in hard, then did the same with the other foot. He next put in the other ice axe and delicately shifted his weight off of one foot and kicked it in at a higher level. He moved up, repeating the process again and again. The ice looked dark blue and nearly vertical. If it had been higher, Chouinard would have put in an ice screw — a piton that is literally screwed into the ice — for protection. But his confidence in his technique was such that he simply went on up to the top. I watched anxiously, knowing that there could be no checking a fall on ice like that. Chouinard made it look as easy as walking up a path. When he got to the top, he lowered a rope so that the others could climb up more easily. I watched for a few more minutes and then, shivering with cold, retreated to the truck.

A little while later, I spotted Robinson climbing the icy side of the gully alone, and soon afterward, Chouinard and the rest came along and we headed back to June Lake. I was ready for lunch and the warmth of the indoors, but such matters seemed to be far from Chouinard's mind.

"My favorite place to climb is Scotland in the winter," he remarked. "The weather is bad every day, and you know it's going to be bad, so you go out in it anyway. Your hair freezes, your beard freezes, and you come home like an icicle. You're always only a few miles from the pub. The climbing is one foot on ice and the other on rock. That's what I really like."

Lou Reichardt. *Photo by Geoff Tabin*

A Climber of Genius

LOU REICHARDT

By Geoffrey Tabin

[From OUTSIDE, October 1989]

It's a chilly evening in Yosemite Valley, and when Lou Reichardt and I arrive at the Mountain Room bar after a day of climbing, the place is jammed. The party doesn't do much for Reichardt, who had attempted to skirt this evening by suggesting we stay in camp and eat Hershey bars for dinner. As we make our way through the crowd of mostly young, mostly color-coordinated climbers, you can't help but notice that middle-aged Reichardt is wearing a patched down coat, torn wool knickers, and thick, black-framed glasses held together by paper clips and tape. He looks like a theoretical scientist. He is.

"Look at Hubel's and Weisel's work on the importance of visual experience to normal cortex development," he tells me at the bar, commencing a forty-minute review of contemporary neurophysiology. That none of the nearby patrons add their two cents is no surprise. But you'd think somebody would at least recognize Dr. Louis French Reichardt, arguably America's foremost Himalayan mountaineer.

Reichardt has climbed three 8,000-meter peaks, a feat that only three other Americans — John Roskelley, Carlos Buhler, and

Chris Pizzo — have matched, and he's the only American to summit both of the world's two tallest peaks, Everest and K2. Moreover, he climbed Everest by way of the East Face, an approach considered suicidal from the time it was first surveyed in 1921, and reached the top of K2 without supplemental oxygen — another first. He's also thought to be the only climber to lug a backpack to the summit of Everest with the airline luggage tags intact and the first to read *The Universe and Dr. Einstein*, at 27,000 feet on K2.

Until recently, often upon the solution of some monstrous scientific problem, Reichardt would simply hang up his lab coat every three years or so and hike into the mountains to tackle something absurdly difficult. Months after he solved the long-standing mystery of how a cell differentiates itself, he climbed 26,810-foot Dhaulagiri. His widely applauded work on neuronal plasticity preceded an ascent of Nanda Devi, a climb so technically demanding that some characterized it as the best American effort in the Himalaya in nearly a decade.

But alas, Reichardt hasn't climbed a blessed thing for six years. A few years ago, he scratched from an expedition up Kanchenjunga, the world's third-highest mountain, after learning that a research grant might be in jeopardy if he left. He's also passed on expeditions to Cho Oyu, Everest, Broad Peak, and the north ridge of K2. Since climbing Everest in 1983, Reichardt's only adventures have been of the purely cerebral kind, in his neurology lab at the University of California, San Francisco. There, at the nether reaches of the in-vitro frontier, Reichardt lays one brain cell next to another and pursues his field's $64,000 question: Why do similar nerve cells sometimes grow and sometimes not? Why do they fail to regenerate after a spinal-cord injury, yet succeed if the nerve damage is in an arm or leg?

Research in this area is still in its infancy, but Reichardt's previous accomplishments in both cellular biology and brain physiology (his resume runs to fourteen pages) have made him an academic superstar. "Lou is one of the leading researchers of his generation," says Zach Hall, chair of physiology at the University of California, San Francisco. Reichardt has been awarded two of science's most prestigious grants — the Guggenheim and the Howard Hughes — and he recently declined a deanship, an endowed professorship, and virtually unlimited research funds from Baylor Medical School. More than one colleague has mentioned him as a leading candidate for the Nobel Prize. "If I hadn't lost so many brain cells to high-altitude hypoxia," he jokes, "I'd already have been to Stockholm."

Reichardt's long layoff from climbing, however, may be nearing an end. Several months ago, after learning that a National Institutes of Health grant would endow his lab through 1994, Reichardt pronounced himself ready again. "I am an incredibly fortunate person," he says. "If science and discovery are important to you, there could not be a better job. But this is the time to go. I've never been this far from a grant proposal." The challenge of a climbing comeback could be overwhelming, but that's always been the draw for Reichardt. If there has been one clear pattern in his life, it has been his penchant for selecting outrageously difficult problems both in science and climbing. "What is exciting," he says, speaking of mountaineering but perhaps also of science, "is that the challenges almost always come from unexpected places." Would he start back with something moderate, a peak in South America, perhaps, or Alaska? "Maybe Namcha Barwa," he muses electing a 25,445-foot Himalayan giant, the highest unclimbed peak in the world.

Reichardt and I had been teammates on the 1981 and 1983 Everest East Face expeditions, and when I first visited him for this story, I was impressed at how fit his six-foot-one, 180-pound frame appeared. It looked as though Reichardt had been confined to a gym, not the laboratory, for the last six years. Particularly formidable were his hulking forearms, ridged with thick veins and defined by a Harris Tweed jacket a size or two too small. I asked if he'd been working out. "I haven't had any physical exercise in years," he said, smiling. "I've been totally committed to science."

It's moments like these that make climbers wonder about Reichardt. His only regular training is a three-block walk to the bus stop and a one-flight stair-climb to his office, yet on expeditions, at severe altitude, he normally carries what seems to be twice the load at twice the speed of anyone else. Some say he must be a physiological freak, a person whose respiratory system is perfectly crafted for work at altitude. Others contend that his mind simply drives his body past such niggling distractions as tedium, discomfort, and pain. Finally, there's the rumor that Reichardt *does* train — by spending long hours in his laboratory's cold room. He denies it, but a coworker claims to have discovered him in the room wearing only underwear.

Reichardt is a puzzlement for other reasons. While other climbers clamor for donations of state-of-the-art equipment and mountaineering clothing, Reichardt prefers a 1969-issue backpack and a collection of hideous sun hats. He seeks no publicity. He's written no climbing books and just a few climbing articles, and he often mumbles about his deeds as if to make sure he'll never be quoted. ("I just wanted to, well, climb some things," he says of his summits of Dhaulagiri, Nanda Devi, K2, and Everest.) He says so little at times, but clearly knows so much, that it can be unsettling. "Lou is the smartest guy I've ever met, but we don't have much to talk about," says John Roskelley, who's been on four expeditions with Reichardt. Once, while waiting out a storm at 24,500 feet on Dhaulagiri, the pair didn't have a single conversation in ten days. "We weren't mad at each other," says Roskelley. "We just didn't have anything to say."

The same might be said by his scientific colleagues, few of whom see the merit in risking one's life on a mountain or the logic of exposing a brain — especially Reichardt's brain — to potential damage from prolonged stays at altitude. On campus, a distracted Reichardt will often scoot right past acquaintances, responding to a bright hello with . . . nothing. Conversely, a joke from Reichardt is liable to leave lab folks pondering for days. "He has a very elliptical, highly condensed sense of humor," explains

Zach Hall. "He'll say something, laugh, and then move along. It might be hours before you'll get the link he's made between disparate things. It's as if he's three steps ahead of everyone."

The son of a prize-winning architect and a housewife who later became a peace and civil-rights activist, Louis Reichardt was born and raised in Pasadena, California. His parents, both avid backpackers, began taking him along on trips into the Sierra when he was ten. Soon, Reichardt says, "I was wandering off by myself, climbing anything that was nearby. I think it drove my parents nuts."

He attended Midland High School, a tiny, all-male boarding school near Los Angeles. "Lou was tall and awkward, with thick, greasy glasses," says Midland roommate Joe Esherick, recalling his first impression. "No way, I thought, would he be athletic. But he was." Reichardt, Esherick, and a third classmate took a Sierra Club climbing course and made forays to nearby Taquitz Rock. "We were pretty unsophisticated," says Reichardt, an average beginner. "I remember this one long, crazy climb. It was before we started using nuts and things, and at one point I was sixty feet above my anchor. I had no business doing anything like that, but I finally made that damn thing. It made me appreciate the certain thrill in living beyond where someone should rationally live."

Perfect scores on his math SATs and his French boards earned Reichardt a National Merit Scholarship and a spot at Harvard in the fall of 1960. "It was kind of embarrassing," he says. "At Harvard they put me into third-year French. When I came to class they started reading poetry, and I didn't understand a word of it. It was clear I'd scored twice what I should have on the test." Reichardt intended to major in philosophy. "I was never in high school science fairs or anything like that," he says. "I had endless ideas, but I could never get close to the finished product." But he changed his mind soon after taking a class taught by James Watson, one of the discoverers of DNA. "The things he was saying were tremendously exciting. It was obvious that society was becoming driven by science."

75

He joined the renowned Harvard Mountaineering Club but never went on an expedition. "I had school to worry about, and I had to work in the summer," says Reichardt. He did fit in some rock climbing and tried ice climbing during summer vacations back in California.

In 1964, Reichardt went to Cambridge on a Fulbright Scholarship, then to Stanford, where he first attacked the problem of how the myriad cells of a human body, all of which are genetically identical, differentiate to become muscle, nerve, bone, and blood. His academic elders considered the problem of gene expression far too complex for a Ph.D. candidate in physiology. Reichardt persisted anyway, taking on the topic in his doctoral thesis.

It was at Stanford that Reichardt got a reputation as a promising mountaineer and rock climber. He would unwind from an eighty-hour week in the lab by marching fifty miles in a weekend, typically climbing three 7,000-foot summits en route. His fortitude was spectacular, but there was perhaps no uglier stride in all of North America — the result of a college knee injury and his habit of taking one stride to anyone else's two. He also climbed in Yosemite with a Palo Alto crowd that included Paul Gerhard, one of the Bay Area's best climbers. Gerhard invited him on an expedition to Mount McKinley in 1967, the first of three trips they would take to Alaska.

The weather was unusually bad that year — seven people died in a storm that kept most climbers from reaching the top — but Reichardt and Gerhard made it. "Mentally, going to McKinley was a much bigger step than going to the Himalaya," says Reichardt. "It was the first time I was really away from everything." Afterward, Gerhard pushed to get Reichardt on a 1969 American team to Dhaulagiri. Three weeks before the team departed, a spot opened up for him. "I think I got to go because I was the only one without a real job," says Reichardt. "The Himalaya weren't really in my life plan."

The expedition went well at first. But on April 28, Reichardt was on the glacier beneath Dhaulagiri at 17,500 feet, taking photographs while his teammates worked to bridge a crevasse. Later he would write in his diary:

> It began with the noise of an avalanche, then a mutual realization that it might hit us. Then there was silence. No screams, just silence. First came the realization that I was not hurt. It couldn't have been that bad. Then came the discovery that nothing was there — no tents, no cache, no ice ax, and no friends. A moment of hope. It was just a snow avalanche. Hey, Boyd! Hey, Dave! Hey, Vin! I'm alive and OK; here to dig you out. Just let me know where you are. No answers."

Reichardt performed two exhaustive searches, first by himself and later with the expedition members who had been at basecamp at the time of the avalanche — but no bodies were recovered. Seven of the finest climbers in the world were dead. By a quirk of fate, Reichardt, who had been in the middle of them moments before, was left to tell the story. He returned to America and traveled from San Francisco to Connecticut to visit the friends and families of the victims. "I wasn't ready to go back to the research," he says. "I was pretty blown away."

Reichardt resumed his graduate work several months later and published "Regulation of Repressor Synthesis and Early Gene Expression by Bacteriophage and Lambda Virus " in 1972. The dissertation provided a model to explain how one cell develops differently from the next. The understanding of gene expression was radically altered by Reichardt's work, and today it is one of the basics in any medical school curriculum. "I think all of my promotions and appointments still come from my dissertation," he says. "It's the only really important thing I've done." Hall, along with others, thought it worthy of Nobel Prize consideration.

In 1973, Reichardt went back to Dhaulagiri with another strong team. Many climbers were stunned to hear that he was returning to the mountain where he had witnessed one of American climbing's worst tragedies. "Lou carried the heaviest loads,. pushing hard day after day," says Roskelley, who was amazed by Reichardt's strength and intensity. Teammate Jim Morrissey remembers a day when he and Reichardt hiked into basecamp. Subtly, they both accelerated the tempo, turning the trek into something of a race. It ended in a dead heat. The next day, while hiking at 6,500 feet, they learned that a teammate had cerebral edema at 14,000 feet. They took off, and at 11,000 feet Morrissey doubled over sick. As his partner raced on, Morrissey asked, "God, Lou, how can you keep going?" Reichardt put it this way: "Mind over matter."

They pushed on to 24,500 feet and waited out a storm for ten days, then moved into the so-called death zone without supplementary oxygen. On the way down, Reichardt's suspenders snapped and his thick glasses fogged. In a kind of Himalayan Charlie Chaplin skit, his pants fell to his knees whenever he reached up to wipe his glasses. He also suffered a mild case of ataxia, a loss of coordination and sense of balance. Although Morrissey offered help, mostly he observed in bemused wonder as Reichardt stubbornly marched into basecamp under his own power, tail bared to the wind. There, Reichardt diagnosed his ataxia as resulting from a minor stroke in the cerebellum. At that moment, it occurred to him, his vocation and avocation were for the first time in perfect harmony. "In mountaineering there's real discovery, pushing of limits," says Reichardt, who counts Dhaulagiri, his first Himalayan peak, as his favorite. "You live on the edge, figuring out what you need to do to stay on the right side of the line. Science is sort of similar."

In fact, when he returned from Dhaulagiri, life on another edge — the scientific edge — was foremost in Reichardt's mind.

After my dissertation, I could have coasted. I could've stayed in cellular biology for the rest of my life or gone into something new and wild. I decided to go into neurological biology even though I didn't know much about it. It was considered really far-out, the wildest type of biology there was. It was a risk — I might not have ended up under an avalanche, but I could have been left without a grant, which is scientific death.

As it turned out, Reichardt made the right decision, producing brilliant work as a postdoctoral fellow at Harvard from 1974 to 1976 and attracting job offers from the major research centers and universities across the country. He put them all off, at least for the summer, and went to India instead.

The infamous Nanda Devi expedition was a tortured one from start to finish, culminating in the tragic death of co-leader Will Unsoeld's twenty-one-year-old daughter. Reichardt generally stayed out of the number of squabbles that afflicted the expedition and partly for that reason was elected climbing leader. He toiled at shepherding the large, feuding team up the 25,645-foot mountain. Eventually, he, Roskelley, and Jim States — each carrying seventy-five pounds of gear over the route's most difficult section, a thousand-foot sheer vertical buttress beneath the summit area — pushed to Camp Four. When it was time to summit a few days later, Reichardt balked. According to his altimeter, the trio had 1,500 feet to go. It was already midday, and if the altimeter was accurate, they'd probably have to bivouac without any gear. Reichardt trusted the reading and wanted to retreat. The others refused. Against his better judgment, Reichardt made the ascent. The three summited at 2 P.M. on September 1, returned to camp before dark, and proved Reichardt wrong about the altimeter and right about his theory — that the beauty of an expedition begins when things start to screw up.

Harvard, MIT, and Cal Tech had offered posts to Reichardt back in the spring, but only the University of California, San Francisco, agreed to let him take prolonged leaves of absence to climb. "He was the first person I hired," says Zach Hall, who started the university's neuroscience program, now regarded as one of the best in the country. Hall signed Reichardt on the strength of his Harvard work — he had pioneered a technique to distinguish among the many types of brain cells, allowing the neuroanatomists to study rare populations of neurons — but the two had been friends since meeting at Stanford in 1967.

"His stamina is amazing," says Hall. "His style has never been slick or graceful, but he has this tremendous ability to focus his energies and get things done, to cut right through to what's important." The parallels to his climbing style are unmistakable. Reichardt has often said that when he's on the mountain he thinks of nothing but climbing, and when he's in the lab, nothing but science. "He'll appear oblivious sometimes," says Hall, "but it's more that he's recognized that what's going on is not important."

In 1978, an American expedition was gathering for an assault on K2. Americans had been trying to climb the world's second-highest mountain since the 1930s, and although Reichardt was at the crux of his new research, he couldn't say no.

The Karakorum Range suffered from a series of terrible storms in 1978. As the American group trekked in, they met a beleaguered British expedition that had already given up on K2. The Americans went on, changing strategy daily on account of the weather. Reichardt was again the pacesetter. "Without him, we probably would have turned back," expedition member Rick Ridgeway wrote later. When it came time to make a summit bid, Reichardt's oxygen system wouldn't turn on and he fell behind Jim Wickwire, his summit partner. He discarded the seventeen-pound unit, dumped his pack and parka, and caught Wickwire just below the summit. "Tell me if I exhibit any bizarre behavior," said Reichardt, worried that the lack of oxygen would impair his judgment. A short time later the pair walked onto the 28,250-foot summit. "He lacked what, to the rest of us, was the main limiter of our efforts — feedback from the body to the mind," Ridgeway wrote. "Lou's body just carried out the mind's orders."

* * *

LOU REICHARDT

Lou Reichardt is at the helm of the family minivan, calmly piloting his four children home from a church dinner. In the backseat, Anna, Ben, Christian, and Isa, ages four to twelve, are attempting to lever a heavy pack up to the front seat. Cries of "Louie! Louie!" drown out conversation. Seven-year-old Ben begins to scale the front seat when Reichardt spies him in the rearview mirror. "Now Ben, it is imperative that you remain stationary and fasten your seat belt," he says. By the time the Reichardt clan arrives at its modest stucco home in the hills overlooking the Cal-San Francisco Medical Center, the noise has approached the supersonic.

Reichardt's wife Kathy is away this afternoon, and he valiantly attempts to attend to a visitor as the four precocious youngsters spread out. Outside in the driveway, one has inexplicably dropped a rotten Halloween pumpkin on the hood of Reichardt's Toyota truck. Inside, Isa confronts her dad. "Louie," lectures the twelve-year-old, "you have already inflicted severe psychological damage by missing my birthday. Don't you think it would be a mistake to miss my school play?" Reichardt agrees that it would.

These days Reichardt is much more reluctant to take large chunks of time away from his wife and children. "My first priority is my family," says Reichardt, who rarely goes anywhere socially without the gang. "Ever since I became a father, I'm not as willing to stick my neck out."

There are occasional exceptions to this rule, such as Reichardt's trip to Everest in 1981. Hidden in Tibet, the mountain's East Face is its largest and steepest side. It was first seen by Western climbers during the 1921 British Everest Reconnaissance, when George Leigh-Mallory declared it to be unclimbable, concluding that "other men, less wise, might attempt this way, but emphatically it was not for us." The British moved around to the north, where all subsequent Tibetan assaults on the mountain took place.

But in 1981, the Chinese sold Americans a permit to make the first climbing attempt on the East Face, and Reichardt was named the climbing leader. The standard expedition bickering soon erupted into open warfare. Unaccustomed to the role of massaging overamped egos and disinclined to referee the disputes, Reichardt instead showed his leadership by hefting double loads up the mountain. His understated diplomacy failed, and six climbers, including Roskelley, abandoned the effort. Some on the expedition suggested an easier route, but on that subject Reichardt was uncompromising. "There is no greater challenge for a climber than an untested face," Reichardt once said, and clearly he had no intention of substituting anything less demanding. The handicapped squad did find a route up the initial 4,500-foot sheer buttress but stalled from lack of support at 22,000 feet.

Reichardt returned to the East Face in 1983, so determined to climb it that he had actually run "up to five miles in a single day," worked out on pull-up bars, and squeezed a grip exerciser. Led by Jim Morrissey, veteran alpinist George Lowe, and Reichardt, the team quickly worked its way up the mountain. When it came time to choose a summit team, Reichardt was picked along with Carlos Buhler and Kim Momb. Equipment problems delayed Reichardt on the morning of the summit push, and he was forced to climb hurriedly to catch his partners. He finally tracked them down, six hours later, where the East Face merges with the southeast summit ridge at 27,500 feet. From there, Reichardt broke trail through deep snow all the way to the south summit. For the sake of speed, the trio climbed without a rope, knowing what a slip on the exposed ridge would mean. At 2 P.M., thirteen hours after leaving camp, Reichardt, Momb, and Buhler completed the first ascent of the East Face. "Nobody ever believes this, but I never go on any of my trips expecting to reach the summit," says Reichardt, who has been the first to the summit each time one of his expeditions has landed someone on top. "In the case of Everest, I'd never in my life dreamed I'd actually get up the thing."

Reichardt's strength on Everest gave rise to still more theorizing about how he could be so good at altitude. Reichardt disputed the notion that he is some kind of genetic freak uniquely adapted for high-altitude work. "One of the first times I went high, I had a terrible case of altitude sickness," he says. "I was dehydrated when I started the climb, and forgot to bring a water bottle. I had a splitting headache and dry heaves."

Reichardt knows that less oxygen in the air can be compensated for by deeper, more rapid breathing. But faster breathing means you exhale more, losing moisture and acid. Your blood becomes alkaline, a problem that the kidneys deal with by selectively excreting alkaline urine and saving acid. Together, the heavy breathing and the kidneys' compensatory mechanism lead to dehydration. Old climbers' lore holds that at altitude you should "drink until your piss is gin-clear."

Reichardt lives by this rule. "On Everest, I never saw him without a water bottle in his hand," says Buhler. Proper hydration is one part of Reichardt's systematic, ever-logical approach to altitude. He starts his daily carries of supplies before dawn and pushes himself to go twice as fast as most climbers in order to finish his chores early. He then spends the rest of the day melting snow to drink, making sure to shield his head from the high-altitude sun. Never one for small talk, he eschews most expedition socializing to rest in his tent. He often forces down huge gulps of high-calorie food with his liquid, even if he's not hungry. On Everest, Carl Tobin says, it wasn't uncommon to see Reichardt stuff four or five Almond Roca candy bars into already-bulging cheeks. Reichardt says this regimen of maximal exertion followed by concentrated drinking, eating, and rest allows him to work hard each day. And that when it's time for a summit bid, he's both acclimatized and fit.

Reichardt's climbing partners remain unconvinced that it's as simple as he makes it sound. "Lou is a thoroughbred at altitude," says Roskelley. "Put him on a mountain and it's like he was born to run." Physiological research supports that notion. People who acclimatize best to high altitude breathe harder and faster when the oxygen content in their blood drops even a little bit. That explains why marathon runners, who endure maximal exertion with a minimum of huffing and puffing, often fare poorly at altitude. Reichardt, who sprinted in high school breathes heavily with the slightest exertion, even at sea level, giving the impression that he's horribly out of shape. To the contrary, his overactive respiratory response combines with what must be a genetically humongous lung capacity to make him superior at altitude.

Jim Morrissey, a partner on five expeditions, has another theory:

> Lou is unstoppable, not because of physiology, but because of attitude. He's one of the most powerful, capable, and determined mountaineers in the world because he's more focused and driven than anyone else. He also has an incredibly high pain threshold.

Says Reichardt: "Science and climbing are intellectual exercises. There are specific things in each that you just suffer through."

> This is like cancer research ten years ago. It's intense, but the pressures aren't the same as on expeditions, where people will literally hate each other. People aren't scared in the same way. Basically, my job is to figure out how things work, to try and think of good ideas, raise new questions. The stuff I do in the lab is in some ways not so different from, say, the problem of how to get two food bags from Camp Two to Camp Four.

In the six years since Everest, Reichardt's mind has been exclusively devoted to science. Early in his tenure at Cal-San Francisco Medical Center, he did pioneering work with nerve growth factors, the proteins that decide whether neurons live or die. Their existence was cause for much optimism in the scientific community. If scientists could stimulate nerve cells to grow, they could regenerate damaged brain tissue. "Most solutions are only half-solutions," Reichardt cautions about the immense problem before him. The research could occupy a lifetime, maybe much longer, which may be why Reichardt is ready to go climbing again. "One reason he likes to climb," says Kathy Reichardt, "is that when you climb a mountain, the problem is either done or not done."

Since 1983, Reichardt's work-and-family schedule has allowed for exactly one weekend of rock climbing each year. Still, nobody doubts his ability to knock off another Himalayan giant, be it Kanchenjunga or Namcha Barwa. Even with the long respite, he has spent more time above 24,000 feet than any other American. And at forty-six, he isn't unusually old for a Himalayan climber, many of whom reach their prime in their thirties, even early forties. "If you can climb one," he says, "you should be able to climb them all." Reichardt may again prove his mastery over both science and climbing, but that isn't ultimately what he cares to be known for. "My goal is to have children who remember me fondly," he says, the dizzying complexities of two brilliant careers unerringly simplified to the most obvious and important of responsibilities. "There is nothing that gives me more pleasure than being with my children."

Last spring, Reichardt returned to Yosemite for a full week. The object was to relax, but there was something else to do, too. Twelve-year-old Isa Reichardt had told her father she wanted to climb Mount Rainier. He agreed to lead her up the mountain if she met his criteria: first, she would have to hike an advanced trail in Yosemite. Next would come a climb of Mount Shasta, which would reveal her capability on snow and ice. Finally, she'd have to summit Mount Whitney, California's highest peak, to determine how she fared at altitude. While the park burst with early-spring dogwood and a thousand waterfalls, Reichardt timed his daughter as she hiked up to the Yosemite Falls Trail. He reports that she knocked off the three miles and 2,700 vertical feet in well under the allotted time. Mount Shasta is next. Although the preparation may seem excessive to Isa, she should be thankful. They *could* be going to the cold-room.

George Lowe. *Photo by Chris Jones*

Boy George

GEORGE LOWE

By Alison Osius

[From CLIMBING, December 1992]

At 22,800 feet on the North Ridge of Latok I in Pakistan, George Lowe and Michael Kennedy fixed two ropes up a steep seventy-foot headwall and a difficult mixed traverse — the last real barriers to the peak's unclimbed summit. Beyond, a few pitches of moderate ice and an exposed ridge traverse would lead to the top, only 600 feet above.

It was July 1978. That night, as the team of four slept in a snow cave chopped out by George's cousin Jeff Lowe and Jim Donini, a storm hit, dumping a foot of snow. Hoping for a break in the weather, the climbers put off their summit attempt in the morning. The following day, still plagued by whiteout and heavy snowfall, they made a stab at the top, but, cold and moving slowly in the wind and spindrift, they turned back at the end of the fixed ropes.

They had been on the mountain twenty-one days. Everyone was tired. Worse, Jeff, who had become increasingly ill during their stay in the snow cave, was virtually incapacitated by a recurrence of the tropical fever that he'd contracted during the walk-in. He hacked, vomited, and weakened.

Donini concentrated on caring for Jeff. George Lowe, then thirty-three years old and the most experienced member of the party, thought everything through. He and Kennedy were probably still capable of a summit bid, but it would require a long, exhausting day and maybe even a bivouac. The effort would weaken two more, when the team was still faced with a 7,000-foot descent. Without regret, Lowe gave up on the summit. The four waited two more days for the storm to clear, then began their three-day rappel.

"That was my best climb," says Lowe. "It was really great climbing, and we pushed ourselves. It was a small nucleus of good friends. It wasn't competitive." And it was unlike a large expedition, where members may jockey for a chance at a summit. "You're all going to the summit together. It's much nicer."

More than that, the actions brace his own strong beliefs about partnership and responsibility. Asked if he calls Latok his best climb because he is proud of his decision, he pauses and says, "Yes" — which is unusual for him, but we'll get to that.

Three things amaze you when you talk to George H. Lowe III — how much climbing he's done, how much climbing he's done even though he's earned a Ph.D in physics and is a systems engineer, and how much climbing he's still doing.

If completed, the North Ridge of Latok I would have been the hardest route yet done in the Himalaya by a small team employing lightweight tactics. Today, almost fifteen years later, the route remains unclimbed. Still, for Lowe, age forty-eight, Latok is but one large bold image in a long procession of them spanning three decades.

Lowe, a resident of Golden, Colorado, has done the hardest climbs in various disciplines across several eras. In the Wyoming Tetons during the late 1960s he did the hardest winter ascents in the country, such as the North Face of the Grand. In the 1970s, he established the most difficult routes in the Canadian Rockies — the North Face of Mount Alberta, which has been climbed just six times since Lowe and Jock Glidden's ascent in 1972, and, in

1974, with Chris Jones, the still-unrepeated North Face of North Twin (established in atrocious weather, with retreat impossible, and featuring a sixty-footer by Lowe). Other climbers who have been there say that you can't begin to understand the breadth of that achievement unless you walk up and look at that face. In 1977, Lowe did what was then the hardest route in Alaska, the Infinite Spur on Mount Foraker, which has been repeated only once, in 1989. All were done alpine style.

In the Himalaya, after Latok I, Lowe spearheaded the 1983 first ascent of what is likely the toughest route up Everest, the immense Kangshung Face, and led the rotten crux buttress. He attempted the North Ridge of K2 in 1986, and, in 1990, he climbed the Northeast Ridge of Dhaulagiri I, solo from Camp II at 6,400 meters. He has climbed in the Soviet Union, South America, Europe, and all across the United States. On rock, he has done landmark first ascents like the runout Dorsal Fin in Little Cottonwood Canyon, Utah — a stiff 5.10 when the area's top grade was 5.9 — in 1965. He still pulls off impressive climbs like the Nose on El Capitan in a day.

"His climbs were as bold as anything anyone was doing," says Chris Jones, an expatriot English climber now living in California. Jones was Lowe's partner on a number of major climbs in the 1970s. Asked what characterizes George as a climber, Jones immediately says, "Commitment. If he decided he wanted to do something, he wanted to do it." Lowe inspired faith, too. Jones recalls that on the North Face of North Twin, "The only other person I knew that I would have felt equally confident in was his cousin, Jeff."

After Jones and George Lowe met in 1965 in Chamonix, France, they climbed the Bonatti Pillar (Lowe made the first American ascent) on the Petit Dru, and, with two others, tried the Central Pillar of Freney on Mont Blanc, then the most notorious climb in the Alps. "In the very spot where the storm had hit Bonatti [causing four deaths in 1961], it began to snow," recalls Jones. "We got some ropes stuck. We were shaking in our boots, just

from the aura of the thing. The rest of us wanted down, down —
George, I recall, was the most reluctant to leave. He was thinking
of waiting." As it turned out, when the party got down into the
valley, the weather cleared. "We could have done it," says Jones,
"and it would have been a very big achievement."

Lowe has an uncanny natural ability to simply keep on going.
"Other people go up and down, move faster and then slower,"
says Donini. "But George always goes at about the same pace."

It takes a lot to put him off. In 1977, Lowe, his cousin Jeff,
and Kennedy attempted a new route on the North Face of Mount
Hunter in the Alaska Range. They were 4,000 feet up, on a corniced, knife-edge ridge, when Jeff took a sixty-footer and broke
his ankle. With no fixed rope to back them up, they managed a
long, dangerous rappel down in a storm. George and Kennedy
returned and completed the route when the weather broke, then
rested a few days before going onto an even more ambitious new
route on nearby Mount Foraker.

High on the Infinite Spur after several days of taxing climbing, the two were pressed by their aloneness, the size of the mountain, a storm, and exhaustion. "George kept saying, 'Oh, this is
out of control, we're so far out there,' but it almost seemed like a
nervous habit," says Kennedy. "When he was climbing, he wasn't
perturbed at all."

"My strength is probably my determination," says Lowe. "My
weakness — judgment, going on too long."

* * *

George Lowe has patrician features and manner, blue eyes,
and the kind of fine gold skin that tends to fine lines. He is 5'10,"
155 pounds — "150 if I'm in good climbing shape, but I never
am." One of the first things that you notice in talking to him is
that he chronically deflects anything that even hints of a compli-
ment and cringes at taking credit. Sometimes you even want to
give him a shake, tell him it's okay. But that natural humility is

one reason why George Lowe has survived so much for so long. He is very aware of his limits, of caution, of being vigilant about the things that he can control. If he's too tired to climb safely, he'll stop and declare, "I'm going to bivy."

Scientist and climber fuse in his methodology. Trying to find his way off Dhaulagiri two years ago at 24,000 feet on a big face in a storm at night, he "was very hung out." Although afraid, he methodically tried to get down one gully after another, down-climbing until he ran out of snow and his crampons scraped rock. He eventually found the channel that led back to his high camp. "You just have to keep plugging," he says. "You have to work with the problem until you solve it." He makes it sound reasonable — the listener has to fill in the rest, realizing what a supremely exhausting process it would be, requiring the hammered climber to go upward again and again.

He also makes a case for careful preparation. "If you're going to survive in big mountains," Lowe says, "you don't do wild things immediately. You do them after you've learned."

Lowe is a Renaissance man. He can say little about his work, which is proprietary for a private company that does some government consulting, but he hired on with the arrangement to take two months off every year. He has a doctor-climber-pilot wife, Liz Regan-Lowe, a four-month-old daughter, Katie Beth, and two grown children in Alaska, George IV, age twenty-two, and Kara, age twenty, from his previous marriage. He has been a licensed pilot for fourteen years. Lowe talks almost as much about canyon hiking, mountain biking, long ski tours, and river running as he does about climbing. He does every kind of climbing, although not much bouldering or sport climbing. "I like to do everything. Guess that's why I'm a systems engineer," he says.

He constantly makes darting visits to climbing areas, always on the lookout for a good hard route. In their 1990 sortie to Yosemite, he and Alex Lowe (no relation) arrived at night, were racking at 2:00 A.M., slept a couple of hours, then did the Nose on El Capitan in thirteen hours, on sight. Then they left.

Two weeks earlier, he had spent a week in the Valley, during which, among a multitude of other routes, he did the 12-pitch East Buttress (5.10) and the 19-pitch West Face of El Capitan (5.11b). On Half Dome, Autobahn, a dozen-pitch route of mostly 5.10, and (in seven and a half hours), the 24-pitch Northwest Face. "Not a lot of *hard* climbing, a lot of *climbing*," Lowe insists. "I can't do hard climbing!"

He'll fly to the Utah desert three times in a month or from Denver to Zion for the weekend just to do one climb. Throw a Cessna 182 into the equation and you can do a lot. It also helps to bring a nanny, which he and Regan-Lowe do. "I don't have much time. I have to use it," he says.

Hark back to the difficult Supercouloir on Mount Deltaform in the Canadian Rockies, done in 1973 when Chris Jones and Lowe were on their way to the Devils Thumb, Alaska. "We had to stop for a day for car trouble or something," recalls Jones. "A lot of people would have spent the day in the pub, but George would always snatch every opportunity to climb."

Lowe is a quixotic combination of fastidious scientist and *out there* rad boy. He's organized and ritualistic — in a snow cave packed with four smelly climbers, a disaster area of gear and boots and wet sleeping bags, he'll maintain tabs on his own spoon and cup and get perturbed when others stick dirty utensils or fingers into the peanut butter. Yet he's quite unconcerned that big globs of zinc oxide are dropping off of his face.

He is a person of rectitude. Jones, who met Lowe nearly thirty years ago, remembers a cleancut but not socially polished young man with a Mormon background that was peculiar to the others in the Chamonix climbers' camp. "He was different; he didn't drink any beer or wine, I don't think he drank coffee — his habits were quite odd to the British," says Jones. Some have recalled Lowe as the only one who did not smoke pot at certain high bivies.

Lowe is so sharp that you can feel incompetent around him. He mentions Mount Geikie. You say you don't know of that mountain, then fear you should. His convictions run deep. He unself-consciously challenges or corrects others, and his questions can sound admonitory. Yet he is essentially kind and sympathetic. He usually feels a strong connection to his climbing partners and is openly disturbed when he hears about expeditions where the climbers seemed isolated from each other. His keenness can be exhilarating once you relax.

Lowe is humorous, often at his own expense. His shoulders move like a kid's when he laughs. He is reserved, courteous, and then — in the mountains — goes for it.

* * *

George III was one of six children in a Mormon family in Ogden, Utah. His father, George, was a surgeon and his mother, Beth, a nurse. George grew up camping, hiking, and river running with his Uncle Ralph and his brood of eight, which included Jeff, Greg, and Mike Lowe.

Jeff Lowe, who was to become one of George's mainstay climbing partners in the 1970s, climbed the Grand Teton at age seven and has since amassed a lifetime of important ascents. Throw in Jeff's brothers Greg and Mike, each with an enviable record of ascents, and a few other assorted brothers who climbed, and you have a name surrounded by mystique, a name that inspired young climbers to do the routes the Lowes had done.

George first bouldered at age ten or twelve with his Uncle Ralph and did his first roped climbs in 1962 at Tahquitz and Big Rock when he went off to college at Harvey Mudd in Claremont, California. Harvey Mudd is a respected school for studies of science and math, but Lowe didn't like it — too many people, too much smog, and too far from the mountains. He transferred to the University of Utah, where he completed his undergraduate and graduate studies and climbed on school breaks.

Lowe married at twenty-seven, not as young as is common among Mormon families. "But I was emotionally young," he says.

There were times, especially after his divorce during two separate years when he was a single father, when he barely climbed. He mostly went camping with his children. Later, when they were older, he took them climbing on Puppy Dome in Tuolumne.

But Lowe always came back to climbing and these days is constantly planning new forays. He and Liz live in the foothills of Golden, commuting to work in Denver. Their home, located on a quiet, open hillside, is a cabin that Liz calls "hodgepodge," which they intend to redo. Here her collection of Lladro Yadroux porcelain figurines lines the windowsill, while his mountain photos march along the hall. The hall's doorway is topped by a hangboard.

"Climbing with George, you don't miss a day," says Liz. She is a serene person who usually speaks in measured, thoughtful tones, although she also is quite capable of sudden demonstrations of backbone. This evening, recalling a European vacation in 1989 during which the two had climbed in the Dolomites and the Verdon, she does an exaggerated imitation of a conversation between them, herself whimpering, "When do I get a rest day?" and George's ferocious rejoinder, "When I get a new climbing partner!"

"The only rest days were driving days," she says.

He replies, "Those were rest days, dear," and then remembers something significant. "We had a half day in Venice!"

She rolls her eyes. "We did. A half day."

The two met climbing, through a blind date arranged by some doctor friends. Originally from Boston, Liz is thirty-nine, an orthopedic surgeon. Their first time out was "a classic George date," she says. "He picked me up at the crack of dawn. We went to the South Platte, we bushwhacked in, and we climbed until dark. Then we bushwhacked out."

"Not 'until dark,' " protests George.

"We climbed until dark," says Liz firmly. "That's a rule with George," she adds. "It's only a partial-credit day if it's not dark." He blusters but can only laugh.

On their second date, George escorted her on a two-day trip to a place called the Black Hole, White Canyon, Utah, where she found herself swimming 200 yards, pushing her pack through a canyon so narrow that she couldn't see the sky. On another hot date, Lowe took her to climb the Totem Pole in Monument Valley, Utah, where they were arrested for trespassing and fined $100 each.

"If you ever go climbing with George," she warns, "bring a headlamp."

* * *

In 1990, when George and Liz made wedding plans, they decided to spend their honeymoon in Death Hollow on the Utah desert. Then, when Carlos Buhler's partner for the East Face of Dhaulagiri canceled, Buhler called Lowe. Lowe agreed to go to Dhaulagiri, as did Liz (thinking that she was being awfully flexible). The wedding date had been set for early August, and the invitations already ordered when Buhler called and asked, "Can you get Liz to move up the date?" George looked sideways. Liz was watching him. He said, "No." After the wedding, George and Liz had a wonderful walk to the mountain, around its west face. They arrived at the north side and the standard basecamp to find seven expeditions and huge piles of garbage and feces.

Lowe speaks fervently against the trash and against the abuse of natives that he witnessed. Members of one expedition sent their Sherpas back up to Camp IV for their oxygen in one day, saying that they wouldn't pay them if they didn't go. "I want to be with people who want to be on the mountain," says Lowe. "I would rather not climb with people who are paid to take risks on your behalf. If you can't climb the mountain otherwise, you ought to think about what your motivations are to climb it."

Meeting Buhler, George and Liz found him ill with bronchitis. The third team member, Dainius Makauskas from Lithuania, had stepped into a crevasse and torn a knee ligament, the anterior cruciate. Liz examined him and told him that he should not even walk out on it.

Buhler descended to lower altitude hoping to recover. Lowe decided to go up on the mountain solo, although he would have preferred to climb with someone. It was late in the season, however, and all the other climbers had left. He hoped to do a route on the mountain's harder East Face, but due to avalanche hazard decided to take the standard Northeast Ridge. Nuru Sherpa, the expedition's Sirdar, climbed with him to Camp II, and from there Lowe went on alone to the top.

Lowe says that he gave Nuru the choice of whether or not to accompany him to the summit. Sherpas, Lowe says, are very conscious of wanting to progress, to do better climbs and improve their reputations, and, culturally, they feel responsible to take care of the sahibs. Lowe commented, "He said words to the effect of 'Climbing Everest [but not Dhaulagiri] is worthwhile to my career. I think there's too much risk.' And that was fine."

Lowe and his new wife then left the mountain, and afterward Buhler, Nuru, and Makauskas climbed it. Makauskas disappeared on the descent, possibly slipping at a tricky spot on the summit ridge. Buhler and Nuru suffered extensive frostbite. Buhler lost part of one toe, Nuru all of his toes.

Lowe is in some ways more dismayed by Nuru's fate, because he feels that the determined Makauskas had made more of a personal choice. With some delicate circumlocution, he indicates his disagreement with Buhler. "When Nuru saw the condition the others were in," adds Lowe, "he [must have] felt like he had to go."

Buhler responds that when he asked Nuru if he wanted to go up on the mountain again, the invitation did not necessitate a summit bid, and on the summit day, "There was never a point when someone couldn't say, 'I'm going down.'" Nuru, he says, later told him that he didn't turn around because he wasn't cold on the way up, only later, coming down. Still, on the cold summit morning, all were aware of the likelihood of frostbite.

Buhler contends that Lowe himself put Nuru at risk by taking him across avalanche slopes and, several times, through the mountain's icefall.

Finally, Buhler, who has climbed with Sherpas many times, points out that it was Lowe's first trip to Nepal, and he believes that Lowe and many other climbers assume that Sherpas are less-informed mountaineers. "I look at Sherpas more as individuals than as a culture," says Buhler, "and I get a feeling for who is able to make decisions and who isn't."

At a later time, Lowe is asked whether soloing Dhaulagiri was a high point in his career. "Nah, it was pretty straightforward," he says. "In some ways, because of what happened afterward, it was a low point."

After the incident, Lowe, Liz, Buhler, Buhler's mother, and a trekker friend chipped in to pay Nuru's medical expenses and a year's wages. Buhler later hired Nuru to go to the mountain Dorje Lhakpe, where he has since started a trekking business, Sherpa Professionals, with Nuru and another Sherpa.

* * *

Last year, George was invited to go to Gasherbrum IV with Alex Lowe and Steve Swenson but declined when Liz became pregnant. As Lowe sits in his living room with Katie Beth on his lap, both of his stockinged feet under the table bounce with restless energy. Lowe says, he and Liz have agreed there will be no more big mountains for him. "I've said things like that before, though," he adds with a laugh. "But kids are important. I didn't really get to see my kids grow up and" — his voice drops — "I missed that."

"I've evolved," he says. "You find yourself less willing to take risks when you get older. Too many of my friends have died." Dave Cheesemond, Catherine Freer, Nick Estcourt, Mick Burke, John Harlin — all close friends — were killed climbing. When George was only twenty-one, he lost Mark McQuarrie, his partner from many Wasatch climbs. The two were trying a line of flakes up Church Buttress in Little Cottonwood Canyon when McQuarrie, then age seventeen, fell, and the rope cut. That was the only time George considered quitting, and he did stop for a few months. He was profoundly affected, but he was also profoundly driven to climb.

It's a beautiful, breezy autumn day, the leaves alight and shimmering on the trees. I wait for George and Liz at a tiny airport in Glenwood Springs, Colorado. Behind me is an office that doubles as somebody's home. A bathrobe hangs on the back of the bathroom door. Outside are the black runway, a phone booth, a Texaco sign, a pile of branches, and some junked cars.

A random ambulance pulls up and I start worrying. Light planes are one of my favorite phobias. There's a roar, and here they come, circling, angling, bouncing a bit, rolling to a stop — the parents in headphones, the baby with cotton in her ears, a scarf around her tiny head, and outrage issuing from her lips. Four is the plane's limit, so no nanny this trip. I steel myself. We take off.

In bumpy air (thank God for the Dramamine I took), we fly over Grand Junction, and Lowe asks about the climbing there. Below, the earth spreads in layers of chocolate, then rich terra cotta, then cafe au lait with a touch of white on top. In Utah, Lowe points out the Castleton Tower, slim and elegant and separate. "You've never been up Castleton?" he exclaims. I mumble about not having lived in the West all that long.

We follow the Colorado River, which looks like the Nile. A thick band of green lines its rims; the dust of the desert stretches out of sight.

Here is Bryce Canyon, a long corrugated band of cliffs, lit as bright as a lantern by the lowering sun. Its walls radiate warm pink and orange above the moss green of shadowy, folded hills.

Fifteen minutes later, over the oddly shaped white summits and deep narrows of Zion, George points out to Liz a two-day climb he did with Jeff in the late 1960s. "See? With the knob on top?" He lands in St. George, a town clustered around a bright white Mormon temple.

We rent a car, buy food and diapers, drive to Zion, and camp. In the dark, I mess up my tent's poles and inserts, partly because I haven't set it up for half a year. "You haven't used your tent since spring?" exclaims George.

In Zion, the Virgin River has carved a 3,000-foot canyon of Navajo sandstone. Over the millennia, the undercut sandstone has broken off in vertical slabs — the Zion walls are steep.

George has picked a climb for us — the Monkeyfinger Wall, "the Astroman of Zion," a 10-pitch Grade V, 5.11 AI or 5.12b on the Temple of Sinewava. Our nine-ish start, it will turn out, is overly leisurely. George and Liz bid a mushy goodbye.

Lowe climbs steadily, his style not smooth or showy but workmanlike and effective. He claims that he's not a 5.11 climber, but he's up his 5.11 leads quickly. On the 5.12b pitch, he grabs a sling or two without losing much time.

On the second pitch, a brutal, debilitating sun hits us. The climb is hard work — long 5.10 laybacks and jam cracks, pitch after pitch, Friend after Friend. I've done a lot of crack climbing over the years, but the route starts to grind on me. After seconding one pitch, where I had to hang at length in the direct sun struggling to retrieve a buried Friend, I arrive in a belay cave wanting a drink, some food, and some rest before my next lead. I try to speak and for a surprising second nothing comes out; my dry mouth has clogged on a hunk of PowerBar. Almost immediately, George is handing me the rack. I'm dyin,' and we have three pitches to go: 5.10d, 5.11, 5.10b.

The last pitch is rotten and bushy, with rope drag. Going over the top, I'm literally crawling. We start to descend in twilight and are soon in utter darkness, rappelling free, sometimes spinning, hundreds of feet above the ground. It's a black night, with bright layers of stars abruptly cropped by the looming walls. And no moon. Or headlamp.

We do everything painstakingly, checking and rechecking, trying not to unclip the wrong thing. A light shines across the canyon from the beautiful Moonlight Buttress, and I envy those people, imagining their cozy, blissful preparedness. Then, as many a climber has, I think if there's ever a good person to be with here, it's George.

He takes the lead, carrying the pack to make himself heavier to test the belays, which he backs up. I remove the backups. He skips one belay station successfully, and later another, but runs out of rope fifteen feet short of the anchor. Liz, with the baby, drives up just in time to hear the dad's worrisome shout that he has to anchor himself in by feel.

Now I have to get to the interim hanging belay, pull the ropes, and rap past him. I find the station by feeling along the crack during the rappel. George will later say, "Did you back up that belay?" No. "I probably would have," he says. I get it — no extenuating circumstances allowed.

We have some shouted communications with our ground crew of two. I yell down that I'm going to kiss the ground when we reach it. We get down at 10:15 P.M. Liz has been waiting two hours. George, as he often does, talks about how tired and hungry he is, and she, as she often does, switches from being peeved to sympathetic. Personally, I will be tired for two days (not to mention petrified when the plane bounces while landing in the dark the next night). To me, the three-hour rappel has been tense. I can't imagine rappeling under strain for three days. George hadn't been scared. "There's a fair amount of death in the mountains because people give up," he'll say the next day. "If you're careful and keep it together, you just keep plugging and get there." Under the picnic table, his foot jiggles.

Liz and George were to have gone climbing the next morning, but she has bashed her thumb in the car door, so they plan a hike. They breakfast under a big cottonwood tree, whose waving branches Katie Beth likes to watch. "She likes motion," says George. She'd better.

Not for the first time, I try to get Lowe to explicate the nature of what propels him. He vaguely allows for some intrinsic Mormon industriousness and a possible genetic component, then says with more force, "Our parents were always pushing for us to do the best you can do. Even if it isn't great, if it's the best you can do, that's good."

Lowe next speaks directly and with quiet dignity. "I think part of it is insecurity. If you discover something you do well, get good feedback, pleasure in achievements . . . it's very satisfying. Climbing, mountain biking, anything, it's the same sort of reward.

"I was very insecure when I went to college, a social misfit. I was a terrible athlete in school."

"But you were on the ski team," Liz protests from where she kneels on the ground, placing the baby in a chair.

"I couldn't do ball sports," he says. Decades ago, Lowe focused on a sport in which all felt different. Climbers of yore were not jocks, not at all understood by the mainstream. There was cachet in *that*.

Now George, holding the blanketed baby, pulls a pile tube hat onto his head. Liz turns to him, sees his dark gray hair flowing from the top of his hat, and bursts out laughing. "What?" he asks, smiling. She laughs harder. Not knowing what the joke is, Lowe could easily become irked. He only tips his head, his expression sweet and easy. "It looks like you have an animal on your head." He laughs. Lowe, by nature an unrelaxed person, seems to have achieved a state of calmness (well, relative), sureness; and grace.

In a way, it's all caught up. Chris Jones has observed that, in climbing, there was always a sense of great confidence in Lowe. When the two were descending from Devils Thumb in a complete whiteout, George had a very impressive sense of the land. He simply fit in the mountains; he knew that place, and what it was.

Does he ever miss being on the cutting edge, doing things that turned the heads of the climbing world? "I miss it a little bit," he says. But he redirects the conversation. "Like climbing yesterday, that was just really pleasant. It was still pushing me physically, but the risk is not there. I'm not sure risk is a good measure of quality."

Lowe is drawing on so much experience that things that are high on many other people's scale of commitment and fear are, to him, low end. The forbidding Diamond Face of Long's Peak, for example, is "just a day out on the crag. Things can happen, but the probability is really small that I'll get myself in trouble up there in summer." Lowe can even say of the Infinite Spur, "I probably would feel more comfortable now, having done some things like that since."

In terms of the lifelong friendships he's gained, Lowe is like certain climbers of the old school. Chris Jones actually gets a little teary talking about his old pal. Lowe seems like one of the group, including Charlie Houston and Pete Schoening, who endangered themselves trying to bring their ill friend Art Gilkey down from K2 and who, now in their seventies, remain the best of friends.

But people can't pass off George Lowe with those measures of reverence, respect, and a tinge of condescension as they do many others who climbed hard decades ago. He is still dragging too much out of climbing.

At one point I ask Liz, "What's George's middle name?"

"Henry," she says, then corrects herself. "Headlamp."

Adrian and Alan Burgess.
Photo from Peter Nichols Collection

Expatriate Thugs

AID & AL BURGESS

By Jon Krakauer

[From "The Burgess Boys," OUTSIDE, August 1988]

S pring has supposedly arrived in the Front Range of Colorado, but the sky hangs low and an icy breeze slices through Eldorado Canyon as Adrian Burgess, a thirty-nine-year-old Englishman living in Boulder, muscles his way up the steep red sandstone of a climb called C'est La Vie. One hundred and thirty feet up, he stops at a sloping ledge, secures the rope to a pair of bolts, and belays his three partners, one by one, up to his stance. The last of these climbers is Adrian's identical twin, Alan.

As Alan arrives at the exposed perch, the wind picks up dramatically and a squall commences to dust the belay ledge with snow. Alan eyes the 5.11 microholds that kick off the next pitch, then levels his gaze at Adrian and says, " 'Bout time for the Bustop to be opening, don't you think, Youth?"

The Bustop is a bar that enjoys a great deal of Alan's business whenever he's in Boulder visiting Adrian in between the Himalayan expeditions that have held sway over the twins' lives for the past nine years. Alan favors the Bustop, he says, because it's just up the street from Adrian's home. It probably doesn't hurt that the Bustop offers two beers for a buck during happy hour, and happens to be a topless joint besides.

After an efficient retreat from the walls of Eldorado, the Burgess entourage rolls stylishly up to the entrance of the Bustop in a rusting slab of Detroit iron — Adrian's greatest material asset — to which a bumper sticker has been affixed that reads "A Fool and His Money are Soon Partying." Inside the bar's cavernous, dimly lit chambers, most of the dancers seem to know Alan. Several smile warmly and greet him by name as he leads the way to a table overlooking the runway. Our waitress is a woman named Susan, who Alan first met in Periche, a high Sherpa village on the trekking route to Mount. Everest. Probably nowhere but in Boulder, it occurs to me, would one encounter strippers who spend their vacations trekking in Nepal.

When we sit down, Adrian appears ill at ease, "It's Lorna," Alan tells me under his breath. "Aid's not supposed to come in 'ere." Lorna, the well-to-do niece of a United States congressman, is Adrian's wife of seven years. As soon as the opportunity presents itself, Alan surreptitiously slips one of the Bustop's distinctive matchbooks into the pockets of Adrian's coat, on the off chance that Lorna might someday come across it and demand an explanation. "Want to keep the lad on 'is toes," Alan whispers with a wicked grin.

Fortunately, Adrian is a virtuoso at staying on his toes, and so, for that matter, is Alan. But then, when you're allergic to work, you subsist on charm and the occasional petty scam, and when you spend a sizable chunk of every year dodging death on the roof of the world, you get in plenty of practice.

The Burgess twins occupy a unique niche in modern alpine society. In a subculture that has come to be dominated by clean-living, hard-training, high-profile Frenchmen and Germans and Austrians who pose for Alfa Romeo ads and lend their names to lines of chic clothing, the twins remain low-lying pub-crawlers and brawlers, forever staying just one step ahead of the authorities. They are among the last of a breed of working-class British climbers for whom how much one drinks and with whom one fights have always been as important as what mountains one climbs. Although their names mean absolutely nothing to most of the world, within that small, ingrown, multinational fraternity obsessed with finding harder and harder ways up higher and higher mountains, the Burgess boys are luminaries of the brightest magnitude.

Rail thin and tall, with perennially pale skin, long English faces, and dirty blonde Prince Valiant coifs, Adrian and Alan Burgess wouldn't look at all out of place playing rhythm guitar in a mid-sixties British rock band — the Animals, maybe, or The Who. The twins were born and raised in the working-class village of Holmfirth, at the edge of the vast Yorkshire moors — the same empty, brooding tracts that gave birth to the novels of the Brontë sisters. In the case of the Burgess brothers, their childhood rambles across the moors brought them in contact with rough-and-tumble northern English climbers. These older climbers filled the twins' impressionable young heads with tales of the bold deeds and outrageous acts of Don Whillans, Joe Brown, and other hard-drinking gritstone heroes, irrevocably fixing the course of the Burgess's lives.

The twins took up climbing at the age of fourteen and immediately began to pursue the sport with a vengeance. At the age of seventeen they went to the Alps for the first time and were shortly polishing off many of the most fearsome routes in Chamonix and the Dolomites. They had heard their British elders spinning yarns about legendary climbs like Les Droites and the Freney Pillar and assumed that getting up big-name nordwands by the skin of one's teeth was the norm on the Continent. When they were twenty-four, in 1973, they expanded their alpine horizons by driving overland to India in a beat-up minivan, where they pushed a difficult new route up an 18,000-foot Himalayan peak called Ali Rattna Tibba.

During the early seventies, the Yorkshire lads worked off and on in England's burgeoning outdoor-education racket, conducting Outward-Bound-style courses for juvenile delinquents. "They were what you Americans call 'oods in the woods programs," Adrian explains, "only in our case it was 'oods leading the ''oods in the woods."

107

The twins moved to Canada in the midseventies, where they landed construction jobs in Calgary by presenting themselves as highly skilled carpenters, when in truth all they knew about building was what they had hastily gleaned from a library book the night before applying for work. It was also in Canada that Alan obtained landed immigrant status, with the attendant rights and benefits, by claiming to be an ace VW mechanic, the skills of which no one else in the city apparently possessed. Work, however, even in the outdoors, proved to be a lot less fun than climbing, so the Burgesses decided it was something they could do without. Aside from a few momentary lapses, the twins proudly point out, neither has held an honest job since 1975.

That was the year they began to wander the globe in earnest, pubbing and brawling in the finest Whillans tradition. They were arrested in four countries and reprimanded in many more. In Lima, Peru, they precipitated a slug-fest in a bordello after accusing the establishment of false advertising. In Talkeetna, Alaska, the locals are still peeved about the time the Burgesses and six British cronies absconded with thirty cases of beer from the Fairview bar and narrowly escaped going to jail.

In the course of their travels, the twins also bagged route after harrowing route, from Fitzroy to McKinley, Huascarán to the Howser Towers, Les Droites to Logan to the Grandes Jorasses. "Our lives pretty much turned into one long run of trips," Al reflects with an air of incredulity. "There've been so many that it's sometimes 'ard to tell 'em apart."

The Burgess's string of ascents did not go unnoticed in the British climbing community. As early as 1975, in fact, Chris Bonington considered inviting them on his historic expedition to the Southwest Face of Everest — a route hyped as "the hardest way up the highest mountain in the world." The expedition eventually put Douglas Haston and Doug Scott on the summit, but the twins' names never made it onto the team, most likely, Alan speculates, "because we'd some'ow developed a reputation for occasionally getting a bit disorderly, and Bonington, very much a media man, didn't want anybody along who might blow 'is cool for 'im."

When the twins realized that their "reputation for occasionally getting a bit disorderly" might preclude their ever being invited on an expedition to a major Himalayan peak, they decided to take matters into their own hands. In 1979, they joined forces with a friend named Paul Moores and went to Nepal to attempt an audacious alpine-style ascent of 26,041-foot Annapurna II. They were turned back by hurricane-force winds at 23,500 feet, but that taste of rarefied Himalayan air only whetted their appetites for more of it; the Burgesses have returned to the Himalaya or Karakoram every single year since.

In the fall of 1987 it was Lhotse — Mount Everest's nearest neighbor, the fourth-highest mountain in the world — that received the twins' attention. Nineteen eighty-seven, as it turned out, was not a good year to climb in the Himalaya. Storms ripped through the range with such frequency and violence that not a single climber made it to the top of either K2 or Everest, the first time in sixteen years that the summit of the latter was not attained. The twins were therefore understandably relieved when, on September 27, as they were halfway up Lhotse, the day dawned bright and promising over the Khumbu region of Nepal.

Alan was breaking trail high on Lhotse's southeast buttress, followed on the rope by Adrian and an acquaintance from Colorado named Dick Jackson. The great amount of fresh snow on the peak made the party think twice about avalanche conditions, but the slope felt reassuringly solid beneath the knee-deep mantle of powder. With a dozen Himalayan expeditions under his belt, Alan figured he could tell when a hill was safe and when it wasn't. Furthermore, it seemed important to make the most of the fair weather in a season that had seen so little of it.

At 23,000 feet, the route up Lhotse zigged and zagged through a series of ice cliffs. Alan was leading past one of these seracs over easy ground, casually belayed from below by his brother, when his hypoxic reveries were cut short by a deep, muffled *WOOOMPF!* Alan looked up to see the jagged gash of a fracture line rip across the slope and calve off an immense slab of wind-packed snow, five feet thick and one hundred fifty feet across, directly above his stance. For an instant, the slab seemed to move in slow motion, but as it tore free from the last of its fragile underpinnings and committed itself to the valley, a vertical mile below, the mass of snow began to accelerate with alarming speed. After traveling forty feet, the leading edge of the slab slammed squarely into Alan's chest.

> I tried to scramble on top of it, but there was no bloody way. I went under, and then there was blackness, and all I could think was, "Shit, so this is what it feels like to die." But after maybe three seconds, I suddenly popped back up to the surface, facing downslope, up to me waist in the avalanche, with all this 'eavy snow pulling at me legs. Instinctively, I threw me 'ead back, went into a full arch, and the whole thing slid underneath me.

It was, however, a case of having jumped out of the frying pan into the fire: The avalanche had by that time engulfed his two rope mates and was rapidly carrying them toward the lip of a two-hundred-foot ice cliff. Alan had just enough time to plant his ice axe and dig in his heels before the rope to Adrian and Jackson jerked tight at his waist, threatening to yank him off the side of Lhotse once again. With the weight of his partners stretching the rope tight as piano wire, and Alan's tenuous attachment to terra firma about to fail, his impromptu belay pulled Jackson and Adrian up to the surface of the snowslide, allowing the avalanche to pass beneath them. When Alan finally arrested their tumble, Jackson and Adrian were only ten feet from the edge of the cliff.

The following afternoon, recovering at basecamp, they noticed a lammergeier — a species of Tibetan vulture with a nine-foot wingspan — circling in the updrafts overhead. This was puzzling, for lammergeiers were never seen unless there was a dead yak or other carrion in the vicinity, and there was no reason for any yaks to be near. The puzzle was solved a day later, when the twins accompanied the doctor from a Spanish expedition to the toe of the mountain to search for four overdue teammates and came upon bits and pieces of climbing gear scattered across a large avalanche fan. The missing Spaniards had been attempting to climb Lhotse by a route adjacent to the one taken by the Burgesses and Jackson and had been caught in a similar avalanche on the very same morning. The Spanish climbers, however, hadn't been so lucky: All four of them were swept six thousand feet to their deaths. A thorough search of the runout zone turned up the mangled remains of two of the bodies, which Alan and Adrian helped the doctor bury. "Man," Adrian recalls with a shudder, "that was a 'orrible job." It was not, however, a job the twins were unaccustomed to.

Any alpinist who sets his sights on the higher reaches of the Himalaya stands a fair chance of being party to someone's premature demise. For those who attempt 8,000-meter peaks with the frequency of the Burgess brothers, it is a statistical inevitability. They had both been present in 1982 — Alan as a member of a massive Canadian Everest expedition, Adrian with a small New Zealand team attempting Lhotse from the west — when first an avalanche in the notorious Khumbu Icefall, and then a collapsing serac, killed five of their cohorts. The twins had also been on K2 that ugly summer in 1986 when the mountain took the lives of no less than thirteen men and women. Among them was the leader of their expedition, the acclaimed English climber Alan Rouse, whose companions (not the twins) had been forced to abandon him, comatose but still alive, in a tent at 26,000 feet to save their own skins.

By Adrian's reckoning, more than half of the twins' climbing colleagues have, as he put it, "gotten the chop," the majority of them in the Himalaya. But if the implications of this gruesome tally bother the Burgess boys, it doesn't show. Dealing with risk, walking the fine line, playing a game of ever-escalating brinkmanship —

this is what the cutting edge of climbing has always been about. Those who elect to participate in this hazardous pastime do so not in spite of the unforgiving stakes, but precisely because of them.

Even after the unpleasant business with the dead Spaniards underscored the closeness of their shave with the avalanche in September 1987, the twins gave no thought to abandoning their original plan to climb the Southeast Buttress of Lhotse, traverse its long, spectacularly serrated summit ridge, descend the distant west side of the peak, and then, for a finale, run the gauntlet of the Khumbu Icefall to reach the base of the mountain. Alan actually managed to convince himself that their brush with death had bettered their odds — from then on, they'd be more cautious.

A week after the avalanches, the twins, Dick Jackson, and another Coloradan, Joe Frank, went back up on the peak, only to be stopped at 21,700 feet by even worse avalanche conditions than before. The twins still weren't ready to give up on the mountain, however. They decided that the route that had killed the Spaniards looked safer than their own, so Alan departed for the village of Namche Bazar to get their climbing permit changed to the Spanish line.

"While Al was down in Namche," says Adrian, "this mega storm 'it the 'imalaya, the biggest of the 'ole bloody year. Dumped more than four feet of snow in thirty-six hours." During the second night of the storm, Adrian was lying in his tent at basecamp when the back side of the sturdy dome suddenly collapsed, smashed flat under a mass of snow. Unable to get to the door, he cut his way out to discover that a small avalanche — just a slough, really — had slid noiselessly off the hillside above camp, crushed half his shelter, and stopped a foot short of burying him. His brother's tent, a few yards away, was completely buried beneath six feet of cementlike avalanche debris. "If Al 'ad been in it that night," Adrian gravely postulates, "there's no question what the outcome would've been."

The next morning, Adrian set out for Namche to find Alan. The walk out required breaking trail through chest-deep snow; it took two hours to make the first mile, a distance he'd normally cover in fifteen minutes. After another mile, beneath Island Peak, Adrian came upon the basecamp of a Royal Air Force expedition.

It looked like it'd been 'it by a fuckin' bomb. All the tents were flat, two bodies were lying nearby, all that showed of another body was this frozen 'and sticking out of the snow. The survivors said a fourth body was still buried somewhere, they didn't know where, and that a Tamang porter 'ad gone crazy after the avalanche, thrown off all 'is clothes, and run off into the night. All I could think was, "Oh man, is this shit really 'appening?"

The naked porter was eventually found, frostbitten and hypothermic but alive. Adrian hoisted him onto his back with a tumpline and lit out for Chhukun, the nearest settlement, seven miles distant. Halfway there, Alan appeared, coming up the trail. "Eh up, Youth," Adrian greeted him, "good to see you. Give this fucker a ride, will you?" The brothers ran the rest of the way down to Chhukun together, taking turns carrying the porter, and managed to reach the village in time to save his life.

The Burgesses were finally forced to give up their Lhotse expedition. But before they'd even arrived back in Kathmandu, they were hatching schemes to raise funds for a K2 expedition the following summer. One of these schemes involved convincing *The National Enquirer* that Alan Rouse might still be alive after spending two years in a tent at 26,000 feet (nobody had been back to the upper reaches of K2 since Rouse had been abandoned in August 1986). The twins would return with the story of how he had survived by cannibalizing his fallen comrades and in return ask the *Enquirer* for a modest honorarium — say, ten or twenty thousand dollars. As it happened, the *Enquirer* deal never got off the ground, but the twins managed to get to the Karakoram regardless. At the end of May they set up a basecamp at the foot of K2; as this is being written — if all has gone according to plan — the Burgess boys should be arriving at the summit.

* * *

Then again, they might not be. In scanning their climbing record, one is struck by how often success in the Himalaya has eluded the Burgesses. The twins have tried and failed to climb Annapurna II, Nanga Parbat, Ama Dablam, Everest (twice for Alan, once for Adrian), Lhotse (three times for Adrian, twice for Alan), Cho Oyu (twice for Alan), and K2. The only major Himalayan peaks they've actually seen the summits of, in fact, are 24,688-foot Annapurna IV and 26,795-foot Dhaulagiri. If climbers kept track of batting averages, Adrian would be hitting about .200 in the Himalayan Leagues, Alan a lowly .167.

These unimpressive numbers can be attributed at least in part to the twins' habit of going after very tough routes with very small teams, and on many occasions intentionally making those routes tougher still by attempting the climbs in the screaming winds and unimaginable cold of the Himalayan winter. Paradoxically, the twins chalk up the scarcity of big summits in their lives to a "cautious nature." Alan insists that "among our peer group in England, we've always 'ad a reputation for being careful climbers, for not sticking our necks out that much. Which is why we're still alive, I suppose, and most of them are not."

While both twins concede that dumb luck has a lot to do with who survives and who doesn't in the Himalaya, they also argue that the great majority of mountaineering accidents are preventable. "We look at it," says Adrian, "that most tragedies 'appen because climbers make mistakes. Sure, we're capable of making mistakes, too, but if you keep your eyes open, and don't climb for the wrong reasons, you won't make as many of them."

Alan says the deaths of two of their closest friends, Al Rouse and Roger Marshall (who, in 1985, fell while trying to solo the north face of Everest) are perfect examples of what can happen when people climb for the wrong reasons. Alan explains:

> Both Roger and Rouse died because they were pushing to meet outside pressure. Rouse's situation back in England was such a mess — the woman 'e loved 'ad left him, and a woman 'e didn't love was about to 'ave 'is

baby — that going back 'ome without 'aving summited was something 'e just couldn't face. In Roger's case, 'e was under incredible financial pressure to get up Everest; 'e needed to summit so 'e could write a successful book and pay off some loans that were 'anging over 'is 'ead and keeping 'im tied to the wife and family 'e was trying to get free of. It's 'ard enough making the right decisions at 'igh altitude without having that kind of pressure clouding your judgment"

If caution and mountain sense have contributed to the twins' failures, their critics — of whom there are many — are quick to cite other, less charitable, reasons for the frequency of their washouts. Even the Burgess boys' most vocal detractors grudgingly admit that the twins are exceptionally strong at high altitude — that they seem, in fact, to perform as well as any climber alive in the cold, meager air found at those extreme heights known as the "death zone." But Gordon Smith — an erstwhile Burgess pal from Calgary who accompanied the twins to Annapurna IV, Everest, and Manaslu — maintains that the lads' freewheeling, "What, me worry?" modus operandi just doesn't cut it on 8,000-meter peaks. "There's a lot more to getting up a big mountain than being able to put one foot in front of the other," Smith states matter-of-factly, "and the twins haven't a clue how to organize an expedition. Somehow, something goes wrong on every one of their Himalayan trips."

On the Manaslu expedition, according to Smith, the twins' stubbornness led to critical shortages of important gear, such as snow pickets. On the same expedition, a group of trekkers who'd paid hefty fees for the privilege of accompanying the climbers to the first camp were, upon reaching the mountain, arbitrarily denied the opportunity when Alan became impatient with the novices. Smith feels the twins' shortcomings as expedition leaders stem in part from their trying to do too much. "It's very difficult," he explains, "to be up at the front all day, pushing the route hard, and then have enough energy at night to properly oversee the expedition logistics."

But Smith disapproves of more than the twins' managerial skills. "They know how to be charming when it suits them," he continues bitterly, "but basically they're just a couple of con artists. They don't seem to care how many enemies they make; when they get caught out they just change their friends and move on to a fresh set of marks." If Smith's disaffection with the twins seems rather pointed, it might have something to do with the fact that their last trip together — the unsuccessful attempt on Manaslu in 1983 — concluded with a disagreement over Alan's handling of expedition finances that escalated into a no-holds-barred fistfight in the streets of Kathmandu.

* * *

Spend any time in Chamonix, or Llanberis, or the chang houses of the Khumbu, and you'll come to appreciate that there is no shortage of stories about the Burgess boys, their quick fists, and their brazen scams. "Wherever you go in Nepal," says American climber/physician Geoffrey Tabin, "as soon as the local people see that you're a Westerner, they excitedly ask you, 'You know Burgess? You know Burgess?' The guys are living legends on four continents; Alan's sexual escapades alone could fill several volumes of 'Penthouse Letters.' "

One of the more recent additions to the wealth of Burgess lore originated amid the weirdness and bright lights of Las Vegas, at the annual outdoor trade show. The twins were in attendance, putting the touch on industry bigwigs for funding and free gear for their Lhotse expedition. After a hard day of hustling, the twins made the rounds of the usual parties, where Alan met a friendly native who invited him to have a nightcap in her hotel room.

Alan, Adrian, and Alan's newfound friend were driving down the Strip in Adrian's beater truck, en route to Adrian's hotel, when a low-slung car, carrying several Vegas cowboys, pulled alongside at a red light. Adrian, to make small talk, held up the beverage he'd been sipping and yelled out the window, "This American beer tastes like piss!" in his best Yorkshire accent.

At the next red light, the low-slung car again pulled alongside the twins' truck, and two of the cowboys jumped out. Adrian also jumped out and, being a firm believer in the preemptive strike, immediately punched one of the cowboys. Because Adrian was so drunk, however, he lost his balance while completing the round-house and fell on his face before the cowboy could return the punch. Alan, seeing his brother on the pavement and assuming he'd been coldcocked, jumped out and bloodied the hapless cow-boy's nose (the second cowboy had by this time scurried back to the security of the low-slung car). Alan then collected Adrian, got back in the truck, and roared off down the Strip.

When they stopped for the next red light, the low-slung car pulled directly in front of the twins in a menacing fashion, but none of the cowboys got out. This so angered Adrian that he hopped out of the truck, ran up the back of the low-slung car, and leapt up and down on its roof until the light turned green and the car peeled away.

Unfortunately for the cowboys, though, the traffic lights just weren't turning for them that evening: the next one in their path was also red. Alan pulled the truck up behind the low-slung car, paused for a moment, and then rammed it smartly. Then he put the truck in reverse, backed up a few feet, and rammed the car again.

By now the cowboys realized that they'd made a grave error in judgment in tangling with the Burgesses. The cowboys decided, to hell with the red light, punched the car's accelerator, and promptly slammed into an oncoming vehicle. Alan, disappointed that the fun with the cowboys had come to an end, steered around the twisted metal and broken glass and motored slowly on down the Strip toward Adrian's hotel.

Shortly thereafter, five police cars surrounded the truck with lights flashing and sirens wailing, and Alan was yanked out of the cab and spread-eagled across the hood. The cops said they wanted to ask Alan a few questions about an alleged assault on some local citizens, followed by a hit-and-run accident. Alan politely explained that the cops had it all wrong, that he and his equally innocent brother, who were in town on important international business, were the victims, not the perpetrators, of the assault. And as for the accident, Alan said, the thugs who attacked them had simply collided with another car while trying to flee the scene of the crime.

As Alan continued to embellish upon this theme, the cops warmed up to the story. It had the ring of truth, they thought. They liked Alan. They liked his respectful, Boy Scout attitude and his comical accent, which they mistook for Australian. Alan, in fact, reminded the cops a lot of this guy in a movie they'd just seen, this Crocodile Dundee fellow.

From that point on, the cops were putty in the Yorkshireman's hand. Great movie, that Crocodile Dundee, the cops told him, Alan ought to check it out. The cops went on to say how genuinely sorry they were that Alan had been attacked in their usually peaceful city, and they hoped he didn't judge all Americans by the behavior of a few bad apples. And then they wished him a friendly good night.

* * *

Of all the preposterous twists and turns in the Burgess saga, perhaps none is more preposterous than the pairing of Adrian and Lorna Rogers. Adrian, after all, is by his own admission a destitute, uncultured, thirty-nine-year-old adolescent, while Lorna is as upper crust as they come. Her family has been at the summit of Denver society for four generations; theirs is a world of polo ponies and coming-out parties and very exclusive country clubs, a world where one's children are expected to go to the right schools and marry into the right families. Lorna — an intense, strong-willed, very attractive attorney — did the debutante routine in all its splendor, went to college at Williams, has a sitting congressman, Mo Udall, for an uncle, and likes to unwind by riding thoroughbreds in fox hunts. And in 1981, eleven months after meeting him in Kathmandu's Yak and Yeti bar, she married Adrian Burgess, bad boy of the Himalaya.

When I asked Lorna what she thought of having a husband who was absent four or five months of every year, she admitted she'd been "really miserable for the first couple of years, but now I kind of like it; I like the pattern of coming and going, the way it keeps the relationship from getting stale. I get to have a husband and share a life with him, but I also get to have a lot of freedom. Actually, Adrian being gone isn't nearly as bad as the way these goddamn expeditions monopolize the household when he's getting ready to go."

Adrian has spruced up his act some under Lorna's considerable influence. The renowned honky-tonker and street-fighter, for instance, has lately taken to riding in the family fox hunts, decked out in full regalia. Whillans is no doubt spinning in his grave, but according to Adrian, "It gets a bit exciting, if you want to know the truth. Riding those 'orses is like sitting on a fast motorbike that goes where it wants to, not where you steer it."

There are not yet any fox hunts on the other twin's horizon. Alan remains the consummate lowballer, a grand master of the art of getting by, living proof of Eric Beck's oft-quoted dictum, "At either end of the socioeconomic spectrum there lies a leisure class." Alan, observes his ex-friend Gordon Smith, "has no visible means of support; he never seems to do any work, yet somehow he always scrapes by. It's a bit of a mystery how he manages it, really."

One way he manages it is to spend most of his time, even between expeditions, living in Nepal with Sherpa friends. Alan says:

> I suppose I average about six or seven months a year over there. It's a lot cheaper to stay in Nepal between trips, living on three dollars a day, than to fly back to the West. Of course, to get by on that you 'ave to be willing to eat the same things the Sherpas eat, and eating potatoes and lentils and kurd three times a day can get a bit boring. And that kind of money won't allow you to drink beer, you 'ave to stick to chang and rakshi.
>
> I don't mind dirt-bagging it, though. I've actually come to prefer the Third World lifestyle. When I come back to the West now, I become confused by all the

choices. You really feel the culture shock, the difference between a culture that 'as some depth and one that only thinks it 'as. My gut's grown accustomed to the Sherpa flora, right, so I never get sick over there anymore, but as soon as I come back 'ere — like to Vancouver or somewhere? — BANG! I get the shits, the congested chest, the 'ole bloody business.

By living in high Sherpa villages, Alan is also able to sneak off and climb illicitly, without the hassle of permits, peak fees, or liaison officers. In the winter of 1986, for instance, he and a Sherpa friend ducked into Tibet with their Sherpani girlfriends and managed to come within a day of summiting on an 8,000-meter peak Alan says:

It was all 'ighly illegal, of course, but it was the biggest adventure I've 'ad in the last eight years; it was great. We went super light: just one tent, two mats, and two sleeping bags for the four of us. During the trek over to the mountains, we 'ad to listen carefully for yak bells, and lie low whenever Tibetan traders came up the trail, because they'll sell you out to the Nepalese check posts if they see you.

Over the eight years Alan has intermittently lived and climbed in the Khumbu district of Nepal, he has developed a remarkable rapport with the Sherpa people. Because few Western climbers can come close to matching the performance of Sherpas in the Himalaya, most Sherpas privately condescend to sahibs. "They tend to regard Westerners as chumps," Alan states flatly. Because Alan is unusually strong at altitude for a white boy, and has learned, like a Sherpa, to carry monstrous loads with a tumpline around his forehead, he has earned a rare degree of Sherpa respect. "In some ways," Alan brags, "they consider me a local."

That consideration is at least partly due to the fact that in

June 1987, a twenty-one-year-old Sherpani named Nima Diki gave birth to Alan's son in a bed of leaves at thirteen thousand feet in the village of Phortse. Alan allows, "When I got the letter from a Sherpa friend warning me, 'Nima Diki's looking a little big,' I thought, 'Oh fuck, what am I going to do?' But when I got over there and saw the little guy, I stopped worrying."

It remains to be seen whether the arrival of the child, named Dawa, will finally bring Alan's protracted adolescence to a close — as he prepares to enter his fifth decade — and actually usher him into the world of adult responsibility. He has, however, been over-heard mulling over such adult-sounding dilemmas as whether or not Dawa should go to school in Kathmandu or in the Khumbu.

Meanwhile, Chris Bonington — apparently no longer concerned about the twins' reputation — recently invited Adrian and Alan on a major expedition, scheduled for the spring of 1989, to attempt the only significant unclimbed line remaining on Mount Everest — the notorious northeast ridge, where Britain's two finest Himalayan climbers, Joe Tasker and Peter Boardman, disappeared back in 1982. Because the 1989 expedition will be a typical Bonington extravaganza — involving sixteen western climbers, thirty Sherpas, live television broadcasts, siege tactics, bottled oxygen — and both Adrian and Alan have had unpleasant experiences on big-budget, big-team Himalayan efforts, the twins respectfully declined the invitation.

After participating in Alan Rouse's large and ill-fated expedition to K2 in 1986, says Adrian, "We decided, absolutely, that from then on we would climb only with each other, and never again with a huge team." Owing to the expedition's complex logistics, the Burgesses were almost never ropemates on K2, and were profoundly unhappy because of it.

Sherpas believe that identical twins — *zongly,* they call them — are imbued with exceptional luck. Lucky or not, the power of the bond between twins cannot be overestimated. Their relationship has a built-in intimacy that at times seems almost clairvoyant. Adrian says:

With your twin, you always know just what 'e's thinking, just what 'e's going to do. There's this tremendous
trust: you couldn't lie to your twin, even if you wanted
to; 'e'd see right through it straightaway. On a big trip,
on the other 'and, because of all the expedition politics
you're never in total control of your own climbing.
Somebody at basecamp decides who you should climb
with, when you should go up, when you should go
down. And that's dangerous.

Adrian speculates that Bonington's upcoming Everest expedition is likely to be particularly hazardous in that regard. "Because
of all the money being spent," he explains, "and the direct
involvement of the media, the climb is going to be hyped up like
crazy. And the climbers will start believing all that hype, of course,
and develop a 'go-for-it' mentality. Personally, I think somebody's
going to get killed."

That somebody, notes Adrian, could all too easily be a
Burgess were they to go along. "I've learned to accept death as a
part of life in the mountains," Adrian reflects. "I've even learned
to accept it when close friends die. But I don't think I could handle it if Al died; I couldn't accept that."

It's likely that pride, as well as caution, played a part in the
twins' decision not to join Bonington. On the huge 1982 Everest
expedition, by all accounts, Alan Burgess did more to make the
climb a success — in terms of route preparation, leadership, and
load carrying — than any other member of the team, yet poor tim-
ing and a malfunctioning oxygen mask denied him the opportunity to stand on the summit. That, in itself, might not have bothered Alan unduly had he not seen the postexpedition glory — and
financial spoils — go almost exclusively to those who summited.

According to Gordon Smith, who also did more than his
share of the work on Everest but did not summit:

When we left basecamp after the climb, all eight
climbers still felt very friendly towards each other. Then

we arrived in Kathmandu, and the media started separating us into winners and losers. The guys who got to the top, the winners, received all the recognition — and quite a bit of money as well, from endorsement contracts and the like. The rest of us went back home to find that we had no jobs, no money, no reward. You find yourself thinking, Jesus Christ, I did a lot more work on that mountain than the bloke who happened to summit; is there any fairness in that?

So, the question of whether the twins would be going to Everest in 1989 was an open-and-shut case, or at least seemed to be. A few days after Alan left for K2, however, I received a post-card from him. He'd experienced a change of heart, he said, and decided that he was going to accompany Bonington to Everest after all, even though Adrian remained adamant about not going. Since I'd recently listened to both brothers hold forth at a table in the Bustop about the evils of mega-expeditions in general, and this Everest expedition in particular, I phoned Adrian — who had not yet departed for K2 — to get the lowdown.

"Al's always been a good rationalizer," Adrian offered, "and now 'e's telling 'imself that the route's a lot more difficult than 'e first thought, and therefore warrants the use of oxygen and fixed rope and a massive team and all that other crap. I think the real reason 'e's all of a sudden decided to go is that, basically, going to Everest means three free meals a day and a place to call 'ome for three months." A long, uncharacteristic silence followed. Finally, Adrian said, "Well, that's me brother, isn't it?"

Rick Ridgeway. *Photo from Adventure Photo*

Captain Fun Hog

RICK RIDGEWAY

By Tim Cahill

[From "The Real Indiana Jones," ROLLING STONE, December 1985]

He met his wife at the Yak & Yeti bar in Katmandu, on his descent from Mount Everest. He climbed the world's second-highest mountain, without oxygen. He scaled giant rock spires in the Amazon jungle. He sailed the South Seas and water-skied off Antarctica. He was jailed in Panama and nearly died from typhoid in the jungles of Borneo. His name is Rick Ridgeway, and he knows, well before his time, what it means to die. He considers himself a "fun hog."

Rick and I are fun-hogging it for a few days out on a thirty-seven-foot sailing cutter. Just getting out of the Santa Barbara harbor in a full gale was a lot of fun. The hard beat to windward along the coast, with frigid salt spray flying in forty-degree weather, was ten hours of happy misery for Rick. Presently, we're anchored for the night just under the bight near Point Conception.

There's a little more fun in store for us on this trip. The cutter is crack-jam full of gear. We've got scuba tanks, surfboards, climbing ropes and fishing equipment. "No matter what the weather's like," Rick says, stepping over the gear piled in a bristling mound, "we won't get aced." The only thing we seem to have forgotten is protein of any sort, but Rick figures fish, abalone, lobster, and crab — caught and killed along the way — will complement the dozen or so bottles of fine wine we were clever enough to remember. It's funhog city out here in the howling winds under the bight.

Rick's "ace pal," Yvon Chouinard, is on board with us. It was, in fact, Chouinard who coined the term "fun hog" on a multiple-sport expedition through South America. So that the people of Colombia and Peru and Patagonia might know how to refer to Chouinard's party, he painted PUERCOS DEPORTIVOS — loosely, "pork chops of sport" — on the side of the van he drove. Pork chops of kayaking. Pork chops of surfing. Pork chops of mountaineering

Chouinard is arguably the finest pork chop of ice climbing in the world, and he has made a multi-million-dollar business out of designing and marketing upscale climbing gear and outdoor clothes. Half the outdoor photographers in America would sacrifice an eye to publish a shot in Chouinard's Patagonia and Great Pacific catalogs. Ridgeway brought his cameras and expects to get some good shots of people wearing Chouinard's gear while funhogging the Pacific Ocean — photos that he will sell to Yvon, who will publish them in his catalog.

The two men have made risk sport a paying proposition, and this trip aboard the cutter is a typical if somewhat tame Ridgeway expedition. Call it high adventure for high pay.

* * *

There was a time when we all wanted to be Rick Ridgeway, although the image we had in mind may have been that of Tarzan or Clyde Beatty or Jane Goodall or Edmund Hillary or Richard Halliburton or Dian Fossey or Marco Polo. The desire was born in that shining moment sometime between Peter Pan and the first date — a time when the world seemed limitless and the future of our fantasies glittered before us. Climb the highest mountain, sail the seven seas, hang out with the Pygmies in the jungle (which jungle we didn't know), study lions in Africa — it was all possible. The fantasy flickered and fell dim under a dark weight of responsibility. Periodically, the desire flames into fire, and we label the burning with names that suggest psychological aberration: the big chill, a midlife crisis.

The record of Rick Ridgeway's adventures is fuel for the flame. "I'm a storyteller," he said. Rick has written books about climbing the world's two highest mountains and has worked on award-winning films about the jungle and the Antarctic. He has produced two mountaineering films of his own, and he has written about exotic people and places for *National Geographic* and other magazines.

He was born thirty-six years ago in Long Beach, California, a child saddled with the sort of Dickensian name that seals destinies. A guy named Ridgeway is going to climb mountains the same way a guy named Butkus has to play middle linebacker.

Rick's father owned a scuba shop, and the boy pretty much grew up on the ocean until the old man purchased a pheasant ranch near Lake Tahoe, where Rick began scrambling around on rocks and dreaming of being a mountain climber. When the pheasant ranch burned to the ground, Ridgeway's father didn't handle it well.

"I was about eleven when my dad split," said Ridgeway. "I didn't see him for years, but I did get post cards. They were all from some South Seas island — pictures of bare-breasted women with orchids in their hair."

Rick's mother bought him an Outward Bound climbing course for high-school graduation, and there he began learning the technical aspects of rock climbing. He enrolled in the University of Hawaii, studied oceanography, and lived with his dad, who had settled in Oahu. "My dad'd come home with a bottle of booze and a couple of floozies on his arm," said Ridgeway. "He'd tell me to close the books became it was party time." Ridgeway said, laughing affectionately. "My dad was the kind of man that no matter what he was doing, he was listening to a ukulele song in his mind."

When the silent ukuleles got too loud — after about four months — Rick moved onto a boat down at the yacht harbor. A standout member of the university sailing team, he was invited to crew on a sailboat headed for Tahiti that summer. This voyage was a seminal experience for Rick Ridgeway.

"We had been three weeks at sea," he said, "and one morning, just at dawn, we could see the jagged silhouette of mountains, land. I was eighteen years old then, but I can still see the morning sun fill in the details of the big valleys leading up to the central peaks of Tahiti. Magic: Tahiti at dawn seen through a young kid's eyes." Ridgeway stayed two months, then left for his sophomore year in college.

Back in Hawaii, Rick changed his major to anthropology because, he said, "'I wanted to learn more about the people I had met on some of the more remote islands." He spent his summers crewing on boats that sailed around the world. "I was wide-eyed at this point. Twenty-two years old and looking for one adventure after another. I wanted to think of myself as a modern-day pirate." It was a fantasy that died a hard death in a Panama City jail.

In Central America, Ridgeway met three young men who owned an eighty-foot schooner. They wanted to start a yacht charter service in Fiji. To get the seed money, the four men pooled what they had and ordered $6,000 worth of .22 shells from the rifle range in the American-governed Canal Zone of Panama. They planned to trade shells, illegally, to Indian prospectors in Colombia in exchange for emeralds, which they'd sell to Hindu gem merchants in Fiji.

Before the bulk of the shells arrived, however, Rick and his partners sailed around, fun-hogging it and trading the ammunition they'd been able to buy for food and other necessities. "We traded shells for an ounce of marijuana," said Rick, "with a guy who turned out to be an agent." Panamanian authorities thought they had stumbled onto a ring of big-time bad guys — gunrunners and dope dealers. The marijuana had been long consumed by the time Rick was arrested. "Christ," said Rick, "this gunboat pulled up, and the cops boarded us. My girlfriend and I were alone on the boat They tied me to the mast and stuck a machine gun in my neck, screaming and swearing. And when they couldn't find any dope, they got really mad."

Ridgeway's friends were in the Canal Zone, not subject to arrest, and they eventually sacrificed the boat and all the accumulated cash to pay his legal fees. Ridgeway spent a month in jail. "God," he said, "'it was horrible. I saw five people get killed in that time." One man — "He cussed the guards" — was beaten to death, apparently with rubber hoses. Another man who killed a guard was tortured to death. "We could all hear him screaming," Ridgeway recalled.

> And the whole time I was there, I was facing the specter of Coiba, the prison island. Guys who'd been there told horror stories — guys with no hands telling you about how they made you work in the swamp with alligators. Every week the guards would read a list of names, and everybody on the list had to go to Coiba. Men would break down and cry when they heard their names read. It was a nightmare.

When Ridgeway's friends finally sprang him, Rick took his last twenty dollars to a casino where the roulette wheel was kind to him. He then had several hundred dollars in his pocket and an intense desire in his heart to leave Panama.

* * *

With his degree from Hawaii, Ridgeway finally landed a job as an anthropologist for the University of Manchester. "They were doing a study in the Andes, and I was living in this little Indian village with mountains all around," he said. "Well, I got a hankering to go climbing again. I did two new routes and four big ascents altogether that first season. And I met all kinds of climbers" — guys like Ron Fear, one of America's best high-altitude climbers, a man who had just completed the first ascent of Dhaulagiri II, in the Himalayas.

Ridgeway was twenty-four, and for the next few years he spent his summers guiding mountain-climbing expeditions with Fear in Peru and his winters sailing in Hawaii. The high-altitude guide service wasn't paying for itself, though, so Rick and Fear decided to take clients rafting on a Peruvian river called the Urubamba.

It was there on the Urubamba that a simple miscalculation cost two lives. Ridgeway arrived first, but Fear was delayed and missed the train. While Rick waited downriver, Fear decided to put in, with the clients, at a spot well upriver from their departure. "Ron didn't know about the waterfall," said Ridgeway, with no change of expression. His words came slower, though, in a stumbling cadence.

> Fear went over the falls and killed himself and one of our clients. And it was, uh, it was my first experience with someone real close to me getting killed. That same week I got the news that my main rock-climbing partner in California had fallen off El Cap in Yosemite. And he was killed. All at once. It happened all at once.

Dealing with that sort of grief "gave me pause," said Ridgeway. Still, there was an elemental lesson left unlearned.

> Even though I had two close friends die, I was removed from it. I was saying, "It wouldn't happen to me." Both accidents were the result of a miscalculation, and I thought, "I won't make those mistakes?"

It wasn't until later that I discovered the huge difference between learning to take risks and learning to die. More than that, I learned the real emotion of what it is to die, and I think you only learn that when you come very close to death — when you think you are dead."

But that didn't happen until years later: a final revelation on the remote and deadly Chinese mountain Minya Konka.

* * *

The deserted beach at San Miguel stretches out into an infinity of sand. An elephant seal, half a mile away, slips into the surf. We might be walking through another century, another millennium: San Miguel before the time of man. The incoming tide has tossed thousands of tiny crabs up onto the beach, and a white blanket of seagulls at surf's edge are feeding greedily. They rise before us as we walk, hector us with their shrill cries, then settle down to feed behind us as we pass. It is like walking through a living cloud.

We scramble out onto the tide pools, under the cloud of hovering gulls, and collect mussels for tonight's dinner. Later we'll fish. Just fun-hog out, here on San Miguel: pork chops of seafood and Chardonnay.

* * *

Through his friend Fear, Ridgeway met other climbers, and one of them got him on America's bicentennial Everest expedition. He was on the South Col, at the magic 8,000-meter mark, chosen for the second summit team, when the Sherpa support team quit. A good thing — Rick was suffering from bronchitis but would have surely made a deadly try for the summit.

CBS filmed the Everest climb, and Ridgeway worked with the movie crew. Ridgeway said:

One time, we were way up near the South Col, and one

of the guys was filming. I was helping him when it dawned on me that we were doing exactly the same thing. Climbing. The camera guy was having every bit of the adventure I was, except he was getting paid for it. I thought, "A guy might be able to make a living out of adventuring."

Rick settled down to write a book on the Everest climb, and *The Boldest Dream* sold well. He looked up Mike Hoover, the climber and director of the Everest film, who told him, "All you need is an idea."

"I got plenty," Ridgeway said.

"Give me one."

Ridgeway had been reading about Alexander von Humboldt's travels in South America, and he was fascinated by descriptions of giant rock towers erupting out of the jungles of the Guiana Highlands. Hoover thought the idea sounded good, and Rick drew up a proposal for ABC. Two weeks later, Hoover called up and said, "We got it."

Hoover coordinated the filming, and Rick organized the climb of Mount Autana, the first ascent. The film was a success, and Ridgeway, with his various writing and lecturing and film projects, was beginning to make a career out of adventure.

In 1978, Ridgeway was invited to join an expedition to K2, the world's second-highest mountain.

There was no money in it, but I was disappointed about not making the summit of Everest, and I couldn't pass up the chance. Well, K2 was tough. Not extremely technical, but we had to work our asses off. No Sherpas to support us. From basecamp to summit, we were sixty-eight days on the mountain. All above 18,000 feet. I looked like a concentration-camp victim after the climb. I lost twenty-five pounds. My fingers were black from frostbite. We suffered from hypoxia [lack of oxygen]. There was dissension: personalities just exposed to the quick. But four of us made the summit, three of us without oxygen. It's my major mountaineering feat. It was the first ascent by the northeast ridge, the first American ascent, the first ascent without oxygen.

Ridgeway's book on K2, *The Last Step*, was well received. He earned more money on a slide-show lecture about the expedition. He also learned that the first step in making the business of adventure pay is simply drafting the proposal, and in 1979, the year after K2, Ridgeway watched as Mike Hoover tried to put together a trip to Antarctica. The television people loved the Everest film and asked him — Ridgeway thinks this is a funny question — "What can you do that's bigger than Everest?"

"Climb the highest peak in Antarctica," he answered.

"Is it bigger than Everest?"

"Not higher, but . . . "

"We dunno."

"Okay, we'll get to the peak by dog sled."

"Still not bigger than Everest."

"We'll sail down on an old squarerigger, with the dogs on board."

"Interesting, but . . .

"And we 'll film it live, by satellite."

TV liked that one. Hoover and Ridgeway began organizing the project, but the only usable satellite died and funding dried up. Hoover, however, had put so much work into the preparation that he decided to go anyway, and Ridgeway chose to join him. ABC picked up expenses in return for a short film.

Ridgeway and Hoover took a tourist ship down, hoping to hitch a ride on a supply ship out of Antarctica. They had no reservations.

"Well, we went scuba diving and iceberg climbing," Ridgeway said. Fun-hogging Antarctica. The expedition had inflatable rafts powered by outboards, and Ridgeway water-skied the

Antarctic seas, cutting rooster tails around the ice floes. "And all the time," he said, "it was like the sword of Damocles hanging over you, ready to fall in the form of winter. What if the last ship out wouldn't give us a ride? We'd have to stalk seals. Live in an ice cave for eight months." And die, in all probability.

An Argentine freighter finally got Hoover and Ridgeway out of the ice before winter clamped down on the continent. Hoover's film for *American Sportsman* won an Emmy, and a year later, in 1980, Ridgeway got his first chance to produce his own film. ABC was financing an expedition to a remote peak in an isolated eastern margin of the Tibetan plateau. The mountain was called Minya Konka.

* * *

The day's surf is dismal, but Ridgeway notes, in his journal, the location of a beach that would have great breaks in a south swell. The island of Santa Rosa looks perfect for a sea-kayaking expedition. The diving, in a kelp bed off Santa Cruz, has been exhilarating. We drink a crisp, cold pinot blanc with our dinner of lobster and scallops.

I ask Rick about the framed photos of exotic people and places I had seen in his home. "They're great," he says. "They were taken by Jonathan Wright." Ridgeway stares down into his wine. "Jonathan was one of my best friends."

In 1980, Ridgeway's Minya Konka expedition was the second party of American climbers allowed into China in recent history. They had just set up Camp 2 and were working their way across a crevasse field when their weight kicked loose an avalanche.

> We tried to arrest out of it, but the wet heavy snow was too much. It sucked us down into it. In just a couple of seconds, we were in the middle of an exploding sea of ice. All I remember is looking around, seeing the guys with me: arms, legs, and then only ice boiling all

around. I was getting bashed, banged around, and then I came up again. I could see Yvon's head in front of me, and then the slope got steeper.

We went off a cliff in a sea of ice, and I figured, "Shit, I'm dead. This is it." I was absolutely certain that was the last moment of my life. I could see all the way down below, see the whole valley of Tibet laid out in front of me, and I knew I was dead.

I got sucked inside the ice again, and it just went on and on. I had my eyes open, and all I could see was blue and white. Ice blocks crushing me.

Ridgeway popped to the surface of the slide a second time and saw that he was being funneled down a narrow canyon.

There was tons of ice. I could see Yvon's head sticking up in front of me. And I thought, "I just might survive this thing." I struggled as hard as I could to stay on top and keep my feet positioned downhill. I could see rock on both sides whizzing by as we were blasting down, but the snow all around seemed still because I was moving with it. All this snow that seemed stationary — it was like it was breathing, pulsing, moving up and down like the lungs of some huge monster.

We hit an alluvial fan at the bottom of the couloir, and it started to slow down. Then it stopped. I thought, "Jesus Christ, I must be banged up pretty bad, but I'm alive." So I struggled to get off to the side . . . and the avalanche took off again. We were sliding toward a huge cliff. It was horrible, because for a moment I thought I was going to live and then I was dead again.

The avalanche stopped a second time, right in front of the cliff. I looked around, and Yvon was digging himself out. He was bleeding from the head. Kim Schmitz was moaning off to one side. He had broken

135

his back. Jonathan Wright was next to me, moaning. I was bashed up, but I really didn't seem to be hurt, and I started attending to Jonathan, who was in the worst shape. He had passed out, and I tried to keep him alive with mouth-to-mouth resuscitation. Half an hour later, he went limp and died in my arms.

Ridgeway came back from Minya Konka "not sure I'd ever climb again. I was left hollow. Vacant." It took him well over a year to come to grips with the tragedy on Minya Konka, longer than that to understand what adventuring meant — its value and lessons.

* * *

Ridgeway, Chouinard, and I pull on wet suits, ready for another dive.

One thing I learned on Minya Konka: you don't have to keep upping the odds. You try to control the risks. What we're doing now, it's a good adventure. And I still think the best adventure I've ever had is the first Tahiti trip. I hate to use the word "jaded," but it was a time for me when the world seemed larger than it is. As you grow older and have more experiences, it's hard to recapture the sparkle and magic you had when you were really young. But I look for it, I quest for it.

Ridgeway sets the mask on his face and falls off over the side of the boat. I follow him down into the kelp bed. The massed vegetation on the surface breaks the light of the sun until it looks like the backscatter of headlights seen through a lilac bush on a still summer night. Ridgeway disappears off to my right, and we both search for our own magic, alone, in that silent prism of tangled light.

* * *

In 1981, Ridgeway didn't really do much but think about Minya Konka.

> I couldn't come to grips with the idea of further adventures, because now I knew just what it was to die. I was shoved out over the edge, given a chance to stare into the abyss, then yanked back. That's what it was — a blank abyss. I knew that in my gut. Things just stop, and you rot away.
>
> Then I began to realize that the whole trick is to keep that rotting from happening. Is it worth it to go out there, risking the abyss, for . . . what? The thrill? The lesson? After a year of contemplating it, I started to realize that it was. I must admit, I was lucky. If Jonathan could say whether it was worth it, he'd surely say otherwise. But the way I saw it, my life had been reduced to a handful of seconds, and now I had millions. I realized that everything I was doing had a freshness to it. A magic. The value I'd learned from Jonathan's death, and my own near-death, was that sense of moment. It's an incomparable scale to rate things by, to know what is and what is not a matter of consequence in your life.

In 1982, Ridgeway finished the Minya Konka project, a film about the mountain and the death. It won a Golden Eagle award. He produced an hour-long special for HBO about a group of handicapped climbers. The short movie won awards at the San Francisco and Chicago film festivals. He married Jennifer, promotion director at Chouinard's Patagonia; his daughter Carissa was born a year later. Meanwhile, he was putting together several proposals, most of which he assumed would be rejected. In 1983, every Ridgeway proposal was accepted and funded. It was a remarkable year, even by Rick Ridgeway's standards.

In January, Rick got hooked up with Frank Wells and Dick Bass, two businessmen who, late in life, hatched a scheme to climb the highest peak on each continent. They hired Ridgeway to guide their expedition to Aconcagua, South America's highest peak.

"I got back from that one," Rick said, "and found that ABC wanted me to cover the Bass-Wells attempt on Everest." Ridgeway was the climbing color commentator. He got to stand shivering in front of the microphone in fifty-mile-an-hour winds and say, "If the weather clears, they'll be going for the summit tomorrow. And now back to Bob Beattie in Katmandu."

Coming down from Everest, in Katmandu, Ridgeway learned that the Camel cigarettes marketing department had accepted his proposal for the second Camel expedition — a traverse across the unmapped breadth of Borneo, the world's third largest island. The expedition would trek across jungle highlands and make the first descent of the Kayan River, which rivals the Colorado for rapids and danger. It was there, in Borneo, that Ridgeway came within a day of death.

He was hiking the jungle when the fever hit him. Nausea, vomiting, and cold sweats left him dehydrated. "My fingers had curled over," said Ridgeway. "Even my toes had curled down from all the dehydrated ligaments shrinking. I had severe leg cramps and could barely walk."

The rest of the party had gone ahead, hoping to stumble onto a native village and medical help. Ridgeway and climber John Long were slogging along alone when they came on a huge expanse of burning forest. The local people, the Dyaks, had been headhunters well into this century, and they still use the slash-and-burn method to clear land for their rice paddies. The hardwoods smolder for days, and Ridgeway stumbled through the choking haze, figuring that there must be a village somewhere nearby. He could walk only 100 yards at a time.

The trek took Ridgeway over beds of burning coals in temperatures of well above 150 degrees. Blue flames hissed out of gutted hardwood trees. "That walk," Rick said, "was as tough as the last day on K2."

At the village beyond the burning forest, Ridgeway was taken before the Dyak chief, a jowly, betel-chewing man who held court in a 600-foot long house. The Westerner, clearly, had only a few days to live, and the nearest doctor was 350 miles away — 350 miles by river and on foot. The chief said that some months back a missionary had landed a plane on a nearby grass plateau and had promised to return on Indonesian independence day, August 17. "By happenstance and good luck," said 'Ridgeway, "the date was August 15, and the missionary kept his promise. I was evacuated, but it still took me another three days to get to a doctor. By then I couldn't even walk. I had to be carried. I had dehydrated so much I went into a fetal position and couldn't straighten up."

Back at home in Ventura, California, Rick began putting together a film on the Borneo trip and recuperating, but in November — this is still 1983, remember, the year of Everest, Aconcagua, and Borneo — Wells and Bass asked Rick to help guide and organize their climb of the 17,000-foot Vinson Massif, Antarctica's highest mountain.

They were to fly down from California in a DC-3 that had been built in 1941 and retrofitted with turboprop engines for arctic use. The climb, Ridgeway said, "was a classic *Raiders of the Lost Ark* adventure. Imagine this old rattletrap plane landing on skis 760 miles from the South Pole. A climb in possibly the most remote area in the world, and all of us completely dependent on our ability to solve and anticipate problems." Famed climber Chris Bonington was along on the trip, as was Yuichiro Miura, who is best known for skiing down Mount Everest. The climb took two and a half weeks in fifty-degree-below weather with stiff winds. Everyone made the summit, but Ridgeway admitted, "I was in a little trouble because I still hadn't fully recovered from the typhoid and felt weak. Anyway, we came back, crossed our fingers, and started up the plane. There was a big cheer when we were finally airborne."

* * *

Ridgeway, at the wheel, squints into the glare of ocean and sun, holding a course he plotted a few hours earlier. We are out of sight of land, heading home. "Tighten up on that sheet a little," he says. The wind's behind us, and this is a sleigh ride, a pleasure cruise. Rick treats himself to a beer.

"I suppose" he says, "sailing and climbing are the twin passions of my life." He's interested in putting together a proposal that would involve sailing to several sub-Antarctic islands and making the first ascents of various mountains there.

Nineteen eighty-three was such a busy year — four major expeditions, ten months of travel — that Rick Ridgeway spent 1984 "basically recovering." He finished a new book, *Seven Summits,* and designed a line of high-quality, moderately expensive camping gear for Kelty — the Ridgeway line. And in 1985, just after the birth of his second daughter, Cameron, he did some climbing in Bhutan, in the Himalayas, on an expedition funded by Rolex watches. Recently, he's been at work on a feature-film project.

"I want to start pacing my adventures," Rick says, "to balance my life out and spend more time with my wife and children."

Rick's more rational schedule has also given him time to think about the business of adventure.

> Ever hear of Joshua Slocum? Guy wrote a book about sailing around the world in the 1890s. Slocum had been the skipper of a square-rigged sailing ship, and when steam came in, he refused to convert. He was out of a job, but he found a small sailboat decaying in a cow pasture and resurrected it. Called it the *Spray.*
>
> Before Slocum, yachtsmen had names like du Pont, and they wore suits and ties while their crews sailed the ships. Slocum didn't have much money, but rather than give up sailing, he took off on his own for a great

adventure around Cape Horn and across the South Pacific.

To me, he's the predecessor of a whole brethren of modern-day adventurers. Sailing was his occupation, but when it was impossible to find the adventure he loved in his job, he found it through a risk sport. That's what people do today. I think it's pretty tough to find any occupation that has real adventure to it, something that gives you the satisfaction derived from taking controlled risks, from learning your own limits, from visiting unique places, and from expending the physical effort it takes to get to those places. If people can't find that satisfaction in their occupation, they try to get it through sport. To my mind, Slocum is the first guy to do that.

In the hazy distance, the coastline of Southern California becomes visible. The sun is low, and it explodes off the windows of houses high on the coastal range.

"It's funny," Ridgeway says, "but now it seems there are a few people like myself who've brought the concept full circle. We've attempted to make an occupation out of sport."

The harbor breakwater looms up before us. The course Rick plotted was true, not a single degree off, and we sail safely into the harbor without a turn of the wheel: pork chops of the sea, home before dark.

John Roskelley. *Photo by Greg Child*

A Direct Style

JOHN ROSKELLEY

By David Roberts

[From "The Direct Style of John Roskelley," OUTSIDE, July 1983]

I n the anarchic community of mountaineering, there is no such thing as common consent. But if you asked a random sample of American climbers who this country's best high-altitude mountaineer is, most would answer without hesitation, "John Roskelley." He has climbed in the Himalaya during ten of the last eleven years. He is the only American to have reached the summit of three different 8,000-meter peaks. In addition, he has led the first ascents of four lower but technically far more difficult Himalayan mountains. In an article last year, Reinhold Messner, who is often cited as the world's foremost mountaineer, declared that he thought Roskelley was the stronger climber.

In Europe, Messner is a name comparable in celebrity to a film star, while Roskelley, in his own country and elsewhere, remains relatively little known, even to other climbers. A few years ago the British journal *Mountain,* the most widely read publication of its kind in the world, published an interview with him titled, "Who is this man Roskelley?" Unlike Messner, Roskelley has no real flair for self-promotion. He is, in a sense, a simple and retiring man who cherishes the privacy of his own family. He has spent thirty-four years in Spokane, Washington, and plans to spend the rest of his life there too.

Despite these traits, Roskelley has managed to embroil himself in controversy and to acquire a minor legion of detractors. Out of such notoriety a cartoon persona has emerged: Roskelley as staunch misogynist, as ultraredneck, as cold and ruthless climber out for his own glory. The bitterest imbroglio surrounds his 1980 expedition to Makalu, in the wake of which Roskelley was accused of abandoning a fellow American stricken with cerebral edema so that he could bag the summit in solo triumph.

There is, of course, a paradox here: the man with no talent for self-promotion who has an uncanny knack for attracting criticism. The paradox springs, perhaps, from the fatal combination of two qualities that seem to epitomize John Roskelley. He is one of the bluntest, most outspoken fellows you are ever likely to run across. At the same time, he is, in a certain sense, quite naive. (That naiveté is a key to Roskelley's considerable charm.)

Roskelley tells about one of his pet peeves, "door dings." One day he was sitting in a Spokane parking lot in his new diesel-powered, nine-seater Chevrolet Suburban truck. As is his practice, he was parked sideways, straddling two white-painted slots.

> This cop pulled up next to a little red Porsche. You know Porsches, with those beautiful round bumpers. Anyway, the cop got out of his car in a hurry and, sure enough, put this door ding right in that little Porsche. Then he walked over toward me. I rolled down the window. He said, "What the hell do you think you're doing parking sideways like that?"
>
> So I checked the name on his badge, looked him in the eye, and answered, "One, I happen to know you're out of your jurisdiction here. Two, when I leave this parking lot, there's going to be a note on that Porsche's windshield telling the driver that Officer Collins was responsible for his door ding. And three, the reason I

park sideways is to avoid getting door dings from ass-
holes like you."

Roskelley tells this story not because he thinks it's funny,
which he doesn't, but to illustrate the importance of unceasing
vigilance against the door-dingers among us.

* * *

In March 1983, Roskelley went off to Tibet for an attempt
on the west face of Everest, which he hoped to climb without oxygen, as Messner was the first to do. The world's highest mountain
had already proved a bugaboo for Roskelley: two years ago, as a
member of a large American expedition, he took one look at the
proposed route on the mountain's unclimbed east face and
declared it too dangerous. As it turned out, the expedition failed
far below the top, despite accomplishing some extremely difficult
climbing. Roskelley's nonparticipation caused some hard feelings.
He is returning with a different party this year to attempt the
opposite side of Everest.

"That was a bad year," says Roskelley ruefully. Earlier in
1981, he had also failed on Mount McKinley's Cassin route — his
only Alaskan expedition — when he developed cerebral edema
around 17,000 feet. In 1982, he was brilliantly successful with a
small party on the previously unclimbed Cholatse in Nepal. In
returning to Everest in 1983, however, it was clear that Roskelley
felt that reaching the summit of the highest mountain would not
only give his career a great boost (as it had Messner's), but that he
needed the triumph to bind up private wounds as well.

* * *

Roskelley's father was that rare man who found exactly what
he wanted to do in life. As outdoor editor of the *Spokane Daily
Chronicle* for thirty-four years, he got to hunt and fish three or

four days a week and call it work. At the age of four, John was out with his dad. "He couldn't afford a bird dog," says Roskelley. "I'd drive through the brush and kick up the birds, and he'd shoot 'em." He has remained an avid hunter all his life. "In fact," Roskelley says, "I probably enjoy going after deer, elk, and bear more than I do climbing." The comparison is a logical one, to his mind. "That's where I got so dang fast and efficient [as a climber]. There's nothing more challenging than chasing down a wounded pheasant."

John's father was a Mormon who brought the boy up with strict discipline. In a memoir written for a Japanese mountaineering journal, Roskelley reflected, "I learned many things from my dad, but the two rules I've always tried to follow are 'Do your best' and 'Never give up.' " In grade school, John read the classic mountaineering book *Annapurna;* later, when he was fifteen, his father brought home a review copy of Lionel Terray's autobiography. "I wouldn't say I had heroes," says Roskelley the adult, "but Terray and [Louis] Lachenal did incredible things to me. It was guys growing up and having a good time in the Alps, competing with their friends, the whole camaraderie." At once John enrolled in a basic climbing course offered by the Spokane Mountaineers.

"I went through the course," he recalls, "enjoying it because it meant I could get away from home — it gave me a free rein to do a lot of goofing around. But then I started *liking* it." In the same course was another promising climber named Chris Kopczynski. "Being competitive young kids, we wouldn't talk to each other. Then, on an outing on Mount Shuksan, we met almost on the summit. We were both very speedy and in good shape, and we seemed to have a good time together after we got started talking."

It was the beginning of Roskelley's longest and closest partnership. In the first year, it made for a roughly equal pairing. Soon, however, Roskelley was doing all the hard leads. "I sort of took over at that point," Roskelley explains self-consciously. "We'd get in trouble at times, and it was easier for me to speed out and go. We just had our roles."

During the next nine years, up to the spring of 1973, Roskelley became a very strong rock climber and mountaineer. He made his mark in the Cascades, the Canadian Rockies, the Bugaboos, and Yosemite, where he teamed up with Mead Hargis to make a fast ascent of the North America Wall — then regarded by many as the hardest rock climb in the world. In view of the climbing he was yet to do, however, Roskelley's record was relatively modest. Almost none of the big walls he had conquered by the age of twenty-four was a first ascent. Nor had he electrified any local climbing scene the way Henry Barber was doing almost routinely wherever he went during those same years. Indeed, in 1972, faced with the necessity of making a living, Roskelley essentially gave up climbing.

He had always worked, as a boy with a paper route and in high school in a packaging-and-shipping job. Summers during school he would work at construction or mining jobs (he was a geology major at Washington State). In 1972, he got married, and though Joyce had a steady income as a schoolteacher, John wanted to contribute. "I got a job retreading tires for a local company, on the graveyard shift. I was making $2.80 an hour on some of the hardest work I'd ever done, using old steam molds, burning my forearms on these pipes. God, it was terrible. But I had to have the money."

As 1973 began, Roskelley was, in his own phrases, "hurtin' " for money and "bummed out" about life. One day he was bouldering near Spokane with a talented local climber named Del Young. "I said, 'What are you going to do this year?' " Roskelley recalls. "Del said, 'I'm heading off for Dhaulagiri.' I said, 'Really? God, how'd you get on that?' He said, 'I just applied.' So I said, 'Geez, maybe there's a chance I can get on.' " Roskelley went home, wrote up a "climbing resume," and sent it to the expedition. A month later, just as he was giving up hope, he got a call from Jeff Duenwald, the deputy leader of the party.

"Duenwald asked me, 'Can you go to Dhaulagiri?' I said, 'Sure. Where is it?' I didn't know where it was, how high it was, nothin'. I just knew I had to get out of here."

With only a month's notice, Roskelley had to scramble to get ready. A consequence of his hurried departure was that he ended up borrowing a pair of boots in Kathmandu that were too short for his feet. On the mountain, Roskelley was a leader in the hard climbing that forged a new route up the mountain's unclimbed southeast side. After a knife-edged ice ridge stopped the party cold, Roskelley was one of three to reach the mountain's summit by the "old" Swiss route. The night before the summit, Roskelley sat sleepless, hunched over a stove trying to warm his already frostbitten feet.

"Standing on the summit," he wrote later, "exhausted and feet frozen, I felt none of the elation I had imagined [the triumph] would create. There had been no magic, just hard work and fear. My greatest concern was getting down alive in the ever-worsening storm and trying to save as much of my feet as possible." He was subsequently hospitalized and had two toes amputated.

On the strength of his Dhaulagiri ascent, Roskelley was invited on the large international expedition to the Soviet Pamirs. During an attempt on Peak Nineteen, a camp established by Roskelley and three others was buried by an avalanche. John and his tentmate frantically dug out the other two, but not before one of them, Gary Ullin, had been suffocated. Roskelley returned to finish the route with Jeff Lowe, but he left the Pamirs, as did the rest of the Americans, under the pall not only of Ullin's death but of the deaths of fourteen other mountaineers who had been killed during that disastrous summer.

On the way home, Roskelley spent a few days in Switzerland, where he and Chris Kopczynski made the first all-American ascent of the north face of the Eiger. As was their arrangement, Roskelley led every pitch. Kopczynski's honest account of the dangerous climb, later published in *Ascent*, is sprinkled with exchanges of the following sort: "'We got to move fast, Kop.' 'I'm going as fast as I can,' I bluntly replied."

In 1975, Roskelley wanted badly to be included on the American K2 expedition but was not invited, he wrote in the Japanese journal, "because of personality conflicts with several members of the team."

Instead, Roskelley that year did a hard new route on Huayna Potosí in Bolivia. For the first time, Joyce accompanied her husband to basecamp on one of his expeditions. Roskelley's trips abroad had, of course, put new strains on the family budget. He had worked for two years as a construction laborer on a new Sheraton Hotel in Spokane, then had traveled through seven states and two Canadian provinces as a sales representative for SMC, the outdoor-equipment firm. "Here I was," Roskelley reflects, "driving around like mad, getting fat, not doing any climbing." He lost the job when he had his driver's license revoked for too many speeding tickets.

That December, in her loyalty, Joyce came to his aid with what Roskelley now sees as a life-changing suggestion. "She said, 'Look, you're not happy working on all these other jobs. Why don't you make your living out of climbing?' " Roskelley plunged into his new career. His plan was to support himself by writing articles, selling photos, and giving slide shows. For the summer of 1976, he had been invited on the Nanda Devi expedition to be led by Willi Unsoeld and H. Adams Carter. Carter had been on the first ascent of the mountain exactly forty years before, when Nanda Devi had become the highest summit yet reached. Before he left for India, Roskelley had decided to write a book about the expedition.

In his view, the Nanda Devi expedition was ill-conceived from the start. The party exhibited an extraordinary range of both talent and ambition. One faction seemed to approach the trip as a vacation outing, although the route the group was attempting was an extremely serious one. In the end, it was unquestionably Roskelley who got the summit party of three to the top of the mountain. As was becoming his wont, he led all the pitches on the steep buttress of mixed rock and ice that was the crux of the route.

During the approach march and as the route was being established, Roskelley made no bones about letting his companions know what he thought of them. Now, when other team members wanted to follow up the fixed ropes for a second summit attempt,

Roskelley bluntly told some of them he didn't think they were qualified for it. They included Unsoeld's daughter Nanda Devi, whom Willi had named for the mountain he considered the most beautiful in the world. The Unsoelds, father and daughter, nevertheless persisted. Then, at a high camp above the difficult buttress, Devi had an acute attack of an abdominal complaint from which she had been suffering on and off; before her teammates could do anything, she died.

* * *

As he returned to the states, then, Roskelley felt burdened by strong and contradictory feelings. Partly to purge the traumatic aftereffects of the expedition, he immersed himself in his book. For more than nine months he toiled at it, often writing six or eight hours a day.

He sent it off to a series of publishers, each of which rejected it. Some offered gentle excuses: mountaineering books never sold, no one cared unless it was Everest, and so on. Even such potentially sympathetic publishers as Sierra Club Books and The Mountaineers turned the volume down. For Roskelley, the experience was deeply vexing. "In Britain," he says today, "guys were turning out expedition books on failures right and left. And I couldn't sell a book on one of the most spectacular climbs done by Americans in recent years — and an interesting story to boot."

Six years later, Roskelley's book remains unpublished. As he is the first to admit, he is not a smooth or graceful writer. Still, the book is the equal of a number of American climbing accounts that have been published in the last few years. The failure to publish was, Roskelley says, "one of the biggest disappointments in my life. It was my Everest." The rejection has turned him, perhaps permanently, away from writing; it is the reason, he says, that he will no longer contribute even perfunctory articles to the mountain journals. (The memoir for the Japanese publication is a rare exception.) Today, Roskelley is stingy even with interviews.

Whatever its literary merits, the Nanda Devi manuscript offers some clues to Roskelley's deeper nature. The man's bluntness and honesty are stamped on every page, and they have the effect of exposing the occasional laziness or cowardice of teammates to merciless scrutiny. Most of the other expedition members have apparently not read the book. If they had, all but one or two of them would breathe a sigh of relief that the account has not been published. Because he is always willing to lay himself on the line, Roskelley makes the shirkings or incompetence of others look pathetic.

On the other hand, Roskelley has an annoying habit of second-guessing. Even if he did indeed advance from the start counsel that later would prove to be wise, the constant punctuation of the narrative with implicit I-told-you-so's seems smug. Roskelley's strictures against others are tempered, if not balanced, by occasional spasms of self-criticism. And he can repeat a joke on himself, as when he passes on the nickname of a certain latrine: " 'Le John' — not only because I had helped build it, but as I was later told, [because] 'it also had a cold and heartless personality.' "

The most striking anticipatory I-told-you-so in the book occurs when Roskelley tries to talk relatively weak climber Elliott Fisher out of abandoning the expedition.

> "You know, I'd like to go out too, Elliott. All of us would. This mountain's dangerous, and someone's going to be killed."
>
> "If that's what you believe, then why don't you leave and get off the mountain?" he asked.
>
> "Because it's not going to be me," I replied.

Yet if the narrative is flavored by a constant incredulity that others refuse to heed his good advice, Roskelley remains reticent about his own superb climbing, which allowed the expedition its success. One must read between the lines to gauge the full measure of his skill, as when he admits that as he was nearing the summit, he was breaking trail in deep snow faster than his two companions could follow in his kicked steps.

More subjectively, Roskelley's book reveals an intense perfectionist who holds himself to even more rigorous standards than he does others. If there is a "cold and heartless" personality at work, it is not that of an egomaniac, but rather of a man who knows exactly how to minimize risk. One way to be safe on a dangerous mountain is never to let someone less competent make decisions for you. At the same time, Roskelley seems to have a naive notion that candor and bluntness are the same thing as truth. He is recurrently grieved to discover that his aggressive confrontations with teammates backfire; it is as if, to John, more sensitive or indirect ways of communicating smack of hypocrisy.

Two years after Nanda Devi, Roskelley joined an expedition to K2 led by Jim Whittaker. Again the range of talent and commitment within the team was immense. Often in the lead, Roskelley was instrumental in placing the party in a strong position for a summit attempt; he was also a leader in the faction who wanted to get to the top without oxygen. When success came, Roskelley was one of the four who reached the second-highest summit in the world.

Like the Nanda Devi expedition, however, this one was split by bitter quarrels. Rick Ridgeway's candid book *The Last Step* revealed what some of the squabbles were about. Roskelley had been the most vocal member of a group who thought that Whittaker was endangering everyone by trying to get his relatively inexperienced wife, Dianne Roberts, higher than she ought to go. And Roskelley was the most outspoken critic of Chris Chandler, who, besides being a long-haired liberal, had apparently become involved with teammate Cherie Bech — whose husband, Terry, was also on the expedition.

Press coverage of the expedition was extensive in the Northwest. The Seattle papers simplified the conflict between native hero Whittaker and outsider Roskelley. The *Post Intelligencer* quoted Dianne Roberts as saying, "Oh, Roskelley is such a male chauvinist . . . .He really believes that Himalayan expeditions are no place for women and if women go on them they should organize their own." The *Times* headlined Roskelley as claiming that AMERICAN WOMEN AREN'T AS COMPETENT AS MEN. The *Post-Intelligencer* concluded, "Roskelley has strong opinions about hippies and women. He and long-haired, free-spirited Dr. Chris Chandler were an instant failure in human relations."

The public image of the redneck woman hater was taking shape. Seldom was Roskelley directly quoted. Ironically, his very excellence as a climber may have reinforced the caricature of a macho superathlete intolerant of all human frailty. Thus journalist Laurence Leamer, a few years later, in a reckless and gossipy biography of Willi Unsoeld, would assert blandly, "On a great mountain Roskelley considered other human beings the way he did crampons or climbing rope, as instruments to get the strongest climbers to the summit."

When he is given a fair chance to explain his views about "hippies and women," Roskelley makes a great deal of sense:

> If you go off on your own expedition with two or three couples on some little peak that's insignificant to American prestige, that's your business. But if you go on a major expedition to K2 or Everest, the climbers should be chosen solely on their ability and their willingness to get along. You only get one permit for K2, and Americans have been trying to climb that mountain for years.
>
> If I'm trained and fit, then I expect my partners to be also. It doesn't make sense to risk hundreds of thousands of dollars and everyone's lives on an expedition just because somebody wants to take some woman who isn't qualified to be there. And obviously, if you have an emotional relationship with someone else on an expedition, that takes precedence over good mountaineering decisions. On K2 we weren't worried about the relationship [Cherie Bech and Chandler] were building, we

were worried about losing the other guy. Any time you combine stresses with the opposite sex, you have a high potential for problems.

In the meantime, Roskelley had been working out a personal alternative to the large, expensive Himalayan expeditions that seemed to produce so much acrimony. In 1977, between Nanda Devi and K2, he was a member of Galen Rowell's six-man assault that succeeded on the beautiful, previously unclimbed Middle Trango Tower. But 1979 was probably Roskelley's finest year in the mountains. In May, he and a Sherpa reached the summit of Gaurishankar, a fierce mountain that had repulsed all previous attempts, including those by some of the world's finest climbers. Roskelley led fifty-eight of the sixty pitches on the climb. Two months later, all four members of Roskelley's Uli Biaho expedition made that mountain's first ascent. Uli Biaho is probably technically the hardest climb yet accomplished in the Himalaya or Karakoram. Roskelley broke his authorial silence to write about the climb in *The American Alpine Journal*. At the end of the article he added in parentheses, "First Grade VII completed by Americans." It had been Messner himself who had first advanced the notion in print of a seventh grade. Roskelley's footnote was as close to an out-and-out boast as he is likely ever to make.

A similar success was last fall's first ascent of Cholatse. Roskelley is proud not only of the fine climbing such expeditions have achieved but also of the style in which they have achieved it. Everest ventures can require upward of $400,000 to launch. Cholatse and Uli Biaho cost only $12,000 each, all-inclusive from the United States.

In 1980, Roskelley applied the lean, low-budget, high-motivation approach to Makalu, the world's fifth-highest mountain. The party of four included Chris Kopczynski, Dr. Jim States (who had reached the summit of Nanda Devi), and Kim Momb. All four were friends from Spokane. There were no Sherpas, and they carried no oxygen. At the end of a long buildup, all but Momb went for the summit. Exhausted, States and Kopczynski had to turn back; Roskelley reached the summit alone. He finished his descent in the dark, knowing that to bivouac would be to die. He admits that Makalu may be the closest he's come to "losing it" in the Himalaya, but he says, "That's the time to be ballsy. You might as well be, for the summit push."

Expecting some modicum of recognition for his team's bold ascent in the finest of possible styles, Roskelley discovered instead on his return an unholy furor circulating along the climbing grapevine. It had to do with Mike Warburton, a climber on a totally separate expedition to nearby Makalu II. At a camp at 20,000 feet, he had fallen seriously ill with cerebral edema. Another member ran down to the Spokane party's basecamp. As Roskelley tells it:

> They were already behind the eight ball . . . and their woman doctor had abandoned the party on the hike in to be with her boyfriend. We were resting up to get ready for the summit. I told their leader to go down and get their team's Sherpas. We gave them stretcher poles, a radio, food, and clothing for the Sherpas. States waited for an extra day. As Chris and I went up, we monitored their effort on the radio.

Roskelley and friends were not, however, willing to abandon their own expedition to try and evacuate Warburton, as long as there were Sherpas available who were trained for the job. "My belief is that every expedition has to be on its own," he says. "You cannot rely on an outside source of rescue." The upshot was that Warburton was eventually carried down the mountain by the Sherpas, then hauled on foot for eleven days — against Roskelley's advice that the party call for a helicopter, he says — down to the lowlands. Warburton spent a long time in the hospital in Nepal and still has trouble with one leg.

"When I got back," says Roskelley, "I learned that we were

catching a lot of shit. There was some slide show in California, and somebody started saying, 'Well, God, Roskelley and States should have helped you more.' " Roskelley was never directly confronted, but the rumor spread, intersecting with the "cold and heartless" persona of caricature. This writer heard about the expedition first as a garbled rumor: "Did you hear about Makalu? Roskelley left some guy to die so he could solo the summit."

What Roskelley feels is a kind of underground boycott against him on the part of the American Alpine Club may or may not have begun then. At the club's annual banquet each December, four or five slide shows are given. By tradition, they honor American mountaineering's finest achievements of the previous year. Roskelley was incredulous that his Makalu team was not invited to do a show in Washington in December 1980. At a luncheon meeting, he confronted AAC president Price Zimmerman and program chairman Sallie Greenwood. Greenwood insisted the show had been designed to focus on climbing in China. "I said I couldn't see the logic behind that," says Roskelley. "I brought up Makalu again. Zimmerman stood up from the table, said, 'Not after what you guys pulled,' and walked out. I chased him into the street and told him essentially what had happened [on Makalu]. But there was no use trying to convince that guy."

Zimmerman's recollection of the meeting is not greatly at odds with Roskelley's, although he puts it as follows: "John was being provocative, and he provoked me into saying something like 'A lot of people have questions about the whole episode.' "

Roskelley subsequently resigned from the AAC. Galen Rowell feels there may be substance to the notion of a club boycott. "Last fall," he says, "I was called by the program committee and asked to do a show on Cholatse. I wasn't able to, so I suggested John. They said, 'No, we couldn't have Roskelley, because of his reputation and all the things he's done and all the problems.' 'What problems?' I asked. 'Makalu.'" Roskelley was not invited, and the Cholatse climb was not among the slide shows featured in Boston last December.

Despite his meager earnings, Roskelley continued through 1981 to try to make a living out of climbing. For the last three years during that span his main source of income was slide shows, for which he had finally begun to charge reasonable fees. Even so, he was grossing only $8,000 to $10,000 a year. Joyce's salary as a teacher was what kept the family afloat.

For the last year and a half, however, Roskelley has been retained by Du Pont to give testimonials for its products Quallofil and Sontique. He is extremely grateful for Du Pont's indulgence: the company seems to buy the argument that Roskelley's real job is climbing, so that going off to the Himalaya or even working out is part of what he's paid to do. He feels considerable pressure, however, "to get to the top of Everest or at least continue a successful trend. They'll drop me like a hot potato if I don't."

Despite his scattered failures, at thirty-four Roskelley is riding the crest of an eleven-year "successful trend." As Galen Rowell puts it, "If you try to single out the factors that make Roskelley the best, you come back to one definite fact. He's done more successful climbs." Perhaps the most incredible measure of the man's dominance is that on Nanda Devi, Huayna Potosí, Cholatse, Gaurishankar, the Eiger, and Makalu, Roskelley led all or most of the pitches. Among his technically most difficult climbs, only on Trango Tower and Uli Biaho did he share leads equally. He is not shy about asking to take someone else's lead. As Rowell says, "On Cholatse he was obviously faster and stronger than I was. He said he could take over, and he was right."

Kim Schmitz went to Everest, Trango Tower, and Uli Biaho with Roskelley and says, "Roskelley has tremendous drive. He goes to a mountain, focuses in, and forgets everything else. But he also acclimatizes quicker than anyone I've ever seen. I don't know why. Some just do, and some just don't." Roskelley denies this. "I'm not stronger than other guys, and I don't acclimatize better. I'm more efficient. I don't waste one ounce of energy if I can help it. It's a lot of little things — cooking, getting out of the tent, knowing how to put on your crampons. It's a matter of pushing even when you're hurting."

Another mark of Roskelley's excellence is that he's had surprisingly few close calls in the mountains. Says Schmitz, "He won't take any risks at all." Rowell clarifies: "A lot of top climbers, once they sink their teeth in a challenge, won't turn back. Roskelley maintains a perspective. He's like Messner in that respect." Much of Roskelley's instinct for safety comes from a distrust of others. "If we're not belaying," he says, "I unrope. That's rule number one. That way I don't kill them, and they don't kill me. And very seldom do I trust other people's [rappel and fixed-rope] anchors. I look at 'em very closely." Not having to trust other people's anchors is, it should be said, a luxury that derives in part from leading most of the pitches yourself.

Roskelley is just starting to be widely known. Thanks to Du Pont, his strong, squinting visage, ice in his beard, stares out from the pages of several magazines every month. He nurses a feeling, however, that his climbs have not gained the attention they deserve. "I've gotten recognition from the people who count," he says. "But I do feel that some of the people I've climbed with, once they're back in the United States, haven't given the credit to my feats that they seemed to while we were on the mountain."

* * *

To spend time with Roskelley in his home in Spokane is to gain a much better understanding of the man. In the context of a blue-collar mining and timbering town, as in Roskelley's strict Mormon upbringing, the redneck image that creates so much glee among other climbers reveals itself as basic down-home integrity. As he runs around town doing errands, Roskelley is unfailingly courteous to everyone he meets. He does not even play the small-town boy made good; he is still the small-town boy.

A typical day includes racquetball before breakfast, a seven-mile run at noon, and an hour or two on the Nautilus in the evening. Even driving to the gas station, Roskelley is impatient. He walks fast wherever he goes, and he visibly hates to waste time.

(Galen Rowell's wife, Barbara, recalls a Roskelley visit: "He can't sit still. He can't just come in and relax for a while. He's like a restless, pacing cat.") His hobbies are all energetic ones: hunting, downhill skiing, karate (he's a green belt). When asked if he has any sedentary pastimes, he says, "Working around the house." Sedentary? "Well, you're in one place for a long time."

Roskelley is about five feet ten inches tall, 150 pounds; he looks bigger, perhaps because of his energy. He is quite clearly in fantastic shape. His face is rugged but youthful, with angular, pleasing features; dark, straight hair, cut conservatively; and eyes that brighten when he breaks into his good-looking grin. Women seem to notice him, although even in Spokane his is not yet a recognized face.

Joyce and John have lived in the same suburban house for the past eleven years. The rooms are decorated with keepsakes from his travels, including a gigantic Pakistani samovar. The wall of the den is draped with the hide of a black bear he recently shot. Joyce has a sixteen-year-old daughter by a previous marriage and gave birth to a boy last July. Even though Joyce has been, by Roskelley's admission, the "breadwinner" for many of their years together, he is the patriarch in his own home. "Blood is more important than anything else," he says. "If I go off on an expedition, I know I have a place to return to, people who care for me." His ambition is to make enough money so that Joyce can quit her job and stay at home.

Joyce accepts her husband's supremacy without question. To an extraordinary degree, she is familiar with the minutiae of his expeditions and conflicts, what so-and-so said about John five years ago, how such-and-such newspaper misquoted him. In the *Mountain* interview, she talked about what it was like when John went off on an expedition.

> When he leaves, he has packed and left a mess in
> every room of the house. As I adjust to his being gone,
> a few things get put away until everything gets put away

and then I know that I've shifted gears. Leaving his stuff out is like part of him is still here. . . . One year, the first year he left, I didn't change the sheets the whole time he was gone.

Roskelley has what he calls "a strong value system." The sanctity of the family is a basic tenet of that system. Not entirely in jest, he says that the working men of Spokane — deliverers of packages and the like — are afraid to come to his home because he has let the word get out what he will do to any guy he catches with his wife. He refers to Joyce always as "my wife," never by name. Another basic tenet is honesty — "Regardless of how much it hurts, tell the truth."

Roskelley describes himself as "patriotic." He wanted to join the CIA and tried to go to Vietnam to fight, but he was classified 1-Y for a back injury. "He doesn't hate hippies," says Kim Schmitz, "he hates war protesters." Roskelley abhors the use of drugs and reports that if other climbers smoke pot on expeditions, he's not usually aware of it — "They sure don't bring it around me." His greatest pet peeve, beyond even door dings, is cigarette smoking. He hasn't had a drink since last May, because, he says, he didn't like the way he felt in the morning after quaffing a beer or two the previous night.

Galen Rowell suggests that Roskelley may have learned to bait others with his own straightness. "He loves to get a reaction," says Rowell. "If we're walking along, and I'm talking about stalking some animal to take a photograph, he'll talk about stalking one to blow its head off."

There is, in general, an unmistakable streak of pure aggressiveness in Roskelley's everyday demeanor. He plays racquetball the way he climbs: whaling the ball, all straight shots, hard and low, nothing cutesy with the side walls. As he drives his Chevrolet Suburban around Spokane, he keeps up a commentary for his infant son, Jess, who is strapped into a special harness seat next to him. A small car pulls across the intersection ahead; Roskelley accelerates. "Let's get that little Toyota, Jess, okay? Crunch him up good."

There is also a tender side, albeit guarded. On the eve of his most recent expedition, he bounced Jess in his arms, confessing, "Leaving this guy is going to be the hardest thing about Everest." On the expeditions he writes poetry, which he mails home to Joyce.

After two decades of climbing hard, without a year away from expedition life in the last eleven, Roskelley is showing some minor signs of fatigue. "Physically," he says, "I think I can keep it up for an indefinite number of years. Mentally, I don't believe I can." Nonetheless, he has expeditions planned and applied for through 1987. Eventually, he predicts, "I could conceivably lead expeditions. They seem to pick on older climbers for that. And I've always got hunting. It's just as gratifying as climbing. I can hunt till I die." He imagines eschewing his gun in favor of a bow: "Like cutting off Sherpas and oxygen. Certain animals I've hunted with a gun deserve better from me."

In the *Mountain* interview, Roskelley was asked how he would like to be remembered if he disappeared tomorrow on some climb. "That I was a good husband and a good father," he answered. "That I didn't really let anyone down, and that I was honest to everyone I met."

Roskelley reads very little about climbing. (He is more likely to immerse himself in the long novels of Leon Uris and James Michener.) Other climbers have had little influence on him, and he is reluctant to admit that he might ever have had heroes. But he says, "One person I looked up to more than any other was T. E. Lawrence. He had an incredible story to tell, yet he talked about it in this casual, mundane way. He never really let on that what he did was so important to the world."

Mugs Stump. *Photo by Michael Kennedy*

A Journey of the Spirit

MUGS STUMP

By Michael Kennedy

[From CLIMBING, February 1993]

High on the Cassin Ridge, three climbers considered their options. It was bitter cold and snowing hard, and as far as they could tell, they were off route. Searching for a decent bivouac among the windswept granite cliffs, they were astounded to see a lone figure off to the side, climbing quickly and confidently up into the raging storm.

Carrying nothing but the ice tools in his hands, a liter of water, a few energy bars, a stove, and a parka stuffed in a day pack, Mugs Stump paused briefly to shout directions to the trio. Concerned that he'd disappear into the clouds above and never be seen again, they told him he'd be welcome to share their shelter.

It was early in the morning on June 5, 1991. Mugs briefly considered staying with the three climbers. "I knew how bad it could get up high," he said several months later. "I had to make a conscious decision to keep going." But feeling that the storm wouldn't get any worse, he pressed on toward the summit of North America's highest peak.

Mugs had developed a keen sense of the vagaries of the region's weather from his years of experience in the Alaska Range,

163

so the intensity of the storm came as no surprise. He had also made several previous ascents of Denali, including two of the Cassin, and realized that he now might be climbing into a trap. Although he had already dispensed with the major technical difficulties of the route, the wind and cold could stop him dead in his tracks at almost any point. Nearly 4,000 feet lay between him and the cloud-encased summit at 20,320 feet. And from there he'd still have to make a tiring, 6,000-foot descent before reaching the safety of his camp.

Mugs had started at 14,200 feet on the West Buttress at 9 P.M. the previous night, traversing over and descending the steep West Rib to the start of the Cassin Ridge at 11,500 feet. Near the bottom of the West Rib, he encountered a party laboring up the steep snow, belaying each other and carrying heavy loads. "You're bumming our epic, man," one of them commented as Mugs sped past.

Continuing on in the twilight of the Alaskan summer night, he motored up the Japanese Couloir and the ice ridge above, then tackled the difficult traverse necessary to circumvent the bergschrund below the Cassin's hanging glacier at 13,900 feet. At 5 A.M. he came across a Czech climber bivouacked in the first rock band. The weather had started to go bad, and Miroslav Smid made tea while the two got acquainted. "We are solo brothers," Smid told Mugs, offering him a spot in his tattered tent until the weather improved. After a short stop, though, Mugs continued up the route.

By the time he'd reached the off-route party in the second rock band, Mugs was climbing in a full-scale Alaskan blizzard. Yet there was something oddly serene about the snow drifting silently down the steep granite and the surrealistic gray clouds swirling all around. "I felt very comfortable being up there alone, at home," he said later. Even the distant howl of the wind on the summit ridge seemed less threatening than usual.

His intuition about the storm and his faith in his capabilities paid off. A few hours later, Mugs climbed through the clouds into the morning sun, and soon he was standing happily atop the Cassin Ridge at 20,000 feet. He had spent fifteen hours on a route that even fast-roped parties climb in four or five days. Eschewing the summit, a half-hour of easy walking away, he headed down, taking a short nap in the middle of the "Football Field," the 19,000-foot summit plateau, along the way. Mugs stumbled back into his camp on the West Buttress at 12:30 A.M. on June 6, just twenty-seven and one-half hours after leaving it.

* * *

As long as it was at least a little bit *out there*, Mugs Stump was always psyched for anything — big walls, long free routes, frozen waterfalls, or high-alpine faces. A true climber's climber, he wanted to be on the edge, pushing the envelope of possibility, getting to that rare place where you climb intuitively, fluidly, unburdened by doubt and fear. Although Mugs readily shared his experiences with friends in conversation and letters, he seldom wrote articles or lectured about his climbs. The act of climbing, the doing, was the important thing. The Emperor Face on Mount Robson in the Canadian Rockies, the East Face of the Moose's Tooth and the Moonflower Buttress on Mount Hunter in Alaska, his two big solo routes on Mount Gardiner and Mount Tyree in Antarctica, and his one-day solo of the Cassin were all precedent-setting climbs, but he wasn't primarily concerned with either his physical performance or making history. For Mugs was more than just a superb athlete he pursued his climbing, and his life, as a quest for spiritual enlightenment, a search for the godhead.

Other climbers were stunned by his rapid solo of the Cassin. The closest anyone has come to his time was Charlie Porter, who took thirty-six hours from the top of the Japanese Couloir during the first solo of the route in 1976. But Mugs considered this audacious ascent as just another step along the path he'd been following for well over a decade. Inspired by the enchainments done in the Alps, he'd even thought about doing a super link-up of hard routes on Denali, Mount Foraker, and Mount Hunter, the three highest summits in the Alaska Range. It would be a project of almost unimaginable proportions, involving miles of glacier travel and close to 30,000 feet of elevation gain as well as difficult climbing in harsh arctic conditions.

Before the Cassin solo, he had planned to solo a new route leading up from the head of the remote Peters Glacier to Denali's north summit and, after a rest, go on to the Cassin. "The Fathers and Sons Face [as he had named his proposed route] has become a deep part of me," he wrote in his journal at the time. "It can be done on-sight and solo, and it is extreme and big and at altitude in Alaska — It is the epitome of this type of big mountain climbing." But during a lengthy reconnaissance and acclimatization period on the nearby West Buttress, he became increasingly concerned with the amount of new snow building up on the route. He decided to leave it for another year, opting for the Cassin alone.

"The Cassin wasn't the ultimate," Mugs told me later, as we sat around his ramshackle house in Sandy, Utah. "What it really did was to open my mind to lots of other possibilities." We talked about some of those possibilities, about climbs past and what he or I or our contemporaries might be capable of, about what the next generation of alpinists would do and the potential adventures that would be left for our children.

As always, Mugs was full of plans: for 1992 alone, he had lined up forays to the Black Canyon, Yosemite, Alaska, Baffin Island, and Antarctica. He was in the middle of negotiating the purchase of the house he'd lived in for several years, and he had hopes of getting a concessionaire's permit to guide on Denali. He was as happy and as at peace with himself as I'd ever known him to be.

It was an enlightening discussion, pleasantly interrupted by friends passing through on their way to a ski tour, random questions from other house guests, and numerous trips to Mugs's library to dig out references to certain peaks or faces. Crumpled sleeping bags littered much of the open floor space, and ropes, racks, and ice gear haphazardly decorated the walls. We parted with tentative plans for a climb together, our first in several years.

"Much form and concentration," he wrote to his parents in March after making the first winter ascent of the Hallucinogen Wall in the Black Canyon of the Gunnison, Colorado, with John Middendorf. "Home on the stone. Close to those I love and the 'big force.' " The day before Mugs left for Alaska later that spring, he told me about the Hallucinogen, and we talked about our proposed trip, going over the mundane details of peak fees and the logistics of Third World travel. "Do you think you'll *really* be able to spend that much time away from home?" he asked me, more concerned about how I'd feel leaving my young son for such an extended period of time.

Three weeks later, on a perfect Saturday morning as I packed lunch before leaving for a mountain-bike ride, the phone rang. It was Billy Westbay, an old Colorado climber I hadn't seen in years, who had been to India with Mugs in 1988. He had terrible news. On May 21, 1992, Mugs was killed while guiding two clients down Denali's South Buttress in a storm, the victim of a simple misjudgment and a substantial dose of bad luck. Investigating the route ahead, he'd strayed too close to the unstable edge of a huge crevasse. When it collapsed, Mugs fell in and was buried beneath the jumbled mass of ice.

* * *

Mugs started climbing at a relatively late age — he was twenty-six when he did his first roped climbs in Utah — but his sense of the spiritual potential of athletics started early on. In the mid-1980s, while on the Kahiltna Glacier in Alaska, Mugs wrote in his journal:

I can look back and I remember . . . when I first realized that my life was not going to be as [his father's], an

167

incredible feeling of freedom, realizing a choice that was a part of me. I was lying on the grass end of Dietrich Field watching the clouds pass over the mountains and Mifflintown [his hometown in Pennsylvania]. I had just run about fifteen miles. Something in me so natural created by the push of my physical body. An opening of my mind brought to be part of the beauty of the earth around me. I thought of the abilities I had and how high they could take me, and how close to God, the spirit that is in everything, I felt when using them. I thought then I would probably be a professional athlete. I was fifteen.

Born and raised in Mifflintown, where his parents still live, Terry Manbeck Stump started fishing, hunting, and camping at an early age with his father, Warren, and his brothers, Ed, Quig, and Thad. His mother, Sis, remembers him as a happy and energetic child who nevertheless seemed to live by the adage "question authority." Although sometimes unruly, Mugs was well liked by his teachers and often displayed a surprising sensitivity for one so outwardly tough.

During his first couple of months at grade school, his mother recalls, Terry, as he was then known, would cry and cling to her leg when she dropped him off. He later told her that he remembered being afraid of his first-grade teacher. His father, who worked hard at the family's grain-and-feed business, was usually gone early in the morning, but eventually he became the one to take Terry to school, and the crying stopped. Later, in high school, when his classmates made life hell for their ninth-grade homeroom teacher, Terry told his mother he felt for sorry him. "The way some of those kids treat Duffy [as the teacher was nicknamed]," he told her, "I'd like to hit them."

Mugs played baseball, basketball, and football throughout his school years. He made the honor roll in his senior year of high school and was an all-state quarterback and captain of the "Big 33," a team of the best high school players in Pennsylvania — a state in which people eat, breathe, and sleep football. "I remember when you (Dad) came up to the field in the evening and would stand by the stands and watch me do my drills," Mugs wrote in his Kahiltna journal. "I would push hard for you, a communication we made to each other without saying a word. It made me so proud and happy. Wanting you to know that I loved what you gave me."

He attended Pennsylvania State University on a football scholarship, and his teammates came up with "Mugs," the moniker he's been known by ever since. By the time he'd graduated in 1971 with a degree in recreation and health, Mugs had started in two Orange Bowls. "He wasn't the best athlete on the team," says Joe Paterno, the well-known Penn State coach, "but Terry was very enthusiastic and courageous, a strong leader, and a hard worker." He was also an independent thinker. Paterno recalls that Mugs was the only player he ever had to tell to get a haircut. When he informed Mugs that he had a choice of playing second-string quarterback or third-string defensive back for senior year, an undaunted Mugs told him he'd play defensive back and start in every game, which he ended up doing.

After college, he skied in Aspen, Colorado, for a winter, and then played a year of semi-professional football. Mugs realized that he was too small to make it into the big leagues, and he moved to Snowbird, Utah, in the winter of 1972-73 to ski full time.

Mugs soon became well known for his go-for-it-attitude both on the hill and off — wild après-ski parties being the major form of entertainment in the isolated Snowbird community — and after two years of skiing virtually anything that held snow, he found himself increasingly drawn to the backcountry. He spent his summers roaming the Wasatch wilderness surrounding Snowbird and by the winter of 1974-75 had given up lift skiing in favor of touring. Bill MacIlmoyl, Mugs's roommate at the time and a constant companion both on and off the slopes, recalls, "Mugs's favorite thing was to go up early and lay down a bunch of tracks before the helicopter skiers came out."

As Mugs ventured into steeper and wilder terrain, he sought out local climbers and avalanche experts for advice, and in the summer of 1975, he made his first roped climbs. "Rock climbing is the ultimate spiritual communication with our center — God, ' he wrote to his parents that fall. Climbing soon supplanted skiing as his raison d'être. As he and MacIlmoyl watched the sun come up after a night on the summit of Mount Timpanagos early in the summer of 1976, Mugs said, "This is what I want to do — climb all over, do big routes, really big routes."

A quick study, Mugs soon started to do routes that were hard by anyone's standards. In the summer of 1977, he spent two months in Chamonix, France, climbing classic snow and ice routes. The trip culminated in an epic attempt on the Dru Couloir, then regarded as one of the most difficult ice climbs in the Alps, with Randy Trover, Steve Shea, and Jack Roberts. Starting out with no bivy gear, and food and water for a single day, they got off route and were trapped on the face by a storm for two days. They barely made it off the mountain alive when, in the worsening storm, the ropes repeatedly froze to the anchors. Unable to pull the ropes through any more, the four finally abandoned them on the last rappel. "If we'd started down ten minutes later," said Trover at a memorial service held for Mugs in Utah, "they would have been doing this for both of us fifteen years ago."

The climbs only got harder. In spring 1978, Mugs attempted the second ascent of the Hummingbird Ridge on Mount Logan, Canada's highest peak, with Trover, Jim Logan, and Barry Sparks. After ten days of hard climbing and marginal bivouacs on a new direct start, the four reached the point where the original ascent party had gained the upper ridge but retreated with several thousand feet and many corniced miles still to go. For Mugs, it was nevertheless a pivotal climb. "He came away from the Hummingbird knowing he could do anything he wanted," says Trover.

Later that summer, Mugs and Logan returned to Canada intent on the Emperor Face on Mount Robson. Logan, a very experienced climber from Colorado, had tried the unclimbed face three times previously, and now the pair was determined, as Logan later wrote in the 1979 issue of *The American Alpine Journal*, "to spend all summer if need be in the attempt." They spent two weeks observing their route and waiting out storms from a camp near Berg Lake, then clearing weather prompted them to move up to a bivouac at the base of the 4,000-foot upper wall.

On the second day, sixty-degree ice slopes interspersed with thinly iced rock steps — the most difficult ice climbing Logan had ever done — took the pair to a good bivouac on a snow rib in the center of the face. The difficult mixed climbing continued to an uncomfortable third bivouac on tiny seats chipped out of a seventy-degree ice slope. A storm moved in that night, and spindrift avalanches threatened to push the two off their airy perch.

The final headwall loomed above. Mugs led up steepening ice to its base, then Logan took over the crux lead, a full rope length of intricate aid and mixed climbing on loose rock. It took him eight hours. A few more easy ice pitches and they reached the summit ridge, where they spent the night.

Mugs and Logan had made the first ascent of one of North America's greatest alpine prizes, a route that had repulsed numerous attempts by some of the strongest climbers of the day. The achievement gave Mugs a heightened sense of inner strength and a feeling of the "rightness" of the path he'd chosen. Several months later he wrote to his parents:

> I have felt myself going through some amazing changes on the walls in the last year, becoming totally relaxed and comfortable, feeling like this is the place I belong. It can be so peaceful . . . even in the most extreme situations. Feelings of endless space and time made so real, a closeness to nature. A sense of accomplishment and a sense of worthlessness — a combination that feels so fine.

* * *

Mugs had a recurring dream that he related often to his friends. In it he had just climbed a very challenging new route, sometimes alone, at other times with a partner, but the style was always impeccable: using neither pitons nor aid, he had done it quickly, leaving no trace of his passage. Next in the dream, he went to a pub and was sitting in the corner with his girlfriend when a group of climbers who had just done the same route came in. The climbers were toasting themselves about their seeming first ascent, and after joining their celebration, Mugs would sit back and smile. All that was important, he would say, was his own knowledge that he had done the climb the way he'd wanted to.

The dream represented an ideal that Mugs would pursue consciously and persistently throughout his life. "Doing the extreme is not the point," he wrote to his parents after climbing Fitzroy in 1980. "I care less and less about that, but the desire to climb and be with nature's and the mountain's forces is still there, strong as ever. I don't care about accomplishments. I care about fulfilling dreams of being happy." To Mugs, being happy would mean achieving an egoless state of perfection, "living outside and exercising, moving every day, climbing — just looking." Even at his house in Sandy, he'd sometimes sleep in his van with the doors open.

Although Mugs traveled widely and loved rock climbing perhaps best of all, the snowy expanses of the polar regions are where he came closest to reaching his ideals. He made four trips to Antarctica under contract with the National Science Foundation. He took his work as a safety consultant as seriously as his guiding. "Mugs was not just a one-man climbing machine, he was into doing the best job possible to ensure the science was done," says Paul Fitzgerald, a geologist who worked with Mugs both in Antarctica and Alaska. "Of all the field assistants I've had, Mugs was easily the best, not just because he was the best climber, but because he really got to understand why we wanted to do things the way we did."

Mugs developed a special affinity for the pristine and barren continent of Antarctica and did much off-the-record exploratory mountaineering there, including two of his purest climbs ever, the 7,000-foot Southwest Face of Mount Gardner and the 8,000-foot West Face of Mount Tyree, each solo, without bivy gear, and in a single day. He never said much about any of his climbs in Antarctica (outside of sharing information for a brief report for *Climbing* in 1990 highlighting the Gardner and Tyree ascents), preferring, possibly, to share the memories and feelings engendered by these remote gems with only a few close friends.

Well before his first trip to Antarctica in 1980, Mugs had ventured north, and over time, Alaska would become his spiritual home. "It's so, so beautiful, unique," he wrote his parents in 1984. "Subarctic lands have such a vast, quiet beauty, a stillness I really hope I get the chance to share with you."

The pioneer atmosphere and booming economy of the forty-ninth state also appealed to his free-spirited nature. In the late 1970s and early 1980s, Mugs earned his living between climbs by salmon fishing off the Alaskan coast. Later, he guided extensively on Denali and elsewhere in the Alaska Range. He returned again and again to peaks surrounding the Ruth Gorge, attempting Mount Johnson several times and climbing a host of routes on lesser-known peaks in the area.

His greatest climbs in the Alaska Range, however, were on three of the region's most celebrated mountains, the Moose's Tooth, Mount Hunter, and Denali, the first two just a few months apart in 1981. In March of that year, Mugs and the legendary Yosemite hardman Jim Bridwell made the first ascent of the East Face of the Moose's Tooth, a 4,500-foot wall that had repulsed some ten strong attempts in the previous decade, including one by Mugs and Jim Logan in 1979. Mugs's and Bridwell's was an exceptionally bold effort over five days in frigid conditions and with minimal food and equipment.

After several days of storm, the two started out a bit hungover after "deliberating on whether to wait another day while consuming large quantities of whiskey," as Bridwell wrote in his 1981 article about the route. In contrast to the earlier attempts, which had all concentrated on the central aid line, Stump and Bridwell climbed icy gullies to the right, then traversed back left on sparsely protected ramps to the center of the wall. They tackled the crux section of the climb — seven pitches of steep, ice-choked chimneys — on the second day, then continued up an A4 head-wall and more tenuous mixed climbing on the third. Gorp, coffee with sugar, and two packets of soup were their entire rations for the climb, so when the pair reached the top on their fourth day they were hungry and severely dehydrated.

After a bivouac near the summit, the pair dropped onto a 1,500-foot rock face, aiming for a wide snow couloir that would eventually deposit them at their base camp at the bottom of the wall. As they descended, the rock got worse and worse. They hadn't brought any bolts and wished they had. Ten pitches down, they had no choice but to rappel from a single #3 Stopper. As Bridwell started off, Mugs looked at the anchor and reached toward it, ready to unclip, then dropped his hand. He'd prefer a quick end to a futile wait of a day or two. One more rappel got them to the snow, and two hours later they were celebrating in their tent on the Buckskin Glacier.

Although Mugs would later say that his and Bridwell's climb was, in retrospect, unjustifiably risky and probably not worth repeating, he had no such doubts about his other great Alaskan climb that year. The Moonflower Buttress on Mount Hunter, which he climbed with Paul Aubrey, represented a quantum leap in technical difficulty for climbs in the Alaska Range. Asked ten years later what had been his best route, Mugs said, "Probably the Moonflower Buttress — doing it just like I'd hoped. It was a very aesthetic line, safe and difficult. It had all the elements."

It was also the only climb on which Mugs ever published an article. The story, which appeared in *Mountain* and in the 1982 issue of *The American Alpine Journal,* describes a four-day odyssey, punctuated by precarious bivouacs and the odd pitch of aid, up icy ramps and grooves. Mugs wrote of the final night:

I thought of what I'd done to get here, not just in the last four days but in the years past. I felt part of some great movement, one of an infinite scale, too grand to see but only to feel in the night's wind. . . . In the vastness in front of me, I felt even more isolated. I was a shell, the same as the figure beside me and the mountains around. I felt an aloneness, my thoughts totally my own, creating a peacefulness of beauty and friendships."

"No place to stop, there was no need to stop," he would write about the last pitch of the route, an ice-filled vertical crack he managed to free climb. "Freedom was my catalyst as I deliberately and methodically made each placement. As I pulled over the top and onto the summit slope I was envisioning a crack such as this running for days . . . I didn't want the feeling to stop." A mile and a half of steep snow climbing would have gotten them to the summit of Mount Hunter, but satisfied with the effort, they rappelled the route, reaching the bottom that afternoon. "I climbed to the top of the photo" was Mugs's usual response to questions about why they didn't go to the summit. (Mount Hunter's North Buttress, as Stump's and Aubrey's route is also known, was climbed to the summit in 1983 by Todd Bibler and Doug Klewin. The route has been repeated several times since, becoming something of a modern Alaskan classic.)

Summing up an incredible year, Mugs wrote later in 1981:

My imagination is a gift for my life. The climbs to do are creations to understand what is there, not to be surprised. The more I have done and been with other climbing partners, the more I have learned about myself. I am so lucky to have such a life, to have such freedom — not the political or social, but the freedom that is my spirit.

Climbers are prone to a certain hubris, and Mugs was no exception. At his best, he was generous, supportive, and enthusiastic, but he could also be selfish, insensitive, and moody. More than anything, he wanted to be a good person — humble, open, caring, and, above all, centered — and he struggled mightily with his own ego and insecurities in finding that perfection.

His relationships with his many girlfriends, in particular, were intense and joyful but often strained. "We struggled in the relationship because he could not be owned," says Lynne Romano of her time with Mugs in the past two years. "I finally asked him for more than he could give me, and we were no more." It seemed as though he could relate more openly to women with whom he wasn't intimately involved. Indeed, he counted many women, several of them ex-girlfriends, as his closest friends.

"He was the most important person in my life," says Mona Wilcox, who lived with Mugs on and off in the 1970s. "He taught me everything — about the mountains, climbing, skiing, living." She is happily married to one of Mugs's old climbing partners from Telluride, but she and Mugs regularly kept in touch with each other over the years. "Words just don't fulfill the experience of things like I am trying to say and do," Mugs wrote to Mona in 1985. "I'm glad that you know me and know what I hope to be and feel in my life."

"Mugs had a huge ego — he was the most selfish person I've ever known," says Jenny Edwards, an occupational therapist whose Anchorage house and Talkeetna cabin had been Mugs's base of operations in Alaska since the mid-1980s. The two were incredibly close nevertheless. "I knew Mugs neither as a guide nor as a climbing partner," says Jenny, "but as a spirit sister and soulmate, and loved him with his imperfections as he did me."

Diane Okonek, a long-time friend from Talkeetna, also remembers his sensitive side. "Mugs would always come by and we would spend a few hours catching up on each others' lives," she says of his return to Alaska each spring. "Sometimes we would laugh and sometimes we would cry, and it was always a special time for us

MUGS STUMP

both. I have always thought of Mugs as one of those rare men who was self-confident enough to allow his gentle side to show."

Mugs could be intimidating to those who didn't know him well, but it usually didn't take long to break through that shell. "I have climbed on and off for thirty years and have never met a guide as considerate, capable, and likable as Mugs," says Bob Hoffman, one of the clients who was with Mugs at the time of his death. "He had a gift for bringing out the best in people, for showing them how to overcome fear and do things they felt unable to do."

Mugs was a good mentor and coach, although he could be demanding. "Some days he would be excited that I was climbing better than he. He was proud that my skills were shaped by his actions," says Conrad Anker, Mugs's protégé over the past several years. "Other days he would hold the high ground and rub it in that I was still the grasshopper." The two climbed extensively in Utah, Yosemite, and Alaska, forming a lasting friendship. In an exercise to help develop mental toughness, Mugs and Anker once drove all the way from Salt Lake City to Yosemite without talking. "By being stronger in the mind," says Anker, "Mugs felt one would be better prepared to tackle the big climbs."

* * *

In 1983, Mugs and I spent eight long, difficult days on the West Face of Gasherbrum IV. On our second night out, we bivouacked sitting up in the open as a light snow fell. I stayed up late melting snow and passing hot drinks to Mugs, who was huddled deep in his sleeping bag next to me. But the frigid night air aggravated my already chronic cough, and in the morning, I knew that I wasn't going to be climbing well. Mugs took over the lead without hesitation and got us to the base of the Black Towers at 22,500 feet, the high point of several previous attempts on the face. After we'd chopped out an airy bivouac site from the crest of an ice ridge, he led up a short, difficult chimney and fixed a rope.

177

Good bivouacs were rare on the face, and we knew that the climbing above would be time-consuming. We therefore anticipated staying where we were for two nights. A thin scud of gray clouds veiled the sky the following morning. As always, Mugs gave me the thumbs-up as I started up the next pitch — a rotten, poorly protected overhang that left me gasping. The climbing felt like 5.12, but it probably would have been 5.8 in rock shoes at sea level. Mugs continued on, free climbing and then aiding up the steep, friable rock. He finished the pitch with a spectacular double pendulum, reaching the top of the Black Towers. We'd done what we thought would be the crux of the route, and even though we still had more than 3,000 feet to go, the way ahead was clear. Our two ropes barely reached the tent as we rappelled down in the worsening spindrift.

We settled into "the hang," rationing our remaining supply of oatmeal, tea, soup, and dehydrated potatoes in hopes that the storm would move through quickly enough to allow us to continue. For the first few days we maintained our psyche, but as the avalanches boomed all around, it soon became obvious that we weren't going anywhere but down. We spent five stormbound nights in the cramped Bibler tent before retreating. "I thought I'd never go back to the mountains again," Mugs later told a slide-show audience in New Hampshire.

When we reached the relative safety of the West Gasherbrum Glacier, Mugs strode out ahead, anxious to rid himself of the intensity of the face, to go the last few miles at his own pace. I trudged on well behind him, lost in my own disappointment about the route. A couple of hours later I crested a little bump in the glacier, and there was Mugs, waiting so that we could walk back into basecamp together.

A year later, Mugs, Laura O'Brien, Randy Trover, and I traveled to northern India to try the virgin Northwest Face of Thelay Sagar, a peak that had seen just two ascents at the time. We planned on climbing independently as two ropes of two, but from the start a subtle tension was in the air. We'd had some minor hassles with the Indian bureaucracy over Laura's late addition to the team. Mugs was sullen and uncommunicative with all of us. In particular, he didn't seem to be getting along too well with Laura, who was his girlfriend and climbing partner. A few days after reaching basecamp, Trover had to retreat to Gangotri, the nearest village, for several days to recover from a bronchial infection. To top off our problems, persistent storms battered the peak, plastering our proposed route with snow and rendering it too dangerous to climb.

We turned our attention to the elegant Northeast Pillar, which after several attempts had been climbed by a Polish-Norwegian team in 1983. It had also been our original objective when I'd applied for the permit for Thelay Sagar in 1982, so as a consolation prize it wasn't bad. Laura and Mugs tried it first, but high winds low on the route beat them back. When Trover and I passed them on our way up, all Mugs would say was that we didn't have a chance. "It has been a rough day, and a rough last week," he wrote to his parents at the time. "I've been very frustrated lately and going through the usual questions of the value of what I pursue at times like this."

Trover and I made the climb despite the continued bad weather. It was a hard-won summit, my first after four trips to Asia. Trover had put in a stellar effort for his first climb in the Himalaya, especially considering his earlier illness and relative lack of acclimatization. We'd pushed hard all the way, especially on the descent, knowing that the porters were scheduled to arrive the morning we would return to basecamp.

But when we got there early on September 15, camp was empty. No one had waited for us or left us any food or even a note. We were disappointed and angry, but not too surprised, given Mugs's moodiness over the past weeks. We stashed our climbing gear in a couple of duffel bags under a boulder and trudged down the valley. Late that afternoon in Gangotri, Laura ran up to us full of smiles and hugs and questions about the climb. Mugs, who was cooking some eggs on the porch of a teahouse, barely glanced up.

We moved to another basecamp nearby to try Shivling, but

Trover and I were burned out, so we headed home. Mugs and Laura stayed on for a few weeks and didn't manage to accomplish anything. Our trip to India ended on a sour note, and we three drifted apart from Mugs for a while. "I thought we'd never speak to each other again, let alone climb together," says Trover, who had learned to climb with Mugs and had been one of his best friends.

Each of us eventually made our peace with him. "Mugs and I knew each other well enough that we didn't need to say anything," says Trover. "Just going climbing together was an acknowledgment that we were friends and that things would work out." The rift wasn't easily healed, but the two eventually became closer than ever. "The last three years were the best time for our relationship, despite the fact that we did almost no climbing together," says Trover, who with his wife, Adrienne, now has a three-year-old son, Eric. "We became his surrogate family. The way Mugs latched onto Eric was incredible — I think he realized it was as close as he'd ever get to having children."

When I had left India, I'd thought that Mugs had simply gotten too full of himself. He seemed to feel that his obvious talent and drive somehow made him a better person than the rest of us, and that the world owed him something. He had even expressed some bitterness over the fact that we'd paid for the entire trip out of our own pockets, forgetting that it had been largely a matter of our own choice not to seek sponsorship.

In retrospect, it seems to me that Mugs underwent something of a spiritual crisis at that time, that he lost sight of his chosen path. Success in the mountains didn't come as easily as it had for several years. He made two more frustrating trips to India to try Meru, for example, as well as three attempts on the East Buttress of Mount Johnson in Alaska. They were the only two routes he returned to that many times. Others with whom I've spoken have commented that Mugs seemed out of sorts for a lengthy period of time in the mid to late 1980s. A letter he wrote to Mona Wilcox in 1985 while he was recovering from knee surgery confirms this impression:

It's been good to have this quiet, still, sedative time here to catch up on some thinking ways, reading and going into my spirit some, to try and reach some understanding about myself [that has] slipped away the last couple of years. I haven't felt as centered as I used to.

In the end, Randy, Laura, and I gained a deeper understanding of both ourselves and of Mugs, and developed a stronger and more complete friendship with him, as have many who were close to him as he grappled with the vicissitudes of his life.

* * *

We all struggle to balance our inner yearnings with the demands of the world. Our lives are littered to one degree or another with unkept promises to ourselves and others, but we hope that our existence has a purpose beyond the self. It was this search for a deeper meaning that always preoccupied Mugs.

In December 1991, Mugs went back East for the first time in several years to visit his family and friends, and at Christmas his father told him he was facing some serious potential health problems. Mugs later wrote:

What a month this has been with the closeness to death. Many thoughts about the fullness and happiness that is held with our friends. I do in my personal (and selfish?) self find a lot of peace and happiness in this drifting way with climbing and the mountains. But it is so good to see those close to us and give our time to those we love.

Earlier in December, Mugs had stayed by the bedside of Gavin Borden as he succumbed to the final stages of cancer in a New York hospital. A wealthy heir and publisher of college textbooks, Borden had been Mugs's best client, but more than that, he had become a true friend. His death affected Mugs deeply. He wrote:

> The feeling of love and caring for others seems to be a natural part of us, yet so many times we don't let it out. "I guess one way I keep a positive outlook is by trying to keep aware that we are all of the same place. When I look into Gavin's eyes or my dad's eyes and I see the fear and worry, I just wish I could somehow help them have peace.
>
> Our lives are so wonderful and it's all we really know. We want to keep its joys, but there must be such an amazing awakening in death. I can't imagine that the supreme God is not realized, or at least in a way there is a true awakening that we are all a part of it.

Jeff Lowe. *Photo by Beth Wald*

A Mountain of Trout

JEFF LOWE

By David Roberts

[From MENS JOURNAL, May 1992]

Climbing hard all day, Jeff Lowe forced the route through a wilderness of false leads and frustrating dead ends, but darkness caught him short of the ledge he had hoped to reach, stranding him in a vertical labyrinth. He was left with no choice but to carve a makeshift cave in a fan of snow plastered against the steep rock, then crawl inside. Wet cold and physically spent, he lit his balky stove and began the task of turning pot after pot of packed snow into drinking water.

In the middle of the night the storm hit. A heavy snowfall poured out of the black sky, and as the snow gathered, it set loose spindrift avalanches that filled Lowe's cave and threatened to smother him. All night he lay in his sleeping bag, pushing and pounding the wall of his flimsy bivouac sack to maintain some breathing space inside the cave.

A lifelong tendency toward claustrophobia compounded Lowe's distress. As he grew drowsy, he would be seized with panic. Ripping open the door of the bivouac sack, he would gasp fresh air, allowing snow not only to spill inside the cave but to fill his sleeping bag, where it melted and soaked his clothes.

By morning, Lowe was in a perilous situation. It was February 28, his ninth day on the North Face of the Eiger. He had climbed 4,500 feet over those nine days, but in the 1,500 feet of frozen limestone that sill hung above him, he was sure he would find the hardest passages of all. His food was almost gone. He could not stay warm at night. And he was on the verge of exhaustion.

This, Lowe knew, was how climbers died on the Nordwand. In just such a way the audacious Toni Kurz had come to grief, his rappel jammed on a knotted rope; or Stefano Longhi, left behind by his partner to freeze to death after a bad fall; or Max Sedlmayer, climbing hopelessly toward the avalanche that would pluck him from his life.

Getting down from so high on the North Face, in the midst of a storm, would take a desperate effort, if it was indeed possible at all. At the moment, with avalanches thundering over the cliffs above and sweeping the fan of snow, descent was out of the question: Lowe could not even escape his snow cave.

Hunkered inside his claustrophobic hole, alone in a gray universe of nothingness, Lowe brooded on his predicament. During the last few days, with the weather holding, he had climbed so well; at last he had felt in perfect form, as success had dared to whisper in his ears. Now the prospect of failure loomed larger with every hour of snowfall. And if the situation got any worse, Lowe would be in a battle for his life.

No, things were not going right — and the pattern was all too familiar. For a year now, things had been going wrong for Jeff Lowe — major things, disastrously wrong. Bankruptcy. The failure of his marriage. Separation from his two-year-old daughter. He had scrambled to hold it all together, but his despair had peaked in late October, just after his fortieth birthday, leaving him sleepless, his antic mind tormenting him with a parade of furious creditors and disapproving friends. Out of the nadir of that depression had come the decision to climb the Eiger — a new route on the North Face, a clean, direct vector between the Czech and Japanese lines. Solo. In winter. Without bolts.

If he could pull it off, it would be the greatest climb ever accomplished by an American in the Alps. And at a deeper, more personal level, the Eiger might somehow tame the internal voices howling of failure and loss. It would be a way for Lowe to return to his strength, to the thing he did better than almost anyone in the world.

Twenty-four hours after burrowing into the mountainside, Lowe was still stuck inside the inadequate snow cave. As he prepared to spend a second night there, shivering in a soggy sleeping bag, he got out his two-way radio and warmed the batteries against his body. Rousing his support team at the hotel far below, Lowe spoke slowly, his voice seamed with fatigue: "I've got a decision to make, whether to go up or down. It's a tough one." There was long pause. "I don't know how hard it would be to get down from here," he said. "I figure it'll take three days minimum to reach the summit if I go up. And that's only if the weather's good tomorrow and Saturday." Another pause: "I guess tomorrow's going to tell. If I go for it, I'll have to pull out all the stops."

* * *

Had Jeff Lowe been born a Frenchman or a German, he would be a celebrity, sought after for product endorsements and asked to write his memoirs. But in the United States, great alpinists remain as obscure as chess champions.

Lowe, moreover, is a purist. He makes a wry distinction between "expeditions" — large, highly publicized assaults conducted in the spirit of the Desert Storm campaign — and "trips with friends," on which, with from one to three cronies, he can attempt brazen routes on unexplored mountains. From his only Everest expedition, a massively funded attack on an easy route involving fourteen climbers, Lowe came home disenchanted. But on some of Lowe's trips with friends, he has performed splendid deeds on spectacular Himalayan mountains such as Tawoche,

Kwangde, and Nameless Tower. On his ascents of Pumori and Ama Dablam, his only friend was himself.

Climbs like Tawoche and Ama Dablam, however, do not make headlines in the United States. Since his early twenties, Lowe had been one of the two or three best ice climbers in the world. Names such as Bridal Veil Falls, Keystone Green Steps and the Grand Central Couloir — extraordinary ice routes that Lowe was the first to master — can bring an awed hush over parties of cognoscenti, but they mean nothing to the lay public.

In the last two decades, the cutting edge of mountaineering has become "good style," and nobody's style has been cleaner, bolder, or more prophetic than Lowe's. Says Michael Kennedy, editor of *Climbing* and a frequent climbing partner of Lowe, "Beyond a shadow of a doubt, he's the most visionary American Himalayan climber who's ever lived."

* * *

In a family of eight children growing up in Ogden, Utah, Lowe and his three brothers were pushed hard by the lawyer father to excel in sports. He was climbing seriously by age fourteen, quickly developing his skills and managing to survive the usual near-disaster of adolescent ambition. After he spent three years at unaccredited Tahoe Paradise College on a ski-racing scholarship, Lowe became a full-time climber. Meanwhile, he scrounged a living from the kinds of marginal jobs most American climbing addicts resort to — pounding nails, teaching at Outward Bound, and tutoring beginners in the sport.

In 1968, Lowe's older brothers Greg and Mike launched an outdoor-equipment company called Lowe Alpine Systems, which quickly gained cachet for its innovative packs and began turning a robust profit. Fifteen years later, Jeff Lowe started his own company, Latok — named for a mountain in Pakistan that was the scene of one of his most memorable climbs — which sold technical-climbing gear. His first full-scale business venture, it began to collapse in 1987, and Lowe's brothers took over the company's debts to bail Jeff out.

Looking back, Lowe says, "I think part of my business problems stemmed from a feeling that I had to be more than a good climber, that I had to do something more meaningful. And that may come from my father."

As if remounting the horse that had thrown him, Lowe soon joined with Texas entrepreneur Dick Bass to organize the first international climbing competition on American soil, at Snowbird, Utah. Contests on artificial walls had become one of the hottest new spectator sports in Europe, and Lowe was gambling that Americans would similarly embrace the spectacle. In the end, Snowbird '88 was an aesthetic success, but far fewer people than anticipated were willing to fork over twenty dollars to stare at the inch-by-inch progress of European climbing stars they had never heard of.

Undaunted, Lowe incorporated himself as Jeff Lowe Sport Climbing Championships Inc., attracted sponsors and investors, and laid plans for an ambitious nationwide series of climbing competitions to be held in 1989 and 1990. Thus began the downward spiral that in two years sucked Lowe into a whirlpool of failure. None of the events came close to breaking even, and Lowe's debts piled up to vertiginous heights. He began borrowing from future projects to pay off past ones. By the time the final competition of 1990 approached — an event organized by the late Bill Graham, the legendary rock promoter, and to be held in Berkeley, California, in August — Lowe was teetering on the brink of financial ruin.

In need of a quick infusion of cash just to pay his personal bills, Lowe concocted a trip with friends to Nameless Tower, a soaring tusk of granite in the Karakoram Range of Pakistan, to be filmed for ESPN. The big draw for European sponsors would be a summit push pairing Lowe with thirty-one-year-old Parisian Catherine Destivelle, the most famous woman climber on the planet.

The Berkeley competition, which took place while Lowe was out of the country, turned into yet another financial fiasco plagued by dismal attendance. Lowe persuaded The North Face, a purveyor of high-end outdoor gear, to lend its name to the event as the leading sponsor. In order to keep the competition from sullying up its good reputation, the company claims it was forced to cough up $78,000 to cover Lowe's bills. "We believed that when Lowe went to Pakistan, he'd secured his loans," says Ann Krcik, director of marketing operations for The North Face. "Three days before the event, it became evident that Sport Climbing Inc. didn't have the money." Bart Lewis, an entrepreneur who helped market the competition, claims that when the dust cleared, Lowe owed him $40,000. Lowe counters, "That's absolutely insane. I owe Bart not even close to $40,000." Other creditors emerged, clamoring for payment. Says Lowe, "I always emphasized the risk involved. Those who were misled, misled themselves."

On the other side of the globe, meanwhile, Lowe and Destivelle managed to climb a difficult route on Nameless Tower. The film was broadcast on ESPN, but several European sponsors had backed out at the last minute. The upshot was that Lowe came home from Pakistan deeper in debt than ever, owing money even to close friends and fellow climbers who had worked as his support party. For two decades, Lowe had been one of the most admired figures in the tight-knit fraternity of American climbers. Now, around certain campfires and in various climbers' bars, his name began to elicit bitter oaths and tales of fiscal irresponsibility.

By the fall of 1990, Lowe had been married for eight years to a woman he'd met in Telluride, Colorado, where she was a waitress. The couple settled in Boulder, where Janie Lowe became her husband's full-time business partner. In 1988, they had a daughter, whom they named Sonja.

On Nameless Tower, Lowe was deeply impressed by Destivelle's performance. As their teamwork evolved, Lowe realized that with only one or two men had he ever felt so confident climbing in the great ranges. At some point, he and Destivelle began an affair. Because her private life was intensely scrutinized in France, and because she had a longtime partner of her own back in Paris, Destivelle urged Lowe to be discreet about their relationship.

When Lowe returned home from Nameless Tower, "he seemed very angry and distant," says Janie Lowe. "It was as if he wanted nothing to do with me. I asked him if he was having an affair with Catherine. 'No, no, no.' Finally, it came out. I asked him, 'Why did you lie to me?' That hurt so bad. He said, 'I'd promised Catherine. I said, 'After twelve years, you tell me your loyalty to Catherine is greater than your loyalty to me?'"

On September 13, 1990, Lowe turned forty. He was deep in a whirlpool, clutching for flotsam. At the end of October, Lowe declared bankruptcy. As his business partner, Janie took an equal brunt of the misfortune, and their relationship grew more troubled. As she tells it, "Jeff would come home and go straight into his study and close the door. Sonja would say, 'Mommy, why doesn't Daddy want to talk to me?' In mid-December, Jeff moved out of the house, and they began the process of divorce.

"I fell apart, " Jeff says. "I felt hopeless. All I knew was that I couldn't stand it after a couple of weeks. I had to start dealing with things one by one." By early February, Lowe was in Grindelwald, Switzerland, staring up at the North Face of the Eiger.

* * *

Beguiled by the shape of this unfolding drama, Jon Krakauer and I had come to Switzerland as well, to serve as Lowe's support team. Lowe's business woes were common knowledge in the climbing community, and word of his Eiger project had spread far and fast. More than one observer suggested that Lowe might be on a suicide mission. Boulder writer and climber Jeff Long, a loyal friend of Lowe, later admitted, "With all the pressure he had on him, I was afraid he was going to use the Eiger as some kind of exit."

Suicidal or not, the scheme — a new route, solo, in winter, without bolts, on the most notorious face in the Alps — seemed wildly improbable to most climbers. Destivelle later told Lowe that her French friends were of a single mind: "He'll never do it. It's too cold in winter, and too hard."

Jeff Lowe does not look like a climber — an accountant, you might guess on meeting him, or maybe a viola player. He stands five feet ten and weighs about 150; his slender physique seems more wiry than muscular. Clean shaven, he has an open face on which alertness struggles against a natural placidity. He wears the wire-rimmed glasses of a professor. The long, straight blonde hair conjures up the hippie he once thought himself to be. Although his hairline is receding, he combs his locks straight back, as if daring them to retreat further. When he smiles, his eyes crinkle shut, and incipient jowls shadow his jaw. To call his low, cadenced speech a drawl is to suggest a regional twang it does not possess. His voice is rather that of a tape recorder whose batteries are running low.

"For the first five years, we were extremely happy," Janie told me. "I think our problems had a lot to do with having a daughter. When Sonja came along, things changed."

Jeff Lowe commented obliquely on marriage and business. "It's a lack of freedom," he said. "I'm trying to get my freedom back. I could have saved my marriage if I had chosen to. But when I was forced to take a new look, I realized, 'Hey, it's not what I really want.' If I do what I really want — it's a weird thing, but climbing is still at the center." Lowe paused. "The Eiger — even if I succeed — isn't going to make all the other shit go away. I don't expect this climb to make everything right." A grin spread across his face. "It'll just feel real good."

The hotel at Kleine Scheidegg near Grindelwald is a rambling Victorian masterpiece, festooned with tiny rooms supplied by elegant if quirky plumbing, linen wallpaper and richly varnished wood wainscoting, cozy reading nooks, eighteenth-century engravings, and oak floors that creak and undulate like a glacier. For fifty-six years the hotel has been the headquarters for Eiger watching. As he prepared for his ascent, it became Lowe's base-camp.

The hotel is owned and run by the legendary Frau von Almen. She is a handsome woman of seventy with an imperious manner and a constant frown of disapproval on her brow. Checking in for the three of us, I told her about Lowe's plans. The frown deepened. "This is insane," she announced. "It is more than insane — it is mad." She turned and walked away. "I do not like the accidents," she nattered. "Because they are so unnecessary."

To stay in the hotel is to put up with Frau von Almen's tyrannical regime. There was a lengthy codex of unwritten rules, a good portion of which we managed to break. I wore my climbing boots upstairs, Krakauer and Lowe brought sandwiches from outside and ate them in her cafe, I foolishly asked her to unlock the front door of the hotel before 8 A.M., and Krakauer had the nerve to wonder if he might move and photograph a portrait of the pioneers who had made the first ascent of the Nordwand in 1938. There was no way to get on her good side. After dinner one night, I complimented her fulsomely on the four-course repast. "And did your friend enjoy the dinner too?" she asked ominously. "Oh, yes," I answered. She replied, "Because he will not eat like this up on the mountain."

Only Frau von Almen's longtime guests — those who had come every winter for more than a decade and skied innocuously each afternoon — seemed to bask in her approbation. The truth was that she was down on climbers. And this was sad, because her husband, Fritz, who died in 1974, had been the climbers' best friend, watching them for hours through his telescope and exchanging flashlight signals with their bivouacs each night. The Frau still had the telescope but would unpack it, she said, "only for emergency." An old-timer told us that a few years ago some climbers accidentally knocked over the telescope and broke it, then ran away.

On February 11, Catherine Destivelle arrived from Chamonix. Five feet, four inches tall, with curly brown hair, a conquering smile, and a formidable physique, she is a superstar in France, yet fame has left her relatively unaffected. Although they could hardly disguise the fact that they were staying in the same room, at first Lowe and Destivelle maintained a demure propriety. Gradually the handclasps became less furtive, the kisses semipublic.

For a first-rate climber, Lowe seemed woefully disorganized. For days his gear was spread all over his hotel room, but as he inventoried it, he discovered that he was lacking essential items. From Krakauer he borrowed a headlamp, pitons, first-aid supplies, and a crucial pair of jumars for ascending ropes. Destivelle brought him foodstuffs (she swore by powdered mashed potatoes) and a two-way radio.

Destivelle was scandalized by Lowe's preparations. "I can't believe he is climbing with equipment he has never used before," she told us again and again. "I would never do this." Lowe dismissed the problem, omitting one of its causes: He was so broke he had to sell much of his climbing gear and now was dependent on the largess of European companies intrigued with his Eiger project.

On the night of February 18, Destivelle joined Krakauer and me in the bar, where she chain-smoked half a pack of Marlboros. (Ordinarily, she goes months without a cigarette.) At breakfast the next morning, she said that she had dreamed obsessively about an all-out war in which everybody was hunting Lowe. She had spent a fitful, miserable night, while beside her Lowe had slept soundly.

In the morning, Destivelle rode the cog railway up to the Eigergletscher station, where she kissed Lowe goodbye. He put on his skis and headed for the base of the wall.

* * *

On February 19, his first day on the *Nordwand*, Lowe waltzed up 2,000 feet in only two hours. The going was easy but dangerous, a matter of planting the picks of his ice axes in a steady rhythm, of stabbing the crampon points strapped to his boot soles into brittle ice overlying steep rock. He soloed without a rope. If he slipped, he would die. But Lowe was in his element on this nerve-stretching ground. The speed and precision that had made his technique famous among a generation of American climbers spoke in every swing of his axes.

It was, however, still the heart of winter, and this was the Eiger. Over the last six decades, it was the easy start on the north face that had seduced so many alpinists. Between fifty and sixty of the best climbers in the world had died here, in a variety of gruesome ways.

The names of the Eiger's most storied landmarks — the Ice Hose, the Death Bivouac, the Traverse of the Gods, the White Spider — are canonic touchstones to alpinists everywhere. Whether or not they have ever seen the notorious wall, all climbers grow up with a keen awareness of its history. Eight of the first ten men who started out to climb the *Nordwand* were killed trying. The first man to attempt a solo ascent backed off prudently, only to die on a subsequent attack with a partner. The second, third, and fourth solo attempts all ended in death. Early on, the wall acquired its punning German nickname, the *Mordwand*.

Accounts of these disasters built up the Eiger mystique. Every climber knows the tales, as visceral as tribal legends passed on around the campfire: Hinterstoisser falling to his death as he tried to reverse his traverse on iced-up rock; Angerer strangled by his own rope; Toni Kurz expiring when the knot jammed in his carabiner, only a few feet above his rescuers, as he spoke his last words, *"Ich kann nich mehr"* ("I can do no more"). The last words of Longhi, borne on the wind from the ledge high on the face where he froze to death: *"Fame! Freddo!"* ("Hungry! Cold!")

At the foot of a sheer 350-foot rock cliff called the First Band, the climbing abruptly turned hard. As Lowe used his rope for the first time, his pace slowed to a vertical crawl. In three and a half hours, he gained only one hundred and ten feet. On the second day, a dogged and ingenious struggle over nine intense hours won Lowe a mere eighty feet more.

On other great mountain faces, clean vertical cracks, good ledges, and solid rock abound. The Eiger, however, is notorious for limestone knobs that crumble as you grasp them, for down-sloping ledges covered with ice, and for a scarcity of good cracks. The severity of the terrain brought out the best in Lowe as he used tiny metal hangers and the tips of axe blades to "hook" his way upward.

But already there were problems. Lowe had what he called fumble fingers, dropping three or four of his most valuable nuts and pitons, and the pick on one of his ice axes had worked loose. He climbed on anyway, adjusting his technique to the loose wobble of the pick. This meant he could never really swing the ax hard and plant the blade securely into the ice. It was a bad compromise, like driving at thirty miles per hour on a flat tire.

Late on his third day of climbing, he had put most of the First Band beneath him, but the climbing was the most frightening yet. The storms of the last few weeks had glued snow and ice onto vertical and even overhanging rock. Lowe had to shift back and forth between rock and snow, from spidering with bulky plastic boots and gloved hands among the limestone nubbins to crabbing his way up the hollow snow with crampons and waxes. When he could, he placed protection — a machined nut or piton in the rock or a screw in the ice.

At 2:50 P.M., Lowe clung to a particularly flimsy patch of rotten snow. Two thousand feet of cold, empty air fell away beneath his boots. He doubted whether he could reverse the moves he had made above his last protection eight feet below and had no idea whether he could find protection above or climb through the looming overhang that blocked his view of the rest of the gigantic wall. For all he knew, he was creeping into a vertical cul-de-sac.

The boldness of Lowe's choice to go without a bolt kit was now manifest. Throughout his efforts to surmount the First Band, he had been stymied right and left by blank, unclimbable rock. With bolts, it is possible to drill the rock and build a ladder through the most featureless impasse. Every other new route on the Eiger in the last thirty years had employed bolts; the Japanese who had pioneered the imposing line just to the right of Lowe's had placed 250 of them. Bolts also bestow a huge bonus in safety. When a climber is "running it out" — leading into uncertain terrain with bad protection — he never knows whether he can find a reliable anchor before he reaches the end of his rope. Without bolts, a solid anchor can be manufactured where nuts and pitons are useless. Without bolts, the process is like creeping farther and farther out on a lake covered with thin ice.

Lacking bolts, Lowe fiddled with a tiny nut, trying to wedge it into a crooked, quarter-inch crack that split the First Band. Suddenly the snow broke loose beneath his feet. He was falling. In conventional climbing, with two people on a rope, one anchors himself to the precipice and feeds out the rope as the other leads above. If the leader falls, he plunges a little more than twice as far as he was above his last protection, until his partner "belays" or stops him by holding tight to the rope. For a soloist, the belayer is a mechanical apparatus. As one might suspect, solo self-belaying is far less reliable than the kind afforded by a human partner.

When he had started up the wall three days before, Lowe carried a new kind of self-belay device he had never used. Before his first hard pitch, he had not even taken the contraption out of the plastic bag it was sold in. The question now, as he fell through the air, was whether the device would work.

An abrupt jolt gave him his answer — the rig had done its job. Lowe was unhurt. He had not even had time to be scared, but now the delayed adrenalin started to surge. In response, he edged his way back to his high point, where he found another plate of snow to try. Gingerly he moved up it, anticipating another fall with each step, until he stood beneath the rock overhang.

The only way to proceed was to angle left through a weakness in the browing cliff. Lowe made a series of delicate moves on rock until he could plant the picks of his axes on snow above, the left pick wobbling in its disturbing fashion. But here the snow was worthless, sloughing loose under the slightest touch. For a full hour he struggled in place, patiently probing the terrain for its arcane secrets. At last he found a small patch of more reliable snow. He planted both axes, moved his feet up, and stabbed the front points. The snow held. He moved a few feet higher, then surged upward.

He was over the First Band, but by now it was getting dark. Lowe placed three ice screws at his high point, then rappelled back down to the snow cave in which he had slept the night before. He crawled into his thin sleeping bag and pulled the frosty bivouac sack over him. Tired though he was, sleep escaped him. His problems danced mockingly in his mind, their shadows darting from wall to wall inside the cave of unhappiness in which he'd lived for a year. The loose pick on his axe nagged at him, and at the rate he was burning stove fuel, he would run out of gas canisters long before he could reach the summit. And he needed those nuts and pitons he had dropped.

In the morning, Lowe turned on his walkie-talkie and called down to Krakauer and me at the hotel. "Guys," he said in his slow, gravelly voice, "I'm thinking about a slight change of plans." He had decided, he told us, to leave his rope in place over the most difficult parts of the First Band and, while he was still low enough on the wall to do so, descend briefly to Kleine Scheidegg, where he might fix his malfunctioning ice axe, replenish his supply of food and fuel and replace the hardware he'd dropped. Then, in a day or two, he could go back up the wall.

Lowe reached the hotel before noon. "Why did you not tell me before the weekend that you were coming down?" Frau von Almen complained, fingering her room charts. It happened to be Friday. "Now I have to put you in 88, way up on the fourth floor." "That's fine with me," said Lowe. "I know," said the Frau as she walked away. "But you are very simple."

A stack of faxes was waiting for Lowe at the hotel, most of which were from furious creditors demanding payment. These did not appear to rattle his composure, but a long missive from Janie seemed to trouble him deeply.

Having come to admire and like Lowe, I was puzzling over the vehemence of his detractors. Jim Bridwell, who claims Lowe still owes him $3,000 for Nameless Tower, said, "I think of Jeff as a climber and what that used to mean. You used to be able to trust climbers. But Jeff will say one thing and do another. I just think he's disturbed. Either he doesn't know he's lying . . . "

Janie Lowe thought Jeff's problems had been compounded by his pride. "He can't say he's sorry," she told me. "Just a few sentences would resolve his debt with his friends."

One voice in Lowe's defense, however, was that of Jeff Long, who insisted, "These people want Jeff's professional corpse swinging in the wind. I think what they did in investing in Jeff was to invest in his vision. What collapsed, he thought, was a whole vision they shared. The brotherhood of the rope. But what was going on was really just business."

For all her sorrow, Janie was determined to keep the channels open. "We'll always be parents," she said. "We have a wonderful little daughter. For Sonja's sake, I hope we can keep our own bullshit in the background."

One night in the hotel, Lowe had watched the three-year-old daughter of a guest carrying her plate heaped with food from the salad bar. The sight had brought tears to his eyes. "Yeah, I really miss my daughter," he admitted. As Janie pointed out, though, "Yes, he totally loves Sonja. But you know what? He doesn't love her enough to be with her." In his own way, Lowe acknowledged that stricture. "I think I know now," he said in a reflective moment, "that I can't do this sort of climbing and have a domestic side. You're not a practicing father if you're not there. You're maybe a visiting father."

* * *

There had been a snowstorm on the morning of Lowe's descent, but by the following day the precipitation had ceased and the weather had stabilized. The temperatures were strangely warm, well above freezing at the 6,000-foot elevation of the hotel. That was better than brutal cold, except it meant bad avalanche conditions. In the weekend prior to Lowe's start on the *Nordwand,* thirty-one people had died in avalanches across the Alps.

There were, in short, plenty of reasons to give up the climb, excuses lying ready to be seized. But Lowe spent the evening in room 88, sorting his gear in his slow, fastidious fashion. Early the next morning, he returned to the foot of the wall, and by noon he was back at his bivouac cave, at the lower end of the ropes he had left in place. By the time evening fell, he had reascended the ropes and wrestled his 100 pounds of gear up to his previous high point.

Then, boldly, he led on into the dusk. It was not until three hours after dark that he suspended a hanging tent from a pair of ice screws and crawled into his sleeping bag. He was halfway up the *Nordwand.*

"Good morning, Vietnam," he radioed us in the morning. "I just woke up from one of the best sleeps I've had in a long time." When he started climbing again, his route coincided for a few hundred feet with the classic 1938 line. This section of the route, known as the Ice Hose, had been a formidable test to most of the expert climbers who had attempted the *Nordwand* over the years. For Lowe, with his impeccable ice technique, it was almost like hiking. He raced up the Ice Hose and across the Second Icefield and at day's end was bivouacked at the base of the summit head-wall.

Only a little more than 2,000 feet of climbing remained, but it promised to be severe and unrelenting. And as he inched his way up into the dark, concave headwall, it would become increasingly difficult to retreat. Somewhere on that precipice, he would reach a point of no return, after which descent might well be impossible, and the only escape would be up and over the summit.

It was Monday, February 25. The forecast from Zurich was for continued good weather through Wednesday; then a warm front bearing heavy snow was predicted to move into the area. A fiendish scenario began to propose itself. With two days of steady climbing, Lowe might well find himself near or at that point of no return only to get hammered by a major snowstorm.

* * *

Krakauer and I were using the coin-operated telescope at the gift shop next to the hotel to follow Lowe's progress, but he was so high now that we could tell little about his individual moves. On Tuesday night we took a walk. There was a full moon directly behind the Eiger. We caught sight of a pinpoint of light, impossibly far above us, three-fifths of the way up the wall: Lowe's headlamp, as he dug his bivouac site, a lonely beacon of purpose in the mindless night.

Later, his voice came on the radio raspy with lassitude. "Watch that forecast real carefully," he said. "It's going to be a strategy-type thing. If it comes in hard and I'm not in a good place, it's not going to be good."

On Wednesday night, the storm indeed came in hard, forcing Lowe to hole up in the claustrophobic snowcave he'd dug in the vertical fan of snow. It was from this pathetic shelter that he'd wondered aloud over the radio whether to go up or down. After a long, pregnant silence, he confessed, "I don't know how hard it would be to get down from here. I figure it'll take three days minimum to reach the summit if I go up. If I go for it, I'll have to pull out all the stops."

Lowe's miserable snow burrow proved to be a poor place to ride out the tempest. On Thursday morning, he remarked over the radio: "I've never been so pummeled in my life. There's a big avalanche coming down every five minutes. I couldn't move if I wanted to."

At noon, Lowe radioed again. He had managed to get out of his snow hole, but a search for a better bivouac site had been fruitless. The avalanches were still rumbling down, his clothes were soaking wet, and he was cold. It seemed that Lowe had little choice but to descend, and even that would be exceedingly sketchy. Much to our surprise, however, he declared, "I'm going to sign off now and try to get something done." He had resolved to push for the summit.

More than a week before, I had probed Lowe's motives by alluding to the suggestions I had heard of a suicidal impulse. "I think everybody has had thoughts about checking out early," he said. "But I wouldn't do it this way. I'd do it a lot simpler."

* * *

Even if Lowe could complete his route, what lasting difference would it make in his life? Magnificent though the climb might be, was it little more than a superstitious gesture, a way of lashing back at the furies that bedeviled his path? The finest climb ever accomplished by an American in the Alps could indeed bring with it a huge bestowal of self-esteem. And in the chaos that his personal affairs had become, self-esteem might be what Lowe needed most.

He had said: "For me there's no future. All I'm interested in thinking about is now."

Divorce and bankruptcy turned *now* into a crumbling wall between the flash floods of the past and the future. But up on the Eiger, all that changed. The past was the piton ten feet below; the future was that handhold three feet above and to the left. *Now* was what held him to the world, and the trance of grasping its ledges and cracks gave it a glorious breadth. It expanded and became the ocean of all that was.

* * *

Friday, March 1, marked the sixth day of Lowe's second attempt on the *Nordwand,* his tenth day of climbing overall. A south wind sent hazy wreaths of fog sailing over the mountain, but the favorable weather that had blessed the first week of the climb had returned, although another storm was forecast to arrive by Sunday. If he didn't reach the top before it hit, his prospects for survival might be grim. By noon, Lowe had hauled all of his gear up to a distinctive ledge called the Central Band. Only 1,200 feet remained.

Here the wall was scored with ice-glazed ramps leading up and to the left, most of which led nowhere. The protection was minimal, the climbing nasty. Lowe was aiming for the Fly, a small ice field 500 feet above. But now, when he needed to move fast, with the threat of the next storm hanging over him, he was slowed drastically by what turned out to be the most difficult climbing yet. Watching through the telescope, I could gauge how steep the cliff was when I saw him knock loose chunks of snow that fell forty feet before striking rock again. At one point, it took him more than an hour to gain twenty-five feet. The rock had turned loose and crumbly; stone towers, teetering like gargoyles, sat waiting to collapse at the touch of a boot, and pitons, instead of ringing home as he pounded them, splintered the flaky limestone and refused to hold. Bolts would have been a godsend.

Yet on these pitches, Lowe's brilliance came to the fore. He thought of one particular stretch of fifty feet as a kind of never-never land. It was the crux of the whole route to this point. A more driven, impatient alpinist might succumb to dizzy panic here, where the slightest misjudgment could rip protection loose and send him hurtling into the void. With his phlegmatic disposition, Lowe inched his way through the never-never land in a cloud of Buddhist calm.

On Saturday, Krakauer started up the west ridge, the easiest route on the Eiger and the path by which Lowe would descend. Krakauer wanted to camp near the top to greet Lowe and, if need be, help him down. As soon as he skied above the Eigergletscher station, however, Krakauer realized the venture was a mistake. A few days before, he had cruised halfway up the ridge in only two hours, but in the interim, the conditions had completely changed. The storm had blanketed the slope with deep, unstable snow. Without skis, Krakauer sank in to his waist, and even with skis on he plowed a knee-deep furrow as he zigzagged laboriously upward.

At the fastest pace Krakauer could sustain, it would take days to get to the summit. What was worse, the slopes were dangerously close to avalanching; indeed, as he climbed slowly up the ridge, his skis periodically set off small slides.

At 2 P.M., Krakauer came over the radio. "I'm getting the hell down," he said in a jumpy voice. "The hundred feet just below me is ready to avalanche. Watch me carefully. If it releases, it's going to be massive." With a series of slow, deliberate turns, he skied down as delicately as he could. The slope held.

When Lowe next radioed, I had to tell him about Krakauer's retreat from the west ridge. He took the news calmly, even though it raised the specter of serious danger for his own descent. For the first time we talked about the possibility of a helicopter picking him up on the summit.

Lowe climbed on. By early afternoon, clouds had gathered around the upper face, where it was snowing lightly, even though the hotel still baked in sunshine. Pushing himself beyond fatigue, again well into the night, he managed to set up an uncomfortable bivouac just below the Fly. His two-day push from the Central Band had been a brilliant piece of work, but the Sunday storm was coming in early, and 700 feet still lay between him and the summit. He was well past the point of no return.

That evening, he slithered into his dank bivouac sack and tried to sleep. Lowe had two gas cartridges left to melt snow, but his food supply was down to a couple of candy bars. His hands were in terrible shape. The incessant pounding, grasping, and soaking had bruised the fingertips until they swelled into tender blobs, and the nails had begun to crack away from the cuticles. Each morning, his fingers were so sore and puffy that merely tying his boot laces was an ordeal.

Worse, his sleeping bag, thin to begin with, was soaked like a dishrag, and it provided almost no warmth at all. That night, Lowe got not a wink of sleep. For fourteen hours he shivered, waiting for dawn as the snow fell outside his cave.

On Sunday morning, it was still snowing. "Where I am," he radioed, "it's hard to even peek out of the bivy tent without dislodging everything. I'm going to sit here and hydrate." He faced an acute dilemma. If he hunkered down and waited for the storm to end, he could run out of food and gas and succumb to hypothermia. If he pushed upward prematurely, on the other hand, the storm itself could finish him.

By noon he had not moved. At 2 P.M., through a break in the clouds, we saw him climbing slowly above the Fly. As he started to climb, however, he grew deeply alarmed. Something was wrong. He felt weak all over, weaker than he should have felt from fatigue alone. He had been going on too little food, not enough liquids, and insufficient sleep. This was how climbers died on the Eiger. This was too much like what had happened to Longhi and Kurz. After stringing out 300 feet of rope, Lowe returned to his bivouac hole of the night before and spent the rest of the day resting and hydrating and trying in vain to get warm.

Once more, sleep was impossible. Lowe shivered through another night, even though he lit the stove and burned precious fuel in an effort to heat his frigid cavern. The weather had cleared late Sunday afternoon, and the sky was now sown with stars. There was an acoustic clarity. Toward morning, he could plainly hear dogs barking in Grindelwald, miles away and 10,000 feet below. And he thought that he heard something else — a humming, crystalline, harmonic music in the air. Was it an aural hallucination? Was he beginning to lose his grip?

Monday dawned luminous and clear, a perfect day of which he would need every minute. Good weather had been forecast to last through the evening, but a major storm was due on the morrow. We called REGA, the government-run rescue service, and alerted it to a possible need for summit pickup. Then we watched Lowe climb. At 9:15, he turned a corner and disappeared into a couloir we could not see. Two hours later, there was still no sign of him, no murmur over the radio. Although we did not admit it to each other at the time, Krakauer and I each separately trained the telescope on the base of the wall, where we swept the lower slopes. In just such a way over the decades, the fate of several Eiger victims had been discovered.

Lowe had hoped that once he was above the Fly the going would get easier. But in icy chimneys broken by bands of brittle rock, he was forced to perform some of the hardest climbing yet. Normally he never let himself be rushed on a climb: It was one of the secrets of his sangfroid and his safety. Now, however, he kept looking at his watch, and his brain hectored, *Oh, no, hurry!* Ever so slightly, his technique lost some of its famous precision. He felt less weak than he had the day before, but the sense of struggling to meet a terrible deadline oppressed his efforts.

It was hard to place good protection anywhere. Lowe found himself hooking with front points and axe picks on rounded rock wrinkles that he had to stab blindly through the snow to locate. His balance was precarious, and then, just before it happened, he knew he was going to fall. The picks scraped loose: He was in midair, turning. Twenty-five feet lower, he crashed back-first into the rock. The self-belay had held, but he was hurt. He felt as though someone had taken a baseball bat and slammed it into his kidneys.

Oddly, instead of panicking him, the long fall calmed him down. *Okay,* he said to himself, *you've done that. Don't do it again.* He pulled himself together, started up again, and found a way through the dicey hooking sequences despite the pain pounding in his back. At last he surmounted a buttress and reached a good ledge only 400 feet below the summit.

But here he faced a problem. The warm sun had loosened the summit snowfields. Every chute and depression became an avalanche track. One swept right over Lowe, filling his goggles with powder snow, buffeting his body as it tried to knock him from the wall. He was moving faster now as slides shot down all around him. For two hours he climbed doggedly on. During that time, three more avalanches engulfed him. One of them knocked his feet loose, but he managed to hang on with his axes. At 3:20 he called.

"God, Jeff, those avalanches looked bad," I said.

"Yeah, they were pretty horrendous." His voice was ragged

with strain. "I got really douched. I'm totally wet. Am I about a pitch from the west ridge?"

"A pitch and a half, maybe."

"I'm going to call for a pickup. I just want to get off this thing."

We signed off and called REGA. They were waiting in Grindelwald, ready to fly the moment Lowe emerged on the west ridge, a few feet below the top. But a stiff wind had begun to blow a steady plume off the summit. The wind could prevent the helicopter from approaching close enough to execute a pickup or could even cause it to crash.

To our dismay, Lowe disappeared once more into a couloir. The minutes ticked by. At 4:15 he emerged, fighting his way out of the top of the gully, spindrift hosing him at every step. He was only forty feet below the crest of the ridge. We prepared to call REGA, then watched in distress as Lowe stopped at a mottled band of rock and snow, only twenty feet below the ridge. For ten minutes he thrashed in place; we saw him grabbing chunks of black limestone and tossing them into the void below.

In the hidden couloir, Lowe had found it impossible to get in any protection. He had dashed upward, aiming at the mottled band, but when he got there, he found only a skin of ice holding together rocks that were as loose as a pile of children's blocks. When he flung stones aside and dug beneath, he found only more of the same. He could engineer no kind of anchor — neither piton, nut, nor ice screw would hold.

Only twenty feet short of safety, he had run out of rope. His own anchor, 300 feet below, was imprisoning him. In despair, he realized that he would have to climb down at least forty feet to the previous rock band, try to get some kind of anchor there, rappel for his gear and jumar back up. He was not sure he could make that down-climb without falling. What was more, he was running out of daylight.

Lowe got on the radio. Krakauer said what we were both

thinking: "Jeff, if you just dropped your rope and went for it, could you free solo the last twenty feet?"

"No problem," said Lowe. "But are you sure the helicopter can get me?"

If we urged Lowe to abandon his gear and the helicopter failed, he would be stranded near the summit without ropes, sleeping bag, food, stove, or even his parka. He was soaked to the skin. The wind was whipping hard, and the sky had grayed to the color of lead. Tuesday's storm was arriving early.

Krakauer said, "I'm almost positive they can pick you up."

"Let's do it," said Lowe. He untied his rope and draped the end over a loose rock. He was abandoning all the gear that he had fought for nine days to haul up to the 6,000-foot precipice and, with it, deserting his own last refuge.

We called REGA; the helicopter took off from Grindelwald. To be picked up on the summit of the mountain was not a true rescue. More than one previous Eiger climber had resorted to flying from the top when he was far less strung out than Lowe was. It would, however, be a kind of asterisk attached to his great deed. It would not be the best style, and that would bother Lowe. But it was survival.

He sprinted up the last twenty feet. All at once, Lowe had escaped the north face. He stood on a broad shelf of snow on the west ridge, just below the summit. The helicopter spiraled upward toward him.

Still talking to us on the radio, Lowe couldn't keep the shivering out of his voice. Krakauer instructed him that the helicopter would lower a cable, which he was to clip on to his waist harness.

Now the chopper was just above him, hovering in the stiff wind. Suddenly it peeled off and flew away toward the Jungfraujoch. For the first time, Lowe seemed to lose it. He wailed, "What the hell's going on?" Nervous about the strong winds, the helicopter pilot, we later learned, decided to drop off a doctor and a copilot who had been on board so he could fly as light as possible when he made the pickup.

The helicopter reappeared and hovered above the summit, its rotors straining against the wind. The steel cable dangled from its belly. We saw Lowe swipe for its lower end, miss once, then seize it. He clipped in, and the helicopter swept him into the sky. Down at the hotel, the guests and skiers cheered wildly all around us. Lowe was off the Eiger.

The cable wound upward as he rode it toward the open door. The winch man reached out his hand. Lowe climbed through the door and crawled back into the conundrum of his life.

Annie Whitehouse. *Photo by Beth Wald*

A Thoughtful Approach to Mountaineering

ANNIE WHITEHOUSE

By Beth Wald

[From CLIMBING, August 1990]

The recorded voice is soft but determined. "Hi, this is Annie," emerges from a friend's answering machine. "I can't meet you this week because I'm off to Patagonia. I decided to go just today — I'11 be in touch when I get back." Leaving a trail of similar messages in her wake, Annie Whitehouse bolts away on another mountain journey, this time to the wind-blasted Super-couloir of Fitzroy.

The messages echo with memories of ten years of other departures to the big peaks, particularly a trip at the beginning of her mountain career. In 1980, Whitehouse decided to join the American Women's Expedition to Dhaulagiri I only a few days before the team's scheduled flight to Nepal. She had furiously packed her gear in one day in order to make the rendezvous in Denver.

Although only twenty-two at that time, Annie was already an experienced alpinist, with an ascent of Denali and an expedition to Annapurna to her credit. On Dhaulagiri, she faced every problem with quiet confidence and her characteristic wry humor, remaining a calm center in the cyclone of logistics that always threatened to overwhelm the main goal of climbing the mountain.

Fluent in Nepali, she moved naturally between the climbers' world and the native culture of her Sherpa friends. One night during the bittersweet retreat from Dhaulagiri, the expedition women danced, tipsy from local rakshi, linking arms with a swaying line of Sherpas. To the beat of drums and the droning song, Whitehouse taught her teammates the complicated steps of ancient Tibetan dances.

Since that night, her own steps have often taken her back to the mountains and their elusive summits, where Whitehouse has quietly but steadily accumulated an imposing list of important ascents.

* * *

Since 1974, her world has revolved around the peaks of Nepal, Tibet, Peru, Alaska, and the crags of the western United States, where her earliest mountain adventures took place. From 1983 to 1988, Whitehouse held the altitude record (28,000 feet) for American women after reaching the high points on two Everest expeditions, to the West Ridge in 1983 and the North Ridge in 1986. She led a successful expedition to Ama Dablam in 1987, and has either summitted or reached the high point on every expedition she has been on since her major-league initiation on Annapurna I in 1978.

Whitehouse has long been in demand as a climbing partner by men and women alike, both for her mountain skills and for her enduring amiability. But she is quick to admit that she can be a demanding partner. "When I have a goal, like a difficult ascent, I don't have much patience with anyone who could frustrate that goal," she says. "And I absolutely can't stand whiners."

"Annie is as strong at altitude as anyone, male or female, that I've climbed with," says Sue Giller of Boulder, Colorado, a respected mountaineer and Whitehouse's frequent expedition partner. "I don't know anyone else who can actually *gain* weight on the mountain. Eric Reynolds of Grand Junction, Colorado, who has climbed with Whitehouse on numerous Himalayan expeditions, gives a similar endorsement: "Annie has the most tenacity that I've seen in any climber. She has the ability to focus unwaveringly on a summit for weeks and weeks, despite bad weather, setbacks, and difficult climbing."

* * *

In a series of informal interviews, done over intensely black coffee at the local cafe and in Whitehouse's Boulder home as she cooked searing green chiles fresh from New Mexico, she discusses, sometimes bashfully, often humorously, always sincerely, the joys and struggles of half a lifetime of mountaineering.

Whitehouse, thirty-two, is tall and slim; her stylish dress reflects her attraction to varied cultures. Scarves mingle with beaded earrings and, always, bright colors. Her brown eyes reflect her moods, dark when she is serious, glimmering and narrowed when she is amused. Typically, irreverence punctuates even the most profound thoughts; she is quick to laugh at her own misadventures.

Asked about the genesis of her passion, Whitehouse recalls, "When I was about twelve, I clipped out an article about a Chinese ascent of Everest and saved it. I don't know why. I didn't know anything about climbing, but I found it fascinating." That seed of interest sprouted several years later in California. Spurred by her emerging political conscience and thirst for adventure, Whitehouse elected to attend an experimental school in East Palo Alto that offered extensive mountaineering and climbing courses in the Sierras. "I don't know how they let us spend so much time out of school," she says, "but it was a great opportunity to learn, at a very young age, not only climbing, but confidence and responsibility. Our teachers treated us like adults and expected us to be able to make important decisions."

If Whitehouse learned the basic skills of climbing from her high-school instructors, she developed her philosophy of ascent under the tutelage and stern eye of Margaret Young, an experienced alpinist, pilot, and physicist. Young was in her late thirties, had done first ascents in Alaska, and had climbed in Bolivia, Nepal, Afghanistan, Russia, and Africa when she first invited the sixteen-year-old to accompany her on a Sierra ascent.

> She was an intense, intimidating woman, but she inspired me and taught me a lot about both climbing and the mountain world. To Margaret, the surrounding environment was as important as the actual climbing; remembering Margaret, I often remember to appreciate just being in the mountains. She found being a woman and a climber to be easily congruent, an attitude I adopted without question. And from her I learned that you can often get to the top by sheer perseverance, by just putting one foot in front of the other.

Whitehouse soon ventured from the California peaks in search of new summits, new questions and answers. In 1976, she joined a classmate, Margie Rusmore, and their schoolteachers for a trip to Alaska. Climbing as equals with their instructors, Annie and Margie, both aged eighteen, became the youngest female climbers to ascend Denali.

Emboldened by that success, Rusmore applied for a slot on an American women's expedition to Annapurna I two years hence. She was accepted, and the expedition leader, Arlene Blum of Berkeley, California, asked Whitehouse to join also. Whitehouse, by now a student at the University of Wyoming, left school to move to California in order to help prepare for the expedition and also to help nurse Margaret Young, who had been paralyzed from the waist down in a fall from a horse. Although Annie, at twenty-one, was quite young for such a major Himalayan venture, Blum believed that this relative novice would make a first-class climber. "She was a sturdy young woman with determination, endurance, a tolerant disposition, and fine sense of humor," says Blum. The publicity machinery of the Annapurna expedition soon pinpointed Whitehouse and Rusmore as hot young climbers, and although Annie winced at what she felt was unwarranted attention, on the mountain she met all of Blum's and her own expectations.

"It was intimidating to climb with such experienced women, but I wasn't really surprised that I could keep up," she comments. Whitehouse attributes part of her success to another team member and summitter, Vera Komarkova, a Czech climber who had immigrated to the United States. Says Whitehouse, "She taught me how to take care of myself at altitude, how to keep going."

One lesson, however, Whitehouse learned by herself. She had been chosen to join Vera Watson and Alison Chadwick of Great Britain on the expedition's second summit attempt. After a sleepless night spent weighing all of the factors, Whitehouse couldn't resolve her uneasy feelings about the team's odds for success and its lack of support, and backed out of the attempt. Watson and Chadwick went as a rope of two and never returned. Whitehouse, even in the midst of tragedy, was reassured of the validity of her instincts and the importance of calculating one's own risks in the mountains.

The ups and downs of the Annapurna expedition were to influence many of her future trips. "It was very valuable that on my first trip I learned to trust my own intuition," she says. "I was also really psyched about my performance on the mountain. On the other hand, I was not very enthusiastic about large expeditions in general." She was also dismayed by the imperial, colonial style adopted by most large expeditions, which treated the Sherpas and porters like servants.

She also never completely bought into the theory of women's expeditions, only tolerating the idea. "Intellectually, I knew that women climbers were probably discriminated against, but frankly, I never was," she says. "I can't remember a single time that I was prevented from doing what I wanted because I was female, either on the rock or in the mountains." After Annapurna, what appealed to Whitehouse most was a self-contained, streamlined expedition, so she applied for a permit to climb Ama Dablam, a smaller, more accessible and manageable peak.

Although Whitehouse had adequately fit the team-player profile on the Annapurna expedition, she didn't obey every rule. Blum had established a policy forbidding expedition romances, fearing that they could cause rivalries and deflect the goal of the trip. Typically following her heart rather than the rules, Whitehouse fell in love with Yeshi Tenzing, a warm and friendly Sherpa who was the expedition cook. Later, in the United States, the two married.

"I thought very hard before getting involved," Whitehouse says. "To me, at the time, it made perfect sense. I was totally focused on the mountain, on getting to the top, and I didn't want to be distracted, like so many of the other members, by thoughts and longings for home and the people left behind. Yeshi helped me immensely to concentrate on the immediate goals." Although Whitehouse believes that the relationship had its place and time, she concedes that its longevity was less assured. "I lived, and guess I still do, very much in the present," says Annie. "On Annapurna our life together was simple, and I didn't fully consider the future consequences of getting married and living in the United States."

After the expedition, Whitehouse and Tenzing settled in Laramie, where she continued her nursing studies while he worked as a cook. Jealous of their privacy, they hid from the attention generated by the successful Annapurna trip. But not even the sleepy calm of a Western town could insulate the young couple from the personal difficulties they faced as Tenzing accustomed himself to American life and they tried to splice together their vastly different backgrounds and cultures.

* * *

In 1980, Vent Komarkova offered Whitehouse a spot on the women's expedition to Dhaulagiri that would be attempting the demanding North Face. Whitehouse at first was hesitant to accept, having doubts about such gender-defined expeditions in general, and the strengths of the Dhaulagiri team in particular. On the other hand, she was eager to be back among the giant peaks, and in the back of her mind was the hope that a trip to Nepal might solidify her marriage. At the last moment, she and Yeshi packed their rucksacks and left for Nepal.

Even on the flight over, it was obvious that the expedition was an amalgam of strong and diverse personalities, most heading to the Himalayas for their first time. On the mountain, the weather deteriorated, the team grew increasingly divisive, and the Sherpas, sensing problems among the members, lost their usual motivation. Then tragedy struck the troubled expedition as an avalanche swept down the mountain and destroyed Camp II, leaving one member dead and several injured.

At an emergency team meeting, the climbers made a futile attempt to pull back together. "It was at the meeting," Whitehouse remembers, "that I first realized just how polarized the team had become. I guess I'd been just thinking about the actual climbing, and was totally unaware of all the underlying politics and emotions." She adds, "Even without the problems I'm sure our chances for success were minimal." On the long retreat, however, she was already making plans to return to Nepal for her Ama Dablam expedition.

Not only the summit eluded Whitehouse on Dhaulagiri. Although she and her husband spent six months together in Nepal after the expedition, they failed to find the common ground a marriage needs. "When we were married, I had many youthful dreams, such as living with Yeshi in Nepal, dreams I simply outgrew," Whitehouse explains. "I also expected Yeshi, as a Sherpa, to be automatically supportive of my climbing. But he wasn't; he didn't really understand my need to climb." They were divorced in 1982, and Whitehouse moved to New Mexico, where she simultaneously delved into preparations for Ama Dablam and joined the U.S. Air Force.

The military may seem a far cry from the free-spirited world of the mountains, but Whitehouse's enlistment was a carefully weighed decision. "I wanted to cram as much nursing experience as possible into a short time," she explains, "and it was great not to have to worry about money." But she had other reasons, one of them intellectual curiosity. "I grew up in an extremely antimilitary family, but I realized that the military is a huge and important part of our country and our world. I wanted to see for myself how the system functioned."

Although her family was very upset with her enlistment, and Whitehouse herself at times chafed under the harness of rules and regulations, she believes her time in the service was very valuable. "One of the important advantages is that I first started to work as a nurse within the military, where medical treatment is a socialist system — it is free and guaranteed, and therefore often more humane than financially motivated private practice."

During her service stint, Whitehouse launched another dream that had been inspired by her early mentor, Margaret Young, and earned her pilot's license. "From Margaret, I first learned that flying is a great way to get to the mountains. I was also heavily influenced as a kid by books like Beryl Markham's *West with the Wind,* and stories about Amelia Earhart." She was fascinated by the skills needed for flying. She explains:

> You have to use all your knowledge of weather and topography, have the ability to concentrate, make quick decisions, have excellent eyesight and intuition. A pilot needs to be gutsy, but not stupid. A lot like a good climber, who is never completely at ease on an ascent, but always aware, always a bit on the edge, analyzing the situation.

The Air Force had originally supported Whitehouse's Ama Dablam plans and had even considered sponsoring the trip, but it ultimately reneged on the deal. "They decided," Whitehouse says with an ironic laugh, "that they didn't want to be responsible if I died." Frustrated, she had no choice but to transfer the Ama Dablam permit to Sue Giller, who led a successful women's expedition to the mountain in spring 1982.

Then, in 1982, Whitehouse was invited to join the 1983 American Men and Women on Everest Expedition. "For that trip, I was prepared to go AWOL," she says emphatically. "Finally, I felt like I was experienced enough for the route, and as good as any of the members." With much string pulling, she squeezed out of her term of enlistment three months early just in time to join a solid team of climbers on the technically difficult West Ridge.

Whitehouse found the mixed-gender team "a much more natural situation" than either the Annapurna or Dhaulagiri expeditions had been. Another new twist was that on Everest, for the first time, she consciously engaged in expedition politics in order to be picked for a summit bid. "Until this trip, I didn't have a clue how to get a place on the summit team," she says. "But on Everest, Todd Bibler told me, 'Always work really hard and make it obvious that you are totally motivated for the summit.'"

A successful campaign landed her on the second summit team, with Eric Reynolds and Renny Jackson; the trio reached the high point of the expedition before being turned back by high winds. "That summit attempt," remembers Reynolds, "was the first time we'd climbed together, and definitely the most strung out any of us had ever been. But there was an instant unspoken communication between us and confidence in each others' ability. No one bailed out early; we all decided to retreat at the same time."

In her journal, Whitehouse recounts the crucial moments near the summit of Everest:

Above 28,000 feet, the difference between a controlled and an uncontrolled situation is narrow, and we had crossed that boundary within minutes. A strong wind had turned into a violent blizzard, forcing Renny [Jackson] down the rock with freezing hands. For a brief moment, grief gripped my heart. The summit was not to be ours that day.

As a depleted oxygen bottle skittered in the gale down the slope, then plunged down the Hornbein Couloir, bouncing off the ice, arcing into the abyss, she cringed. "I was suddenly terrified, imagining a person taking that ride. 'Ho man,' I resolved, 'Never me, never!' But the thin air and my heavy load left me little time to ponder. It was time to clear my mind, and use it to control my rebellious body."

Waiting for Whitehouse at basecamp after her summit bid was her boyfriend, a pilot from New Mexico. With his presence, Whitehouse felt her mountain sanctuary invaded by a host of personal entanglements and pressures. Despite rocky relations on the trek out, followed by a temporary separation, the two married in 1984. Asked about those years, Whitehouse, a very private person, hesitates and finally answers slowly:

> It was a mistake, but I married Mike because I was tired of fighting — fighting Mike and his demands, fighting against the expectations of my family, friends, and society. Everyone closest to me was holding their breath, waiting for me to settle down, have a family, and live a "normal" life. I'd been climbing for about ten years. Maybe, I thought, they're right. So I gave in.

From 1984 to 1986, Whitehouse redirected her energy from the high peaks in order to spend weekends fishing or playing soccer rather than climbing. Her climbing partners stopped calling. Although her husband had originally supported Whitehouse's climbing and her trekking business, that soon changed. "He seemed to like the idea of having a wife who had once done all those exciting things," she says, "but when it came down to my actually leaving for Nepal without him, it was a completely different story."

ANNIE WHITEHOUSE

Each trip to lead treks became more of a struggle, even as escape into the mountains became more and more essential to Whitehouse. Finally it became obvious that she could not abandon her climbing and the mountains. From these early turmoils, Whitehouse has learned what she needs from a relationship. "My marriage and its failure was an important turning point in my development as a climber," she says, "as well as in my personal life."

In 1986, Whitehouse journeyed to Tibet as a member of a small, alpine-style expedition to Everest's North Face. Climbing without Sherpa support, she once again reached the high point on the mountain. The following year, she finally realized her dream of leading an alpine-style expedition to Ama Dablam. "The Ama Dablam trip was alpine in the purest sense; we were three teams of two climbers [Reynolds and Stewart, Bibler and Mike Dimitri, and Whitehouse and Clay Woodman], and five of us reached the summit with no Sherpa support."

The summit day of November 24, unfortunately, occurred a week before the official beginning of the winter season for which the permit was granted. In an unusually stringent display of bureaucracy, the Nepali government banned all of the summitters from climbing in Nepal for five years. Whitehouse says that when she asked the Ministry of Tourism for an explanation, she was told that the individuals had been dealt with severely because they were well known and could be used as an example to make others pay attention to regulations.

Thus Whitehouse directed her energy elsewhere, journeying to Peru in 1988, where she and Charlie Fowler tried new routes on Huandoy East, Tellaraju, and Chacaraju, attempts that were frustrated by bad snow. With Bibler and Reynolds, she began engineering plans for a return to the Tibetan side of Everest in 1989. The trip, led by Reynolds, aimed for a pure alpine-style ascent of the North Ridge. The gear was assembled and packed when political strife in Tibet first delayed the climbers' visas, then closed the country's borders completely. In discussing the foiled expedition, Whitehouse, who sports a "Free Tibet" sticker on her briefcase, is suddenly very serious and thoughtful.

It was a terrible disappointment. We put two years of our lives into preparing for this trip. But . . . while we lost our trip, the Tibetans were losing their lives. It's a helpless feeling, having an attachment to the people and the land and not being able to do anything.

As the situation in Tibet worsened throughout the spring, she and Bibler gave away their expedition food, started plotting new projects, and went on a crag-hopping tour. Although Whitehouse has rock climbed since her high-school days in the Sierras, it is only recently that she has pushed her skills into the higher grades. "For years I climbed [rock] at a really low standard, just for pleasure," she says. "But then, during the 1983 Everest expedition, I ran into some technical climbing — about 5.10 — on the Lho La, and I couldn't do it. For the first time I saw rock climbing as a goal in itself."

Climbing with Whitehouse on the rocks near Boulder, you can see the same momentum that gets her up Himalayan peaks also propels her over tricky 5.11 cruxes and through nerve-racking runouts. Her all-out go-for-it attitude has inspired some spectacular ascents, and equally sensational whippers. "In the mountains you get so used to not having any gear, so if I have any pro in the rock at all, I assume I'm safe," she says jokingly.

But when she pulled a hold off the top of a route at Cochiti Mesa, New Mexico, in 1988, she found out that this is not always the case. Her pieces ten feet below ripped, barely slowing her earthward plummet, and the rope just caught her as she simultaneously hit the ground and her belayer sixty feet below. Whitehouse badly sprained an ankle, her belayer had a broken collarbone, and Annie's local reputation suffered quite a blow. Other legendary falls include a long flier off Jules Verne, but her boldness and determination have also fueled flash ascents of numerous 5.11s in Eldorado Canyon and at crags throughout Colorado, New Mexico, and Texas, as well as new-route attempts on the Diamond Face of Long's Peak in Colorado, and as far afield as the seaside limestone of Thailand.

Last summer, Whitehouse began to crack the 5.12 barrier and continues to progress on both sport and alpine rock routes. Although she now occasionally "works" some routes prior to red-pointing them, she is most interested in on-sight ascents. "Going back to the same route three or four times seems too much like going to the office," she says. For her, "the office" can be either the steep trails of Nepal, where she leads trips through her small trekking company, Tashi Takia Treks (named for the eight auspicious signs in Tibetan Buddhism), or the maternity ward in the Boulder hospital where she now works. "Working as a nurse provides a human element to my life, an opportunity to give something to people," she says. "It helps to balance the single-minded self-absorption of my climbing."

Diverse interests have always been important to her; increasingly important is a home to return to after the rigors of travels and ascents. Before she moved to Boulder in 1987, Whitehouse experimented with a more migratory lifestyle, climbing as much as possible. "It lasted one and a half years," she says. "I just can't live out of boxes and storage closets for the bulk of my life. I also couldn't live in Nepal all the time — I'm not nearly that eccentric."

Money, of course, is ultimately a concern for Himalayan climbers. Sponsorship is tough to come by in this country, especially for small expeditions. Whitehouse believes that what she sees as a corporate preference for large, high-profile ventures hinders Americans at the cutting edge in the Himalaya. "Huge expeditions like the Snowbird, Cowboys on Everest, or Northwest Everest Expeditions aren't doing anything new, or advancing the sport, but they get the money and the exposure."

Still, Whitehouse turns down invitations to join the big expeditions, preferring to focus on her own alpine vision. To sell herself and her dreams, she has had to fight her reclusive tendencies and learn how to market herself. "It took me a long time," she remembers. "It goes against the grain of mountaineers to see ourselves as commodities."

Together with Bibler, Reynolds, and Sandy Stewart, she raised the full budget for their star-crossed 1989 expedition and is herself partially sponsored by Thor Lo, a thermal sock company. Her fear is that "by the time you've really figured out how to sell expeditions, you're over the hill."

However, the next hill Whitehouse may be going over is Everest; she plans to return to Tibet and Everest's North Face in the spring of 1991 with Bibler and Reynolds on a permit reissued to replace the one that was cancelled. She also hopes that the Nepalese ban will soon be lifted, and she will be free to pursue her many goals in the Nepal Himalaya. "We feel like we've paid our dues," she says. She wants to continue her steady evolution toward increasingly technical, hard, and fast alpine ascents.

Now, just back from Patagonia, Whitehouse calls with news of the trip. How was it? "Good," comes the slightly hesitant answer. She elaborates, "Argentina and Patagonia are completely wild, like Nepal was ten years ago." But how was the climb? "Oh, we didn't get up it," she answers quickly, then adds, "but I think we could have. My partner thought there was too much snow up high."

Whitehouse seldom glosses over a situation, and she talks about her partner's lack of commitment. For a moment, frustration taints the conversation, but her voice quickly regains its enthusiasm. "But I felt great — before we started, I didn't know what to expect. Fitzroy had always been such a forbidding mountain, with a nasty reputation. I was sure it would be a struggle, that I'd be in over my head." Her innate modesty cracks with excitement. "But I wasn't! It was well within my capabilities — I'm sure I could have climbed it." She begins talking of return trips, other routes.

She quotes Beryl Markham to explain her need to come back again and again to the world's highest places. " 'Why risk it?' I have been asked — I could answer, 'Each to his element.' By his nature, a sailor must sail, by his nature, a flyer must fly." Whitehouse must climb.

Carlos Buhler. *Photo by Michael Kennedy*

Solving the Riddle

CARLOS BUHLER

By Jonathan Waterman

[From CLIMBING, October 1989]

I magine Camp III on the unclimbed East Face of Mount Everest in 1983, and the climbing team waiting for the daily radio call. The day before, rumor had come up that an unknown woman had joined the trekking group due into basecamp. There, six male climbers had immediately taken baths. Finally the radio sputtered, "Carlos, you'd better come down. Your mother is here and she's looking for you."

Carlos Buhler was more surprised than anyone. His mother, Julie Dougherty, age 57, seldom hiked, never camped out, and had never visited Tibet. She had told Carlos that his first ten years of climbing were her "dark ages"; she was afraid he would get killed. She hadn't heard about the Everest trek until a week before it left. Her husband had said, "You'd better get over there," so she signed up. Now Buhler rappelled down and walked across the glacier to greet his mother.

Today Dougherty accompanies her son to basecamp on every one of his Himalayan climbs, sometimes twice a year. "While over there, I worry about myself rather than staying at home and pulling the covers over my head and worrying about Carlos," she says.

Dougherty doesn't want to know about the mountain's history or specific hazards until the climb is over, and even then the knowledge is very difficult for her. "Each one is a success only because he comes back in one piece" is her definition of mountaineering victory. "The fact that he reaches the summit is immaterial."

Yet Carlos Paltenghe Buhler has succeeded on a triumvirate of 8,000-meter peaks, has climbed another three score of significant summits worldwide, and has become the most accomplished North American climber in the Himalaya. Unlike his hard-driving predecessor in that role, John Roskelly, Buhler is a person of gentle understatement: He claims that he is a generalist, that his climbs are big walk-ups.

The facts are different, however. The year after doing Everest's steepest route, the East Face, Buhler confronted Roskelly's magnum opus, the West Pillar of Makalu. He also attempted Gasherbrum IV in 1983 (the same year he summited with oxygen on Everest's East Face), Everest again in 1986, Annapurna IV in 1979, and Kungyang Kish in 1981.

Even Buhler's "failures" shine. Makalu was a huge climb for such a small team of relative uninitiates, while Gasherbrum IV and Kungyang Kish involved new routes on seldom-climbed peaks. Buhler tried Everest again in order to summit without oxygen, and on Annapurna IV he brought down a sick Sherpa instead of summiting. Like his mentor Willi Unsoeld, Buhler says he is interested in process, not product.

Buhler has also mined the Himalayan mother lode of success: a new route on Baruntse (23,687 feet) in 1981; a new route in winter on Ama Dablam (22,318 feet) in 1985; becoming in 1988 the first American to climb Kanchenjunga (28,169 feet, alpine style); and a five-day, alpine-style ascent of Cho Oyu (26,906 feet) in 1989. His partners comprise a Himalayan Who's Who, including Martin Zabeleta, Peter Habeler, Dick Renshaw, Michael Kennedy, Sharon Wood, and George Lowe.

Buhler disparages the notion of trying to climb the fourteen highest mountains in the world. Although his calendar is usually cloud-filled with two 8,000-meter peaks a year, Buhler has also set his sights on 6,000- and 7,000-meter peaks like the Nameless Tower in Pakistan, Changabang in India, or Menglungtse in China. Elsewhere, particularly in South America, Buhler has put a sizable dent into the oceanic anticline known as the Andes. He has eagerly pursued Paragot's three great routes, succeeding on Aconcagua's South Face and Huascaran's North Face; Paragot's third was Makalu's West Pillar. Buhler has also done new routes on the West Face of Extremo Ausangate, Carhuaco Punco's West Face, and Huascaran Sur's Northeast Face. He has routinely tagged classics such as Cerro Torre (three months before Kanchenjunga), Huandoy, and Huayna Potosi.

Nonetheless, he says he lost his breath when he read last year's *New York Times* article dubbing him a "superalpinist." Buhler will concede to being a superorganizer, but otherwise, he considers himself a pinch hitter, uninspired by 5.13 climbing, and unable to run up the hills faster than anyone else.

Buhler believes that his forté lies in knowing when to turn up what he refers to as "the volume." On the crags and while hill running, he can crank himself up to moderate levels. At home he prefers a low setting, just loud enough to stay motivated. Once he is acclimated in the Himalaya, however, something happens. His mother senses the oscillation and leaves basecamp immediately; Kennedy says Buhler changes overnight. Up goes the volume, on go the crampons, and the soft-spoken soul becomes a driven, uncompromising pilgrim until he's through with the mountain.

Buhler has never really left Everest or, for that matter, any of the peaks of his toil. Suspended on his apartment walls in Bellingham, Washington, are three pictures from the 1983 Everest climb. Each morning Buhler rises from his fouton on the floor and confronts a self-portrait on the right-hand wall, grinning an 8,000-meter-wide grin while standing on top of the world. During his climbs he is an exacting scribe, and his journals fill several huge boxes in the closet. He pulls out the Everest journal and, play-acting each passage with unbridled and tin-eared enthusiasm, he reads:

Oct 2, Sunday 1983. Today was a fine day for me. We broke trail today up to Camp II . . . But the most wonderful thing that happened was that my body responded to my will with such success.

I've been chosen to make up the first summit attempt team. This is absolutely unbelievable for me! The boy who grew up . . . pudgy and non athletic as I was . . . I'm honored today, not because I'm the strongest member or the most experienced, but still out of an incredibly experienced group of guys I've been selected as competent as the rest.

Oct 10. Ten and a half grueling hours of trailbreaking to the top . . . terrible snow conditions left us pretty wiped. We ran into the seven Japanese trying Everest without oxygen. . . .

It was all kind of a dreamish day and I realized at the time that Laurie and Martin had been there, and Hillary and all the others. Yeah, reaching the top, I sort of realized a few hazy thoughts about all those things. But it was 2:35 and mostly all's I could think about was taking the necessary photos and going with the descent. I didn't look around much at the view and just had to get photos. . . . My moment to be the highest soul standing on earth.

It is not uncommon for climbers to use Everest to clear the way, to fell the biggest tree, then start looking for the sky. After the 1983 climb, Buhler thought about returning to school but beat back societal preconceptions of Everest being the culminating point in a climbing career by proceeding with his "lesser" climbing plans. In his wallet, he carries a hard-creased quote: "The people who succeed and do not push onto a greater failure are the spiritual middle-classers. Their stopping at success is the proof of their compromising insignificance. How petty their dreams must have been."

Five months after Everest, Buhler arrived at the base of the hardest route up the fifth highest peak in the world (three photographs of Makalu also grace his apartment), with three partners and no oxygen. Solving the riddle for this climb, he claims, came from listening carefully to experienced climbers like George Lowe and Lou Reichardt on Everest.

Makalu turned out to be his Armageddon. He refers to the mountain as "his most important watershed," because here he realized how to climb huge peaks with a few friends. For two years, he and Sharon Wood had raised thousands of dollars and chased down innumerable logistics. Once on the mountain, Buhler, Wood, Dwayne Congdon, and Charlie Sassara were equally strong, but because of the coming monsoon and the dynamics of load carrying, only two people could attempt the summit. Although Buhler had hoped to avoid the disparities that the Everest climb had created, Sassara and Wood were forced to carry to the Makalu high camp so that Congdon and Buhler could try for the summit. (Sole had developed a retinal hemorrhage.)

Above the pillar, Buhler saw something that looked like a tent bag. As he got closer, he realized it was the remains of Karel Schubert, who had died in 1976. Buhler passed without stopping, without telling Congdon, not wanting to "freak myself out." He was acutely aware of the risks of climbing above 27,000 feet without oxygen, because he had passed some slow-moving Japanese on Everest who never made it off the mountain. Soon enough, he and Congdon couldn't see more than fifty meters through the blowing snow. The duo realized they would have trouble getting back down the snow-covered rock bands, so within 100 meters of the top they turned around.

"It was a feeling of emptiness. We'd just missed it. Now it's much easier for me to look back and feel good about having completed the West Pillar, and I'm really glad that we had the sense to turn around. It was the right decision, and I didn't struggle with it at the time."

In basecamp, he wrote in his journal: "Last nite I went out and bayed like a coyote on the moon to Makalu. I like it here. I feel changed. Even after nearly two and a half months out here, I feel no hurry to return anywhere. I like the food, I like the sun, I've given up on the mountain."

Nevertheless, the mountain haunted him. For two years after Makalu, Buhler relived the summit day, heavy with failure. He found consolation by visiting Fritz Wiessner, who had turned back within 300 meters of K2's summit in 1938.

Buhler will concede that the main reason he wanted to reach the summit of Makalu was to receive outside recognition for the project — a stamp of approval. A similar pattern had unfolded after he had reached the summit of Everest, due cause for celebration. Buhler had been unhappy that some teammates looked at him as if he hadn't deserved to be chosen for the summit team, as if he hadn't done his share of work on the mountain. Three years later, he tried to reach that summit without oxygen. Then, in 1985, he and Michael Kennedy established a classic winter route on Ama Dablam; afterward, Kennedy drank Star beer in Pangboche and relaxed, but Buhler couldn't kick back. He was obsessed with his phrasing of a telegram to the Ministry of Tourism, describing their success.

Buhler clearly wants to be remembered for his accomplishments. Kennedy says that Buhler blows his horn a lot less than most proficient climbers and that he's also realistic about which of his accomplishments will be remembered. Buhler claims, "I'm never going to be breaking new terrain. I'm never going to be Voytek Kurtyka or Reinhold Messner. I can only tell you what I get out of it. If I started trying to make some sort of plan for what mountaineering is, that's a good way to get killed."

Buhler is different, complex, dream-torn. Most climbers respectfully watch as the Sherpas perform their prayer ceremony, but Buhler focuses, asking many questions while setting up the prayer flags and arranging the juniper twigs to be burned. Once he is on a peak, Buhler becomes a fierce zealot, unwilling to give up his lead. Yet in regular life, he touches people on the shoulder as he talks to them, hugs men goodbye, and sends his friends cards painted with flowers. Speaking recently in front of the august and male-dominated American Alpine Club, he repeatedly emphasized words such as "wonderful," "beautiful," and "companionship" to describe his survival epic on Kanchenjunga.

"I don't think I've ever been successful with guys that have a lot of male energy," Buhler says. "I'm not a very macho person. There's a side of me that's pretty touchy-feely. I can sit and talk to someone about what's really going on in my mind about the world, and risk, and love."

Is he for real? Who is this man, with his graceful humility and the usual male ego, his female sensitivity, and the drive of Ahab?

* * *

Rumor circulates that the thirty-five-year old Buhler subsists on a trust fund, but true or not, it is immaterial in the face of his frugal lifestyle and his self-employed work ethic. His earned income is about $20,000 a year, mostly from hard-won corporate lectures, guiding, or ski patrolling. Otherwise, the organization and planning of his numerous expeditions is a full-time profession for Buhler.

His two-room basement apartment is wreathed with Nepalese Katas scarves. Family photos are taped to the refrigerator; other decorations include two Chinese watercolors, a Nepalese purse, four Spanish medallions, a key to the city of San Francisco (from Everest '83), and a 14-karat gold pen engraved "Kanchenjunga." There is no television. Above his bed, next to the Everest photo, hangs a picture of his mother's cattle ranch in New Mexico.

Considering that he is a serious person, Buhler smiles a lot — a glamorous, straight-toothed, full smile. Crow's-feet fan his temples; a vein pulses beneath his left eye. In one hand he works green putty back and forth. During dinner he doesn't finish drinking the beer someone gave him. Nor do liquor, drugs, or coffee figure into his habits.

The phone rings constantly. A climber calls and asks if Buhler will help guide some clients up the Japanese Couloir on Everest. Holding a hand over the mouthpiece, Buhler says to a visitor, "This guy's nuts. Do *you* want to guide Everest?" A moment later a friend — Javier Escartin — rings from Spain. Buhler laughs with elevated animation, speaking rapid-fire Spanish, agreeing to mail some American overboots and lithium batteries.

Indeed, one of the most influential chapters of Buhler's life was when he spent two years in Spain, first as a high school student, then when he enrolled in the Economic Science Department at the University of Barcelona in 1972. He figured that he would really learn Spanish by getting away from Americans. Although he had attended the National Outdoor Leadership School and spent a season climbing in the Alps, it was in Spain where Buhler learned the true passion of the sport. Having joined the cross-country ski team, he bumped into Escartin at a ski meet in a small village; the two had met on the Matterhorn the previous summer. They climbed in the Pyrenees, then at Montserrat, and became close friends. Later, Escartin and his friends invited Buhler to Annapurna IV.

"Because of his exposure to the different culture," his mother says, "he was able to conclude that you can't evaluate someone by your own standards; you have to find out what their standards and goals are. Consequently, he is very aware of South American and Asian peoples, their hopes and desires."

As for Buhler's own background, his immediate lineage is German, but his great-great grandfather was a Basque. Carlos' father died when Carlos was ten years old. During summers on his mother's ranch, his father figure was (and is) the Mexican ranch foreman, Rafael. "He taught me a lot of things about life," Buhler says. "Taught me how to shoot rifles, drive pickups, set traps, how to walk."

After Spain, Buhler ended up at Huxley College in Bellingham, pursuing a degree in environmental education and human ecology. He spent his summers climbing. For the winter of 1974-75, in what might be either the ultimate climbing boondoggle or the mark of Buhler's developing philosophy, he proposed studying relationships in climbing. He was given the green light to "study" on Mount Hood, Mount Owen, Mount Cline, Mount Assiniboine, and Mount Robson. Based on his journal and those of his partners, he wrote a thirty-page paper, "Interpersonal and Group Relationships as a Function of Mountaineering Stress."

He graduated from Huxley in 1978 and began his intensive focus on South American climbing. The following year, Huascarán became one of his finest Andean accomplishments.

> The North Face was a fight for my life. I was doing all of the leading. I worked on this pitch at 21,000 for two days. I was bringing Don up and I was pulling, and he was yelling, and I was pulling, and he was yelling louder, and I started letting the rope out — I had been pulling with all my might. He got up and was just white.
>
> He said, "God, my harness had unclipped from the rope and I was in this corner and while you kept pulling on it, I was holding onto it with my hands!"

The day before, the pair had dropped the pack with stove and food. Finally, they crawled off the summit, half-alive and hallucinating, and were nursed back to health by some Japanese climbers.

By this time, Buhler felt that no other activity he had found linked body and mind the way mountaineering did. "Climbing in the Himalaya is really a study in interpersonal relations — not climbing. The amount of time you actually spend climbing compared to the amount of time planning is the most inefficient expenditure of your time that you can imagine."

Despite his emphatic doctrine of camaraderie first, over the course of a long weekend interview, he forgot the leader's name from one important expedition and the doctor's name from another. A turning point in his early climbing career involved dragging a schoolmate up the Eiger's Mitteleggi Ridge in 1972 and getting hit by lightning — but he has forgotten this companion's name. Ditto for a partner he towed up the Piz Badille and with whom he suffered a miserable bivouac. Forgetfulness perhaps, or perhaps Buhler is driven to climb for more than just friendship — for reasons he cannot understand.

In 1984, Buhler applied for a permit to climb Kanchenjunga (26,168 feet). He found little information on "Kanch" in this country, other than the epics of the Germans, and he was continually rebuffed by partners who could not make a commitment. Finally, Peter Habeler and Martin Zabeleta signed up.

Habeler insisted the mountain could be climbed with a small team, and furthermore, that the group needed to hire two Sherpas to carry loads. Based on the bitter experience of his friends having to donkey loads to the high camp on Makalu, and his tutelage in the Kennedy school of "light and fast" on Ama Dablam, Buhler was ready to put everything he learned to the ultimate test. Although Buhler feels otherwise, Kanch is probably his finest climb to date.

"A big team has a lot of slack and competition," Buhler says. "It's kind of a duel thing — you're there to work as a team, but to get your shot at the top, you've got to be better than others. I'd rather hire a couple of Sherpas so that there is no question as to who is going up and who wasn't."

The group arrived at basecamp on April 3, 1988, with no oxygen, a small amount of fixed rope, and two Sherpas. They shared the North Face with a Basque team, leapfrogging over one another, frequently beaten back by storms.

Buhler wrote in his journal that he wanted Kanchenjunga desperately, but he'd remain composed if he didn't reach the summit.

These trips are much easier than the early ones. Is it me, or the situations and circumstances? Is it Mom coming to basecamp? Or climbing with friends like Mike Kennedy, or Martin? No, something else is happening too. I'm more at home in these foreign places. More able to see why I'm here. I feel a better understanding of how relationships work.

These are my trips now as well. I put them together, my own recipes. My people, with the same dreams that I have.

By May 2, they fixed ropes and established themselves beneath the summit at 7,450 meters. The next morning, at 4 A.M., the three of them left for the summit. "I went through a tremendous range of emotions," Buhler later wrote. "At times I found myself elated to be so near the summit of such a huge mountain. Then I became utterly discouraged at the situation in front of me. I was frightened by the steepness, by the intense cold drilling into me, and, most of all, by the descent that would have to follow. There seemed to be so many places that I could make a fatal mistake."

Buhler met Habeler descending at 10:30 A.M. Having shot ahead at the start, he had made the summit an hour earlier; Zabeleta and Buhler would take yet another four and one-half hours in the growing storm to get to the top. While descending, Buhler spied an abandoned oxygen bottle and wished he could have some. The pair was plagued by wind and snowfall; Zabeleta had to warm Buhler's feet. They arrived back at the tent seventeen and one-half hours after they had left.

The three climbers descended the next morning in three feet of new snow, bleary-eyed, exhausted, and starving. When they reached Camp III, they discovered that the tents, food, and fuel had all been avalanched off the mountain, so they bivouacked. At 6 A.M., they abandoned everything but their cameras and wove their way down unstable snow.

They reached Camp II only to find that the tents and food there had also been avalanched off. With no recourse now, they were forced onward, falling over in the snow in the most grueling bout of their lives. When they finally reached Camp I, they found that the two Sherpas had survived the Camp II avalanche with broken ribs and a concussion. Buhler's toes were frostnipped, and Habeler was wracked by coughing; Zabeleta struggled in hours later. The Basques never made the summit; later that month, an Indian climber died trying.

After the smoke cleared, Buhler realized that he had learned yet another lesson, when Habeler asked him for whom he climbed. On the summit day, Habeler had put a picture of his wife and children in the tent and spent most of the day visualizing them so that he could make a safe descent. "We connected on this," Buhler says. "Peter and I feel that love and climbing are very intertwined. It went into who you can be for other people." In other words, you have to have someone to love in order to return safely.

Later, in the village of Gunza, Buhler relaxed, ate, read, and listened to the radio. Clearly his attitude had undergone changes since Ama Dablam and Makalu. He was not only learning how to accept failure, but how to put success in perspective.

When Buhler came home, he felt that there was a lot of "hoopla" going on.

> You're a superalpinist, the 7th grade award, please speak at the AAC meeting, and the cover photo on *Summit*. I have to play all that up, I understand that, but these are images that people create and I know there's no magic there, you're not any stronger than anyone else, you don't run up the hills any faster, you don't make decisions any better, you don't swing the ax with any more accuracy.
>
> What gives me satisfaction is when I do a job and things are in control. But I came down from Kanch

feeling that it had gotten out of hand. I got down to basecamp thinking "I can't feel good about this."

Habeler's comment after that expedition was, "I really think Carlos Buhler is now one of the very best mountaineers in the Himalaya, and he is just starting, so there should be a lot more to come." Habeler added that he had taken part in few expeditions that had run so smoothly, largely "thanks to Carlos' management."

In the spring of 1989, Buhler walked into Cho Oyu with his compañero, Zabeleta, and, of course, his mother. More than one outsider commented that the group was more like a family than a climbing team.

"Martin and Carlos complement each other," says Dougherty. "When they're together, they're talking beautiful Spanish, trading inside jokes about themselves and their work. When I'm with the two of them, they buoy me up the way they buoy up one another."

In five days, Buhler and Zabeleta shot from 20,000 feet up the Southwest Buttress to the 26,906-foot summit. Two climbers, no oxygen, no support, no fixed ropes.

During the windy summit day, April 4, Buhler had turned around until Zabeleta found a sheltered spot on the ridge and yelled for Buhler to come back. "I had so much respect for people that turned around," Buhler says. "I was worried about freezing my toes. I thought this was crazy. I didn't have to prove that I could do this."

They continued up, playing cat and mouse with the wind, hiding behind the ridge, watching a 300-foot plume of snow raging off the summit. Fortunately, around midday, the winds abated and they topped out at 2:30 on April 4, mentally exhausted because they wanted to turn back so often. Buhler hugged Zabeleta and said, "Let's get the fuck out of here."

The two have developed a partnership that could be likened

to that of Messner and Habeler, or Boardman and Tasker. They talked about it at 24,500 feet, after the summit. "Goddamn," they agreed in Spanish, "somehow this works out right for us."

"Cho Oyu was a really rewarding experience, because both of us had dreamed of doing it as a two-man team, and we'd never had the courage to do it," Buhler says. (Alan Kearney was to be the third climber, but he remained sick at basecamp.)

In the end, Buhler's contribution to mountaineering will be judged largely by his dedication. He climbs full-time, and when he's not climbing, he lectures about climbing. Buhler denies that he'll ever slow the pace but does concede that he'd like to raise a family soon.

"I know better than anyone that at the blink of an eye, it could be my last trip," says Carlos. "And I also know that I don't think I could go through life shielding myself from that potential blink of an eye, because I like experiencing these very intense interpersonal adventures with my friends. I don't go fooling myself that I'm any safer than anyone else." Nonetheless, Buhler has never been injured or had a serious accident while climbing.

Lhakpa Dorje — Buhler's sirdar and trusted companion from Baruntse, Makalu, Ama Dablam, Kanch, and Cho Oyu — insists that good luck is the single most important safety factor, regardless of the climbing team's strength and experience. So, during Buhler's summit day on Cho Oyu, Dorje hired monks to pray for Buhler's good luck. "Luck," Buhler says, "doesn't allow you to get a big ego."

Buhler left for K2 in May 1989.

I'm not putting faith in karma. I don't go to the mountains thinking I had good luck on the last one, maybe I'll have good luck on this one. I watch my friends getting killed every year. I go through my address book and it's just one more name after another that's gone. So many, so many people were making the same kind of decisions that I would make. A big part of it is having experience, like Martin and Peter. I spent a lot of time thinking about K2, talking to Kurt Diemburger about why that riddle didn't get solved right.

I'm also taking a very careful look at whether it's worth the risk. But I'm not going to do the West Face of K2. I don't know how much satisfaction I'd get out of climbing K2 by a new route and then having my partner slip off during the descent and die. What good is that? I'd rather try things within my own ability. I understand there's no great achievement in climbing the Abruzzi.

However, I am trying very hard to limit myself, to curb my diet. You just can't do it over and over and over and expect to come out alive.

Naturally, both Zabeleta and Dougherty went to K2. Like Dorje, Buhler's mother utters her own private mantra, even though she doesn't know which day he'll try for the summit.

"I try not to perceive any danger at all. I'm aware that no matter how skilled or how good his judgment, or how committed, there are certain factors you can't control. But Carlos is doing the thing he wants to do, and I take enormous satisfaction from this."

Like one partner, who on a mountain relies on his faraway wife and children, Buhler feels that his mother contributes to his success because she gives him the strength to go on when he's tired, the incentive to get down safely. So, while Habeler climbs for wife and kids, Carlos Buhler climbs for community, deed — and mom.

Ed Webster. *Photo by Jonathan Waterman*

The Survivor

ED WEBSTER

By Jonathan Waterman

[From CLIMBING, October 1990]

S everal hundred wide-eyed people stared at Ed Webster and the slides of his climb on Everest as he flicked through them, but he was oblivious. He remembers pounding on the lectern and describing "how I was angry that I might die on the descent. I was reliving it, spitting it out." He also told the audience that the day on Everest when he found that he would lose parts of his fingers to frostbite "was one of those days where I felt my life pivot. That I would never be the same."

The standing ovation brought him out of a daze that night. Webster's oration had transcended its setting, a hall rented in Atlanta, Georgia, by the American Alpine Club for its 1988 meeting.

Back in Colorado six weeks later, at the beginning of another slide show, Webster suddenly grew ill and had to lecture from a chair. Seven surgeries and amputations over eight months had finally taken a toll. Webster subsequently canceled a half-dozen planned lectures.

Several disconcerting months floated by. Webster felt disconnected, and claustrophobic in public. He'd go to a movie and have to leave. Even simple daily chores were too much. He felt like a war survivor, while doctors and friends suggested that these were symptoms of post-traumatic stress syndrome.

"Driving around town, I had to really pay attention so I didn't pass out," says Webster. He had begun to feel that he was losing control of his body and thought of himself as a cripple, an invalid. "Or I'd be thinking *Italian* in a conversation, but I'd say *Swiss* instead."

* * *

Webster's fascination with climbing big mountains began in 1972, when Ed and I piled into a station wagon with five other Explorer Scouts. In the prime of our adolescence, we flashed moons out the back window as we were driven to a lecture given by the British expedition leader Chris Bonington in Boston. At the show, we were rapt at Bonington's storytelling prowess. Ed was totally absorbed by the pictures of the Himalaya, and that night his eyes radiated an inconcealable youthful need.

In short order, Ed read every Himalayan climbing story that he could find. He thought the all-time classic was *Annapurna,* describing Maurice Herzog's landmark climb and the amputation of his frostbitten fingers and toes during a grueling train ride back to Kathmandu. The superhuman stories in *Mountain Magazine* also captured Ed's and my imagination. There was Walter Bonatti retreating from a storm on Mont Blanc, Herman Buhl falling through a cornice and dying on Chogolisa, Layton Kor dragging terrified partners up the Black Canyon, John Harlin's fatal attraction to the North Face of the Eiger, and Reinhold Messner's brother, Gunther, dying on Nanga Parbat. These climbers inspired us. We longed to suffer as they had, to shiver until dawn in lofty aeries.

But before this happened we had to learn how. Lexington, Massachusetts, is not a rock-climbing mecca, but Ed made do. Two hundred yards from the busiest expressway in New England, he discovered a fifty-foot pile of metamorphic offal that had been dynamited and scraped out of the ground by highway crews. He mapped it out, pried off countless flakes, and climbed every conceivable and not-so-conceivable route. He even wrote a guidebook to "The Canyon," initiating a pattern that he would carry on into adulthood.

One Friday night in Ed's basement, while our peers "cruised chicks" and shot beers, we straightened rusty pitons and sharpened our ice axes in preparation for the weekend's adventure. We slept fitfully until 5 A.M., then got up and hitchhiked to New Hampshire. Late that afternoon, we slogged up Mount Washington to a cabin inhabited by tatterdemalion, dope-smoking hardmen.

Next morning, under rime-feathered spruce boughs, we hiked to Huntingtons Ravine and got blasted by the wind. Black, house-sized boulders shrunk beneath the soaring blue bulges of ice. We pulled our hoods tighter and left the Goldline in Ed's pack, for it was too cold to bother with belaying. The hardmen from the cabin turned back, but we knew better: Buhl, Bonatti, Herzog, Harlin, Kor, or Messner wouldn't have fled.

The two of us moved spastically up the ice, gripping our axes tightly when the wind threatened to pluck us off. Suddenly, my axe popped and I was falling eyes just out of Ed's reach. While trying to self-arrest, I dislocated my shoulder. Then, sliding toward a meeting with the boulderfield, my tibia bent, split, and came apart with a dull snap that erupted into an eyeful of fireworks. I cartwheeled to a stop.

Ed climbed down. We splinted my leg to an axe and bound my shoulder with webbing. We scoffed at calling a rescue and decided that this was our own responsibility — after all, real mountaineers always took care of themselves. We especially didn't want to be written up in an accident report.

We developed a system for getting out: Ed would support me by my good arm, and I'd hobble to the next boulder to rest. The ball of my humerus grated outside of the shoulder socket. We heard people coming, so Ed propped me against a tree. When they appeared, Ed prattled on about the wind while I contrived a smile. Eventually, we caught a ride back down the mountain in a Snowcat and hitched a ride home in an unheated Volkswagon.

* * *

During high school, Ed spent most of his time either climbing or in the darkroom. His photography teacher complained that he photographed only climbing. In the art department he won an award for sculpture, but to Ed, his most important achievement was getting articles published in *Climbing* magazine about his new routes at Crow Hill and in the Adirondacks.

From mapping his work at the inconsequential and squalid Canyon to a photocopied "buildering" guide to the high school, Ed always let others know of his accomplishments. Our fellow Explorer Scout and climber Jeff Pheasant jibed Ed relentlessly. "Webbie," said Pheasant, "it's amazing you can free climb so well with such skinny arms." Pheasant viewed climbing as a very personal endeavor, something you did for fun, recreation. But to Ed, it was different. He wanted to sleep, eat, and drink climbing. Seeing his routes in print was a verification of his identity.

Subsequently, his stories and photos would appear in magazines around the world. His photos became covers for *Ascent, Climbing, Summit, Iwa To Yuki, Mountain, Alpin, Alpinism and Randonee, The American Alpine Club Journal,* and numerous books. His letters to friends — scribbled or neatly typed on expedition stationery — were postmarked from itinerant perches in the Canyonlands, Eldorado Springs, North Conway, and the Khumbu.

Following the predictable course of many other single-minded rock stars, Ed majored in geology at Colorado College. Somehow, he still found plenty of time to add to his list of first ascents. Back then, obvious lines on virgin rock weren't a rarity, and Ed was happily obsessed.

In 1976, with Earl Wiggins and Bryan Becker, he did the first ascent of the mega-classic Supercrack in Indian Creek Canyon. The following year, Ed soloed D-1 on the Diamond of Longs Peak, using only nuts. Otherwise, he fired off the first ascent of the Primrose Dihedrals on Moses Tower in the Canyonlands, as well as a four-pitch variation to The Cruise called the Scenic Cruise, and the first ascent of the Hallucinogen Wall, both in the Black Canyon. Back on New Hampshire's Cathedral, with Henry Barber, he did the first free ascent of Women in Love, and, on the neighboring cliff, Whitehorse, he did the first ascent of the Last Unicorn with Pheasant. These climbs put Webster's name within the geography of North American rock climbing. In guidebooks from east to west, his name still appears with the frequency of punctuation.

Ed's makeup also included sharing both the minutiae and the deepest, darkest secrets of his life. For example, within ten minutes of meeting a stranger, Ed might spontaneously divulge the intricacies of his love life, the dilemmas of his career, the reason he once visited a psychiatrist, or the new route he climbed over the weekend.

Partners had trouble drawing a bead on him. Jim Gilchrist, an occasional companion of Ed's from Boulder, thought him lacking in confidence because during an approach or at the base of a climb, Ed would appear uninspired. "I'm overweight," Ed would say, "out of shape. I don't know if it will go." But Gilchrist also notes that Ed became unstoppable once he actually started up the route. "He would throw off blocks, bang in pins," said Gilchrist, "no way he was going down."

In that age of more macho attitudes in the climbing world, one can only picture his less-sensitive partners' mortification as Ed talked freely about whatever crossed his mind, which wasn't always climbing. It might have been health, gardening, or poetry. He showed a sensitivity, a need to emote, a raw streak that struck some partners as slightly feminine.

But the aspect of Ed's personality that really raised the hair on fellow climbers' necks was his ardent route reportage, particularly in a time when such self-promotion was considered egocentric, even blasphemous. Typifying the rift between Ed and other stoically silent climbers, while Ed was hanging off the Hallucinogen Wall for two weeks in 1981, Muff Cheney, down in Colorado Springs, joked, "Ed's probably already got the article written."

Bryan Becker spent most of the 1970s putting up new routes with Ed throughout North America. Their relationship grew to be extremely competitive. "The glory factor was important to Ed," says Becker. As others did, Becker teased Ed constantly, chiding, "The credit will read 'Photograph of Ed Webster by Ed Webster,' right?" whenever Becker conceded to take a picture of his partner with Ed's camera. "I had to play the hard-ass," Becker says. "You couldn't let Ed indulge himself." But although Ed's ego played a part in his self-promotion, his journalistic endeavors were also in many ways an innocent open marriage with climbing, with a love of life that he wanted to share with the world.

As Ed stepped into the 1980s, his father, a physics professor at Harvard, demanded that his son address how "he was going to butter his bread." Apparently unconcerned, Ed changed his major to anthropology, an even less marketable field than geology. And when he graduated from college, the only employers who received his resume were guiding schools.

Ed's travels and guiding ranged from Utah sandstone to California walls to New England ice to European limestone. At this point, he was hardly a seasoned alpinist, but he pulled off a spectacular success on Canada's Mount Robson, third-classing a direct variation up to and along the storm-washed North Face with Becker. While fending off cabin fever during one dreary winter in North Conway, Ed researched, wrote, and self-published a guidebook to New Hampshire rock climbs. The book was successful. Even his father — who had loaned him the money for the printing — whistled a different tune after his son, now an author, promptly repaid the loan, with interest, from his book earnings.

* * *

In June 1983, Ed met Lauren Husted, a petite, blue-eyed, brown-haired twenty-one-year-old. She would soon change his life. Recently graduated cum laude from the University of Vermont, Husted was a fanatical woman of letters, always writing in her diary, seeking publication, and reciting the poetry of Keats.

The two quickly became very close, living under the same roof and sharing similar interests, taking long road trips and reading verse aloud together. Under Ed's tutelage, Lauren became an accomplished rock climber, and the pair established numerous new routes together, including Western Union on the Bastille in Eldorado Canyon, Sparkling Touch on a Spire by the same name in the Canyonlands, Slip Sliding Away on Lumpy Ridge, and All's Well That Ends Well in the Black Canyon. Ed trusted Lauren completely, on and off the rocks.

In a foretelling letter dated January 1984, Ed wrote of a mutual companion who had died:

> It's quite strange thinking of old friends who are no longer with us. They always will be, in my minds' eye, and that's where I find comfort even though often times (at least in climbing), I know they died a terrible death. [Dr.] Pete Thexton's was particularly hard [Thexton died from high-altitude cerebral edema], in that he was about the most well-rounded climber I'd ever met, a role model for me . . . his death seemed so illogical.

That spring, Ed expressed his own interest in expedition climbing. He felt it was time to make the step from waltzing up sun-kissed cliffs to battling with wind-torn, 8,000-meter peaks, as was his inspiration twelve years before. Lauren fixed him with her gentle eyes and said, before breaking into tears, "I'll die before you go to the Himalaya."

Exactly one year after they met, Ed and Lauren descended into the Black Canyon to attempt a new route. They completed the climb up to the final easy section and decided to unrope. It had been twenty-two pitches, the longest ridge climb Ed had ever done. Lauren was climbing behind Ed when he heard her cry as a hold broke loose in her hand. She disappeared from Ed's view, falling 200 feet into S.O.B. Gully. Ed was at her side within minutes, but an hour later, she lay dead in his arms. It was Ed who had to make the phone call to Lauren's parents. And it was Father's Day. "That was the lowest point of my entire life," Ed says. "I'll have his cry of anguish echoing around in my head forever."

Back home, Ed tried to reassemble his life. He named their route, Lauren's Arete and renamed two other routes. All's Well That Ends Well, which Lauren had named, became A Midsummer Night's Dream, while Slip Sliding Away turned into Graceful Dancer. He went through her Keats books and found highlighted sections that spoke to him: ". . . a deepening sense of the precariousness of life, its brevity, and its unpredictability." And in Lauren's diary, there was a poem about falling, slipping, losing grasp, and going into the blackness. "Almost," he said, "like she had left it for me."

He expressed his torment in a letter written at the time:

Ah god — I had another torturous morning. I delivered the new issue of *Denver Magazine* to Lauren's eighty-six-year-old grandmother, containing Lauren's last published article [on Colorado peaches] and a tribute to her. "Why didn't you use the rope?" she kept sobbing. I wish I knew.

I really have, I think, come a long way in the past two months toward resolving my demons over what happened. I do not feel guilty; Lauren made her decisions herself. They weren't the right ones in retrospect — but she hated it when I babied her on a climb. She demanded I respect her judgment, for better or worse.

Ed soloed Castleton Tower and left a register on top dedicated to Lauren. A month later, he rope-soloed a new route on the

Diamond, naming it Bright Star after her favorite Keats poem. "I still cannot believe I did it alone!" he wrote in another letter. "Such a hard-won jewel, a gift for Lauren. That is my fond desire — to make her proud of me, each and every day. If I feel I succeed in this task, I can (somehow) live without her. Doing the Diamond and Bright Star was a big step in that direction."

Putting the past behind him entailed not only doing the big new routes, but meeting the giants of climbing. Via the mail and telephone, Ed had tried to become friends with one of "the legends" for nearly two years. Then suddenly, Layton Kor knocked at his door and asked Ed to go climbing. Kor had been out of climbing for some time, so Ed showed him how to place nuts in Eldorado. Then, in Clear Creek, the two freed a route that Kor had put up twenty years before.

Finally, they returned to the Black Canyon and established two new routes, Wheel of Life and Gothic Pillar. Ed faltered when he saw the ledge that Lauren had died on. But Kor, the doorstop for Ed's emotional barndooring, summoned a ghost from his own past and described how John Harlin's death on the Eiger had affected him. Kor believed that climbers take responsibility for their own actions, so it's wrong to blame oneself for someone else's accident. But he suffered over Harlin's death just as Ed was now suffering over Lauren's.

Kor gave him precious insight. "He could always see the lighter side of a potentially dark situation," Ed wrote, " — a trait of a survivor." So Ed became a survivor.

* * *

The winter after Lauren's death, Ed accepted an invitation to the West Ridge of Everest and became engrossed by training and expedition logistics. Although he claimed he hadn't thought about Lauren since soloing the Diamond, friends were sure she still weighed on his mind. One friend urged him, "Bright Star was for Lauren, Everest is for you."

251

At high altitude for the first time that spring, Ed was more turtle than tiger of the snows. He had a sore throat, couldn't sustain a pace, and fell asleep at his zenith of 24,500 feet. Robert Anderson, an American living in New Zealand, was the strongest team member, pushing out the fixed ropes and making the first summit bid with Peter Athans.

As a member of this nineteen-member, twelve-Sherpa team, Ed got a glimpse of big-expedition politics and dichotomies. While the leader Dave Saas was a clean-living Mormon, the *bon vivant* Jim Bridwell led another faction of the team to new heights of debauchery, partying heartily at basecamp. The lack of communication among the various members became apparent: The lower camps were being cleared on the same day that Anderson and Jay Smith were making the second summit attempt.

Ed was also appalled that the Sherpas didn't always clip into fixed ropes and was relieved that none of the team was killed. "A lot of the climbers thought me to be overly safety conscious," Ed says. "I don't know if you can be too safe, unless it kills an inordinate amount of time." Nonetheless, he became known as "the Turtle," always bringing up the rear.

Ed was the last to leave the village of Tengboche. As he stepped out of the outhouse, a helicopter landed and out jumped a Nepali. "You must show Billy Squier the mountain!" he said. So Ed flew up to Mount Everest with the rock-and-roll star, then on to Kathmandu. As the rest of the expedition waited anxiously in seedy Lukla for their delayed flight, Ed relaxed, bathing for the first time in months amid the gold-plated fixtures of Kathmandu's opulent Yak 'N Yeti Hotel. When his teammates finally caught a plane a week later, they were shocked to find "the Turtle" waiting for them in Kathmandu.

* * *

In August 1985, his friendship with Anderson was cemented during their ascent of a new route on the Diamond. Ed led all of Hidden Diamond (5.11+ when he and Peter Athans freed it a month later). Anderson and he discussed big, unwieldy expeditions and the lack of communication on their West Ridge trip. Later that winter, Anderson mentioned he had a 1988 permit for Everest.

"I became more and more interested in climbs with a lot of risk, a great amount of uncertainty, and physical endurance," Ed says. "I reached a point where I wasn't at the pinnacle of rock-climbing shape anymore, and there had to be something other than big-wall climbing or aid climbing."

Indeed, "the Turtle" had not distinguished himself at altitude, but he did succeed in catching the Everest bug. In 1986, he was hired to photograph Roger Marshall during his solo attempt on Everest's North Col route. While Ed would not attempt Everest, Marshall gave him carte blanche to climb anything else, "so long as you don't get killed."

At basecamp, they listened to radio broadcasts about the mayhem on K2, as the redoubtable British alpinist Alan Rouse and twelve other strong climbers died from altitude sickness, climbing falls, and storms. On Everest soon after, Victor Hugo Trujillo, a young Chilean who Ed had befriended, died in a cornice avalanche below the North Col.

Nonetheless, while Marshall rested during a short break in the monsoon, Ed attempted the East Face of Changtse. Within thirty feet of the Northeast Ridge, steep shale repulsed his best efforts. A day later he took a more direct line up tenuous snow, then traversed to the final ridge. After eleven hours of climbing, he became the first American to reach the 24,780-foot summit; it was also the highest peak yet soloed by an American.

"That was the greatest day of my life," says Ed. "Watching the sun rise over the top of the Himalaya, looking right at Everest. You could see Cho Oyo, Kanchenjunga, Jannu, Nuptse, Pumori. Climbing Changtse was like going to heaven and visiting with the angels for a day."

While descending, Ed began hallucinating, thinking he saw geologists taking samples from the glacier. So he sat down on his pack and ate. After fifteen hours on the go, he staggered past the glacial grave of Trujillo. Ed heard, "Hola, Hola!" And there was Trujillo, waving his hat in congratulations, giving Ed the thumbs-up with a big grin. Then, according to Ed's diary, "Trujillo melted back into a pile of rocks."

Ed arrived back in basecamp, having soloed up and down 4,500 vertical feet in sixteen hours. The next day he heard that Renato Casarotto, a well-known Italian climber who Ed always thought to be invincible, had been killed while soloing K2. "I felt lucky to get away with it." Ed says now, "I'd never do something like that again." Marshall, however, had missed the lone weather break, and with the competitive fierceness of a player who didn't grab the brass ring, Marshall shunned Ed. (Marshall was killed in 1987 while making another solo attempt on Everest.)

Several weeks later in Beijing, Ed ran into Anderson. Ed talked of his coup, and Anderson immediately invited him to the Kangshung Face of Everest. A month later, Ed accepted.

* * *

Organizing for Everest was full-time work. Although the expedition hired an agent and secured corporate sponsorship, Sherpas, winches, and oxygen weren't part of the game plan. Anderson, Webster, Paul Teare (Canada), and Steve Venables (UK) would climb the steepest route on Everest by fair means or not at all.

"Four against the Kangshung?" Charles Houston said, "You're mad." John Roskelly told them the biggest avalanche he'd ever seen had come down the Kangshung Face. Even Reinhold Messner told them that he thought it was too dangerous.

Mimi Zieman, a medical student, came to basecamp as the team's doctor. Joe Blackburn, a disciple of Ansel Adams, was their photographer. Pasang Norbu, who accompanied Ed and Marshall in 1986 (and buried him in 1987), was the expedition's Sirdar and cook. Although Anderson was the titular leader, no decision was final until all agreed to it.

From the beginning, this expedition was different for Ed. Climbers and support crew treated one another with absolute respect; they became a family. Although all possessed the giant egos and toughness to confront this difficult route, they also solicited one another's feelings, performed impromptu skits, planned an eventual reunion, and celebrated Ed's birthday with peals of laughter (and a bottle of Scotch).

"Ed's a very caring person, despite his ego and aspirations," said Blackburn. "I sensed his humanity while he was photographing Tibetans, in his ability to make them open up." Teare, who had climbed only once in Eldorado with Ed six months before the expedition, became another fast friend. Although team members didn't meet Venables until Kathmandu, they welcomed him into their family like another son.

From advanced basecamp, while packing for the face, they watched a serac avalanche plummet a mile off the Lhotse Wall, within spitting distance of their climb. "Good," Venables said, "it didn't clobber our route." Then the work began. For the following month and a half, they avoided snowy weather and linked a passage protected from avalanches.

"Ed's technical expertise really pulled us through," Teare said. "He was adamant about the proper rigging of fixed ropes, which proved to be right on after we'd traveled up and down them a dozen times."

On one occasion, Venables took the sharp end of the rope up a rock headwall coveted by Ed, but typifying their smooth team relations, apologized for hogging the lead. Then came a gully exposed to serac fall. Describing "Big Al" in the *The American Alpine Journal,* Ed used a metaphor that only a physicist's son would craft: ". . . climbing up the side of a nuclear accelerator tube. The idea was to avoid being the smashed atom." Other cruxes came and went, and the leading was shared.

After resting for several days at basecamp, the team reascended to 23,000 feet, where they wrestled with a fifty-foot-wide crevasse. Now "inside Everest," Ed hammered in a piton and a huge ice chockstone exploded. He narrowly missed being crushed by falling ice. But with the overhanging crevasse wall now safe, he aided up. By the next day, they'd rigged a Tyrolean traverse across the crevasse, and the way was clear to the summit.

After another stormbound rest at basecamp, the four alternated trail breaking up to the South Col. At 23,500 feet, another serac vibrated, crashed loose, then roared by Ed like a delivery van. Panic stricken, he turned and yelled to his companions, "Why does this always happen to me?"

During a blustery bivouac on the South Col, Teare contracted high-altitude illness. Some awkward moments passed as the other three tried to decide who would accompany him down — until Teare crouched at Ed's tent. "I can get down on my own," Teare said. "Just make me proud. Okay? Get to the top!" He descended alone.

At 11 P.M. on May 11, 1988, the three started for the top, unroped and without packs. They separated and traveled alone. At dawn, Ed was captivated by a sunrise more serene than any he had ever photographed. After a quick internal debate about removing his mittens, he yanked them off. As soon as his hands, protected only by thin glove liners, touched the camera metal, his fingers burned with cold. Even after he put his camera away and mittens back on, he could not rewarm them.

Two hundred feet below the South Summit, Ed hallucinated about purple-robed monks pacing back and forth, chanting amongst a multitude of colorful prayer flags. Then he passed out. When he awoke, the monks were gone.

Venables continued his lone trail-breaking odyssey toward the Main Summit, while Ed realized that if he climbed any higher, he would never come down. He settled for a high point thirty feet below the South Summit, higher than all but one mountain on earth. That night, he and Anderson bivouacked in an abandoned tent at 27,500 feet, while Venables, in a superhuman effort, reached the top, then bivouacked in the open. When Venables returned the next morning, the other two were amazed that he was still alive. The threesome then descended to the South Col, where they spent their fourth debilitating night above 8,000 meters. In all of mountaineering history, relatively few teams have spent so many consecutive nights above 8,000 meters without oxygen and lived to tell the tale.

Then began the fight for their lives. Ed broke trail downhill in several feet of dangerous new snow. Anderson and Venables plummeted into out-of-control glissades and lost their ice axes; their rope had been left at the South Col. Finally, at dusk, they reached Camp II at 24,500 feet and fixed hot drinks.

The next morning was an agony of torpor in which no one could move. Ed took two hours to stuff his sleeping bag and thought of his mentor, Fritz Wiessner. "You've got to fight it," Wiessner once told Ed when describing his own battle on K2 in 1939, without oxygen. Then Ed thought of his present girlfriend, Randa Hessel, and how horrible it would be to end yet another relationship in death. "There's no way that I'm going to die on this climb," Ed thought. "I am going to keep going, no matter what."

He chided Venables, "You're not going to be famous unless we get down alive." They left at 3:45 P.M. Ed tripped, began sliding, and barely stopped himself from falling into a deep crevasse. And because progress was dubious with the impending night, they decided to return uphill to their open bivouac. The three climbers staggered back up the mountain like walking dead. Ed figured that they would die if they couldn't reach advanced base the next day.

At 10 A.M., Ed started breaking trail, again. Hours later, as darkness fell, Venables began rappelling and digging out the fixed ropes. For Ed, with frozen fingers and only one crampon, that night and its 2,000-foot descent seemed to last forever. By the time he'd finished rappelling a few hours before dawn, his frost-bite blisters were broken and shredded. Teare walked up and escorted him down the last bit of glacier. Once he reached advanced base, Zieman administered oxygen and bandaged his fingers.

All three climbers were frostbitten. But when Zieman took Ed's bandages off a few days later, she saw shriveled, charcoal-colored digits. Everyone tried to be encouraging, but in the tent that evening, Ed told Blackburn, "My whole life has been climbing, but now it's just a total wash." He fell into deeper and deeper despair.

When the group left basecamp, everyone signed the frontispiece of Ed's book, *The Mystery of Mallory and Irvine,* by Audrey Saukeld and Tom Hozel. Zieman wrote, "Keep warm and keep being warm." Pasang scrawled, "I am very happy this time." When Ed asked what Pasang meant, the Sherpa responded with a huge smile, "No one die this time."

* * *

Almost two years later, I stand in Ed's kitchen, while he makes us tuna sandwiches (refusing my help) by palming the halves together, then cutting awkwardly with a knife. Ed, who has spent the last twenty years of his life climbing, cracks a joke about how he can't pick his nose anymore.

In his bedroom there is a Picasso *(Starry Night),* and two Van Gogh prints are posted to the wall. The second edition of his guidebook, shaped into a six-by-five-foot foundation, supports his bed mattress. Behind the computer is a picture of a bandaged Ed with Messner in Lhasa. Messner had assured Ed that his frostbite was not as bad as it looked and that he would be able to continue climbing. At the same Lhasa hotel, Ed met Chris Bonington, sixteen years after his Boston lecture. Bonington concurred with Messner that Ed should take some time off and write a book.

So Ed has labored on his Everest book for two years. He has published accounts of the climb in four magazines. Shortly after his article appeared in *Sports Illustrated,* he got a fan letter from a California football coach who wanted Ed to come stay in the spare bedroom and eat barbecued steaks.

On Ed's shelves are more than a dozen Everest books, including Venables's recently published tome about the Kangshung Face.

On the cover page, the normally reticent Briton had written: "To Ed who made us all get down alive from the Neverest Buttress. Best wishes and good luck with the fingers."

A framed "Certificate of Achievement" holds an important position near his bed. At first, the typed print runs rampant with cliches: "In recognition of a job well done, Ed Webster is hereby awarded this certificate for outstanding perseverance, courage, and success on a new route up the world's highest mountain, without oxygen and overwhelmingly nasty odds — snow-mired yaks, chang-crazed porters . . ." But down in the margin, Anderson had penciled in: "I never thought a footstep or a friendship were more important — Thanks for both on Everest and after."

The phone rings — it's an Everest-bound climber, looking for oxygen masks. Then Norbu Tenzing, the son of Tenzing Norgay, calls and inquires about Ed's fingers. It seems that every direction Ed turns, Everest haunts him. He talks about the mountain in the manner that normal people talk about a job, a lover, or a son. Everest demands no less, particularly from one who has borne the mountain since boyhood. "It's taken so much of his life," Teare says, "he needs to move on." Although Ed wants to go back to Everest, he is not willing to risk his life again. Ed says:

> I've had some experience with people dying. I've seen what it was like for Fritz [Wiessner] to die, getting progressively weaker, having seizures and strokes until he was so infirm that he couldn't even recognize his own family members — I can imagine what that's like. But I don't want to die in the mountains. If you die in the mountains, you lose the game.

Although he has led some difficult climbs since he was injured, he is still wracked by health problems that he attributes to his time above 8,000 meters and seven surgeries worth of anesthesia. Nonetheless, Ed has learned how to be a survivor. He shows me a letter from his doctor in Boston to a doctor in Denver: "I am pleased that Mr. Webster is doing well and I am sorry that he has not given up the idea of serious mountain climbing."

But the doctor's diagnosis is off. "As soon as I start feeling better, my mind goes off on these tangents about the climbs I had planned before I had been hurt," Ed says. "I can gauge my health by how much dreaming I do about climbing." Furthermore, an indoor climbing wall that he built at the Westminster, Colorado, recreation center may well be his saving grace.

That evening, Ed goes to work there and I am amazed at his transformation. Climbers gather in small groups, until three score queue up at the thirty-foot-wide pink flagstone wall. They know all about Ed, while Ed knows many of their names. There are even grade-school children, trailing Ed like the Pied Piper. He checks their knots and shouts encouragement as they scamper up the wall.

Then we sit on the hardwood floor. The young girl notices Ed's fingernails are missing and his fingers are "weird," so she politely asks what's wrong. Without hesitation, he explains his Everest climb. The kids watch his fingers instead of his eyes while he talks. He mentions that he lost some toes, and when they demand further show-and-tell, he asks, "Should I put myself on display?" I shrug, and as he pulls off his sock, I look away. The girl says, "Yuck-o!" and then our laughter rights it all.

I have forgotten my rock shoes, but since our feet are identically sized, I wear his Sportivas. On the wall, I peel off at a crux move, and while Ed holds me, he points out the hold that I missed, belays me up, lowers me.

Then Ed climbs it. Every climber in the gymnasium watches — despite the fact that he created the wall and has memorized each rugosity. We all watch. When he tops out, one has the overwhelming urge to applaud.

Greg Child. *Photo by Mark Wilford*

The Natural

GREG CHILD

By Jonathan Waterman

[From CLIMBING, June 1993]

Watch the video of Greg Child atop K2 in 1990, and you'll notice that something is wrong. Everyone knows that high altitude puts you into a tongue-thickening, brain-stalling torpor. But the video shows Child leering at the camera, announcing the date, time, and his exact elevation — "eight thousand, six hundred and eleven meters" — so crisply that the viewer wonders if it was all a hoax, filmed at sea level. Never mind that he had waited a long twenty-five minutes in impending darkness and storm for the cameraman, Greg Mortimer. Never mind that a bivouac would have fashioned two more frozen lumps onto the summit topography.

Of course, K2 had been climbed before, by Americans, but not by Australians. Sydney-born Child calls himself "a resident alien." Whatever the case, between 1986 and 1990, out of eleven different attempts, no climber of any nationality had summited on K2.

With myriad 8,000-meter peaks ascended every year, it is difficult for even informed climbers to single out climbs of merit. Undoubtably, many would overlook that Child, Mortimer, Steve Swenson, and Phil Ersler set off in "sporting" style: sans Sherpas on a seldom-attempted, technical route, with an herbalist healer instead of a licensed physician tending to their frostbite, approaching on camel from the barrens of China.

To prepare, Child first attempted a wildly corniced ridge on the unclimbed Menglungtse in China. Then he spent a short two weeks at home in Seattle, a time that most climbers might dedicate to some legs-and-lungs training. Not Greg.

"I hate running," he says. "I'm not an aerobic athlete; a VO-2-max test would be depressing. Sometimes I ride my bike around Lake Washington, otherwise I go to the Vertical Club and throw weights around and pull my carcass up plastic."

Although Greg denies it, climbing stellar routes on K2, Gasherbrum IV, Shivling, and Nameless Tower — to name only a few — plainly reveals his genetic propensity for places high. Any climber who has hit the hypoxic wall between 20,000 and 26,000 feet knows how rare it is to be able to perform there, especially without an oxygen mask.

And while, as a freelance writer, Greg knows the slap of rejection slips, he has plenty of writing work. Like high-altitude climbing, writing apparently comes easy to Greg, and he seems to love it. Somehow he returns from high altitude with brain cells intact, and in "a day, maybe two" fires out such wry and candid prose as the K2 story he published in the February 1991 *Climbing*.

Despite Greg's present calm, his life has held tempestuous passages. Descending K2 nearly killed him; he experienced a stroke on a high peak and recovered only to watch his partner die; he survived two near-fatal falls from roadside crags; and his youth was a stormy ocean indeed.

Greg has a loyal mob of confederates ranging from sport climbers to alpinists to writers to armchair mountaineers. None of them take offense at his cutting wit, sprayed mercilessly upon both fools and friends. His routine jaunts to the Himalaya would imply that he is a bachelor, but he has been happily married for a dozen years to Salley Oberlin, who supports him and spends vacations cragging with him.

In this day of climbing specialists, Greg's breadth shines like Florence Joyner-Griffith's sweep of the 1988 Olympics. His vita speaks for itself: first ascents of Yosemite walls, new 5.13s in Washington, an unclimbed ice couloir in Canada, Himalayan peak climbs, and a portfolio of international pub crawls that most accomplished, assiduously trained rice-cake eaters could not follow.

Mark Wilford, a respected alpinist and boulderer, says: "Greg's one of the best all-around climbers. He can boulder hard, he can aid climb well, he can free climb, and he can move at 8,000 meters. And yeah," Wilford adds, "there's something about failure; he doesn't like a skeleton in his closet."

* * *

In the living room of Greg and Salley's Seattle house, an eclectic collection of Jane's Addiction, The Smiths, and Neil Young albums are balanced by Tchaikovsky, Strauss, and Beethoven. The only clues of an alpinist's presence are the chilly thermostat setting and, on top of the piano, a five-by-seven photo of Greg on top of K2, smiling about the incoming storm. Their second-story bedroom is as spare as his best prose; there are three potted plants, two novels on their bedtable, and, with the exception of a Calgary Climbers Festival poster, the white walls are bare.

The basement, however, is a climber's lair. It looks like an avalanche hit the Alpine Club library. Climbing books and magazines bury Greg's word processor, pictures of high spires and steep cracks deck the walls, and stacks of photocopies and files for his various writing projects clutter the floor. God help his tentmates.

It is no surprise when Greg, back upstairs, describes their decision to avoid the American Dream: glued to the television, raising babies, or frazzled by mortgage and bills. Thanks to Oberlin's business talents — her company, Online Press, produces computer software manuals — they own their house free and clear.

During dinner, Greg explains the importance of economic autonomy for Himalayan climbing. Such trips are expensive, but sometimes paying your own way is better than being beholden to a sponsor and feeling pressured to perform. As if to contradict himself, he also explains how important it is to honor your sponsors. His slightly graying, close-cropped black hair reveals a wrinkling brow above brown eyes; his stubby fingers clutch a glass of cabernet. The dinner conversation revolves more around climbers than climbing, and later, more around literature than climbing stories. He raves about reading *Granta*, England's cerebral literature journal.

Greg frequently defers to Salley, a striking, tall, blonde counterpart. She is articulate, soft-spoken, and confident. He listens to her with obvious respect.

In another conversation, Greg is asked about a rumor that circulated in 1988, saying that Salley wouldn't stand for his upcoming Makalu trip. He says, "Salley never told me no, only 'I wish you weren't going.'" Greg guards his relationship with Salley carefully. Nonetheless, his honest prose about the dangers of Himalayan climbing and about his friends dying over the years doesn't help his marriage. "You can't pretend that death doesn't happen," he says. "Salley's not deluded when I'm away."

"It affects your life because of the possibility of something bad happening," says Salley. "We both have our own lives. My business takes up a lot of my time. I also fill the void by spending a lot more time going out and being social when Greg is gone."

Greg says, "I know a lot of people whose marriages have fizzled out because of this lifestyle. But she is very accepting of it and understanding of what makes me tick."

Greg often talks about a friend who died by his side in the Himalaya. "People ask me about [Pete Thexton] at slideshows. I was uncomfortable talking about it for a long time — but now telling aspiring young climbers about it seems to give them important perspective."

In 1983, the Himalayan veterans Doug Scott, Don Whillans,

Al Rouse, Andy Parkin, Roger-Baxter Jones, Jean Afanassieff, and Steve Sustad trekked into the remote Baltoro Glacier in Pakistan to attempt two 8,000-meter peaks. Greg Child and Dr. Pete Thexton, both veterans of 6,000-meter Indian peaks, blithely tagged along.

"Typically," says Greg, "Doug got together some of the best climbers in Britain and threw in a few neophytes." Thexton and Child had to perform. "There was this hierarchy, climbers ascending through the ranks." And where were they going? Greg spits out rancorously about his friends' eventual fates, "Nowhere!"

The team first attempted smaller peaks in order to acclimatize for their primary objectives, Broad Peak and K2. Scott, Child, and Thexton made the first ascent of the 18,724-foot Lobsang Spire, thanks to Greg's drill and skyhook techniques up the blank 100-foot-summit spire. While astride the final knife-edge, a lammergeier flew by, then a kestrel. As Scott rappelled off, Child told Thexton an old legend about a third bird being the precursor to misfortune. Pete laughed and started down, but Child said nothing when a crow rose on an updraft.

Climbing Lobsang started an ideal friendship. Thexton's wry British humor and Child's lighthearted acumen made them inseparable cutups. They spoke of climbing together in Yosemite and the Alps, while Child dreamed of K2 — *if* Broad Peak worked.

"A great warmth radiated from Pete onto me," Greg wrote in his book *Thin Air*. "His small kindnesses and carefully chosen words told me that I was at last breaking through [his] carefully guarded barrier."

A week after reaching their basecamp below K2, the team split into pairs to climb Broad Peak. On their third day of plodding up the mountain's snowslopes, Thexton and Child moved for the summit with pounding headaches. Just below 8,000 meters, Thexton ebulliently pointed out an unclimbed ridge on Gasherbrum IV. Child supposed it to be their future together.

Hours later, on the false summit, the oxygen deficit caused Child to suffer a stroke, paralyzing his right side. He convinced

Thexton to descend. Child passed out briefly, then threw up. Thexton helped him down. Thexton, a physician, understood high-altitude sickness, and for the moment, their safety seemed assured. As Child recovered, Thexton suddenly started having trouble breathing and his lips turned blue — symptoms of pulmonary edema. The wind howled, the sky darkened, and as Thexton weakened he fell repeatedly. Child began dragging then lowering Thexton, who then went blind with cerebral edema. Child pleaded, "Don't lose it now, brother. Please." They reached help and their friend Whillans at the 24,500-foot-high camp after a twenty-two-hour day.

Child collapsed, dreaming of pastoral places. At dawn, Thexton awoke and asked Whillans for water but as the cup was pressed to his lips, he passed away. Child tried to force life back into Thexton's body, giving his own breath to gurgling lungs, rhythmically pounding his palms against the still chest, but as Greg wrote, "he would have none of it."

A Swiss team radioed the news down the mountain, and Scott told Thexton's waiting girlfriend, Beth Acres. Child staggered down utterly wrecked. At the bottom, Rouse helped him into camp. Baxter-Jones held Child tightly. "I was shell shocked," says Greg. "It was really, really upsetting. When you die it negates the whole game. You haven't just fucked yourself, you've hurt lots of other people — that's when it becomes irresponsible and tragic."

Pete Thexton's death changed everything. It forced Child to be "analytical about risk taking;" this would save his own life at least once. As Greg says, "He taught me a lot by dying."

"He had a special relationship with Pete," says Salley. "He really loved him. Every once in a while something will come up — we'll be talking about pulmonary edema, or hear about someone dying — and you can see that love for Pete cross his face."

At first, the bitter turn of events made Child promise never to return to the Himalaya. He even came close to quitting climbing. "Broad Peak was a total botch-up — too high, too fast. I learned all the things that could go wrong without being killed myself."

GREG CHILD

More of Greg's companions from Broad Peak (and other Himalayan trips) — Roger Baxter-Jones, Alan Rouse, Georges Bettemborg, Geoff Radford — would die in the mountains. Don Whillans also died but at home in his sleep, of a heart attack.

Greg now says that it happened a long time ago and the hardest parts are gone. He appears less at peace when asked about the death of his father, with whom he had been seeking a reconciliation. Looking down at the floor, Greg says there was "unfinished business" when his father died.

* * *

Greg was "whelped" (as he is fond of saying) in a rough section of Sydney called Brighton-Le-Sands, mockingly named after a French riveria by Australia's first white settlers — British convicts — who landed in 1788. They shortly abandoned the arid shore.

Two centuries after the penal colony, the residential beachfront slum invites comparison to south-central Los Angeles. Several of Greg's peers died from heroin overdoses; the survivors who didn't wreck their lives had factory jobs to look forward to. For Greg, the ticket out was climbing.

But the teenaged Greg's first foray into hazardous diversions was the collection and study of Australian snakes — often venomous. One day, while he was testing his reflexes with a lethal tiger snake (much more venomous than a rattlesnake), it latched onto his index finger, although one fang only glanced off the nail. Greg flung the snake off and tried to suck out the venom, then began retching. Riding home on his bicycle, he passed out. As he came to, being carried past his distressed mother, he tried to hide his reptilian hobby by saying, "Must've been that cheese and gherkin sandwich you made me for lunch, Mum." But his terrified young pals ratted on him. Listening to his parents scream at each other about their wayward child, Greg, vomiting blood, kept his head in a bucket and concluded that catching snakes had lost its glamor.

269

When Greg was sixteen, his essay writing won a high school award, but he never bothered picking it up. His real interest lay in the Blue Mountains, which he substituted for home, at least on weekends. One day in 1973, Chris Piesker joined Greg at a belay tree, 100 feet off the deck. When Greg reached out to grab a stopper from his partner's harness, an anchor failed.

Flying through the air, "I couldn't get a fix on things," he wrote in Canada's *Alpinism*. "My vision was blurred. Air was rushing past me." Child augured into the ground, shattering his ankle and breaking his shoulder, nose, and ribs. He also sustained numerous lacerations and bruises, a concussion and internal bleeding. He took solace in a nearby black snake, shedding its skin. Greg wrote, "Watching the snake emerge, renewed and glossy, had a vital opiate effect on me." Chris rappelled off the lone stopper.

After being screwed together with enough metal to "set off the airport metal detector," he suffered an unhappy year at home. He fought constantly with his father, but weekend climbing made life bearable. "Then I'd go back to school and uniforms and rules. And *Dad*," says Greg. "I hated it." The moment he graduated from high school, he enrolled in "the University" of Arapiles — the preeminent Australian crag. He would spend the next two decades climbing.

Like the rest of his young peers, he lived on the dole. In 1975, Kim Carrigan, Mike Law, and Greg began pushing the free-climbing standards, "touching 5.12 without knowing what we were doing." When the American "Hot" Henry Barber, who had climbed hard routes all over the world, visited Australia, it changed Greg's life. Climbers, he learned, must travel.

Greg moved to Yosemite Valley. "Climbers had a different attitude then," he says in Americanized Aussie. "It was a *mahk* of your climbing ability to see if you could get really *hamm-ahhed* at night and still climb *hahd* the next day." Then Henry introduced him to Salley Oberlin — who created computer software books but lived for climbing — in the Mountain Room Bar.

"I thought he was shy," says Salley, "but really kind. He also listened when his friends talked to him, and he cared about their feelings. But he had another side too, a fun-loving, carefree side, and I needed that in my life."

Greg alternated living with Salley in Berkeley and in the shadow of huge granite walls. On El Capitan, he made the first ascent of Aurora (VI 5.10 A5), renowned for thin-seam copperheading and hook moves up friable flakes. He also made the second ascent of Iron Hawk (VI 5.10 A4) and the Pacific Ocean Wall (VI 5.9 A4).

Zenith (VI 5.10 A5), Magic Mushroom (VI 5.10 A4), Mescalito (VI 5.9 A4), and an early free ascent of the West Face (VI 5.11b) of El Capitan followed. His story about these test pieces, "Coast to Coast on The Granite Slasher," mentioned no ratings, and the narrative is more philosophy than deed. "Slasher," Greg's first published piece, was reprinted as the lead article in the anthology *Mirrors In The Cliffs*.

Greg composed "Slasher" in Salley's apartment, where he discovered a typewriter. In hunt-and-peck style, he hammered out the story and mailed his "worthless ravings" off. He was too embarrassed to show the story to Salley, but she found a hidden copy.

"When he talked with his [then] strong Australian accent," says Salley, "I could only understand three-quarters of what he said. But when I read ["Slasher"] and saw his talent to communicate, I was moved."

To read Greg's prose, more than anything else, is to understand this climber-anarchist's philosophy. "Never trust the written word," Slasher begins. "At best it's a second-rate account of reality. How can you duplicate the enormity of the moment?" Greg had no idea he would become a writer, so for this story at least, he elevated climbing into a singular art form.

He wrote about the Pacific Ocean Wall: "We were modern Michelangelos working gently and carefully, each placement a crucial work of art, copper and chromolly on granite." "I felt so frail and dependent on technology, helpless without it yet at the same time suspicious of its hold over us."

He wrote about Magic Mushroom as a celebration of spring. Climbing passages are sparse, and he recounts instead tales of hummingbirds fluttering at belays, ice melting and falling from the rim like diving birds, and a frog nestled in an angle pin. On another day or another climb, he upholds naturalist traditions, whether observing and commenting upon snakes, eagles, or the minutia of life that many climbers overlook.

"He's really opened my eyes to snakes and lizards," says Salley. "He finds spiders in the house and makes them into pets or puts them into jars. He demands that these little creatures not get stepped on, or that they get escorted outside."

In 1980, Greg and Salley got married. The next year, Doug Scott invited Child, then a total novice to alpine climbing, to attempt the unclimbed East Pillar of Shivling (21,467 feet) in India, with the Frenchman Georges Bettemborg and the Australian Rick White. Reaching this pillar in the Garwhal Himalaya and climbing it took many days longer than they planned.

"I was pushed out of everything familiar into a sink-or-swim situation," Child says. He and White burned down a large part of their tent when their stove exploded two days up the route, and they ran out of food. And after the hard-won summit, just as Scott told Bettemborg what a good effort the pair had put in for their first Himalayan climb — White tripped. Scott and Bettemborg watched the roped-together novices cartwheel 700 feet down the West Face.

They were miraculously unhurt. As Scott and Bettemborg caught up, breathless, White quipped, "Looks like we found the fast way down."

After surviving this fall, Child somehow figured dying in the mountains wasn't going to happen to him. And he became enamored of his cavalier, veteran partners — "idealistic and nihilistic all at once." But Broad Peak changed all that.

In 1984, still haunted by the Himalaya, Child tried to climb

Fitzroy in Patagonia. It is a place, he wrote, "that eats men for-ever." All the while he dreamed of "friendly El Cap." In Peru with Steve Swenson, he flashed up Huascarán's West Rib in three days round-trip from Huarez (most climbers take a week). In Canada with Doug Scott, he climbed a virgin 5,000-foot ice face on Mount Colonel Foster.

In 1985, he made the first ascent of El Capitan's Lost In America (VI 5.10 A5) with Randy Leavitt. Clearly, he still knew how to go for it, but his life seemed empty without big mountains. So that year, Scott lured Greg back to the Himalaya; dysentery, however, knocked out their Rakaposhi and Nanga Parbat plans.

When Greg returned from Pakistan, he wrote "The Trouble With Hunza" in a gritty, stream-of-consciousness, self-effacing style, rather than as a we-came, we-saw, we-conquered climbing piece. He became captivated by the "cloying heat," the smells of fish and dead cows and open sewers, the "Heironymous Bosch-scape of belching chimneys and coke ovens." A Pakistani cook, Rasool, became one of his best friends.

Pakistan had become his second home, and he dove into planning for the next year's expedition to Gasherbrum IV's unclimbed Northwest Ridge. "G4" had first been climbed in 1958 by the accomplished Italians Carlo Mauri and Walter Bon-nati. Since then, despite eight more attempts, no other climber had reached the 26,000-foot summit. To Greg, the mountain was a prime objective because of its bladelike symmetry and its high-altitude technicality. And knowing that G4 was 75 meters shy of being a coveted 8,000-meter peak made it all the more appealing. For Greg it was a statement: a peak smaller but more elegant and challenging than its big neighbors.

One more incentive electrified Greg's mission. G4's North-west Ridge was the line he and Thexton had discussed climbing some day during their last day together on Broad Peak. In *Thin Air*, Greg titled the Gasherbrum chapter "Unfinished Business."

In 1986, seven teammates, nursing a paltry budget, jostled up into the Karakorum with hundreds of other climbers. That summer would go down in history as the most wind-blasted, snow-laden, and subzero season ever experienced by Himalayan climbers. On K2 alone, thirteen climbers would die.

Continuing storms, deep snowfall, and difficult climbing slowed Child's team, and it took nearly two months of work to get in position for the summit. Eventually, Child, Tim McCartney-Snape, and Tom Hargis bivouacked without sleeping bags just below the summit in a scratched-out snowhole. Child watched Broad Peak framed in the entrance and thought of Thexton. He shivered violently. McCartney-Snape sang boisterously, while Hargis spit and coughed all night, eventually cracking his ribs. At first light they emerged edemic and weary.

After several hours and a tricky, verglassed traverse, they reached the summit and clasped hands. Reversing the summit ridge, McCartney-Snape followed Child, who had thrust an axe tip into thin ice behind his boot. While Hargis soloed on ahead, McCartney-Snape started prying a piton from a crack with his axe. Suddenly, McCartney-Snape cartwheeled backward while Child braced himself and awaited a "grand tour of the West Face."

Miraculously, the rope snagged over a small rock horn. That and his minimal belay allowed Child to hold the fall. McCartney-Snape emerged from below five minutes later, thumped Greg's shoulder, and thanked him for his life. With their throats parched from thirst and their minds filled with hallucination, the trio slid down over steep marble and limestone, fell asleep on ledges, and ducked the clatter of rockfall until they were safely back in base-camp.

Most of the team hustled home. As the death toll continued on nearby K2, Child, Hargis, and Randy Leavitt moved over to Nameless Tower. After already suffering for so long at high altitude, it was almost inconceivable to confront an unclimbed high-altitude wall. Although Child felt the lure of ambition, he was also accommodating Leavitt, who had been thwarted on G4. Child's expedition partners are clearly the most important people in his life — aside from his wife. Whenever he talks about his climbs, he talks first and foremost about his partners.

"The mountain is nothing without people on it," says Greg with typical understatement. "Often you part expeditions exasperated, but a year or two later, you go back with the same partners knowing there's potential in this human relationship."

On Nameless Tower, they managed to climb ten out of what would have been thirty pitches up the Northeast Face. But the desperate work of hauling, Child's malnourished body and bleeding gums, falling ice, and their fatigued inability to simply climb out of sleep each morning finally convinced them to retreat. Nameless Tower would rest in Child's subconscious as an evasive granite chimera, and despite the glory of G4 (and later K2), returning to this particular crag would become a fixture in Greg Child's climbing for years to come.

* * *

In the mid-1980s, Greg turned his back on difficult aid climbing and, in between trips to the high mountains, returned to his 1970s Arapiles roots: hard free climbing. On the eve of his thirty-fifth birthday in 1992, he climbed Churning in the Wake, a 5.13 at Smith Rock. "The kids below were all amazed that an aging fossil like me could still climb," he says.

"Living in the mountains part of the year and rock climbing the rest of the year is a trying adaptation," Greg says as another understated reaction to a difficult transition. "Friends are always amazed to see me inhaling beer and pasta and cheese to get strong for the Himalaya, and then they see me later at the crags eating rice and seaweed."

Greg showed similar versatility in his writing by publishing several pieces of fiction — a difficult and elusive medium. His first tales, "No Gentlemen In the Himalaya" and "Credibility Gap," explored religion and relationships in Pakistan and Alaska. He also worked and reworked his *Thin Air* manuscript, detailing his experiences with climbing deaths and Third World culture.

After an unsuccessful K2 trip, Greg wrote one more short story, "In Another Tongue," a spare piece about two Balti porters beneath K2. Unlike most western climbers, Greg had formed close personal relationships with Pakistanis. He showed an ear for realistic dialogue and unpretentious narrative:

> "If they do not become rich by climbing K2," the Balti boy asks his uncle, "and they are not already rich when they come here, why do they do it?"
>
> "They answer that question in many ways," the uncle replies. "But I'll tell you that the truth is one of three things: either they are liars and all of them are rich, or they tell the truth and all of them are mad, or they have good hearts and are hunters."

In the final pages of *Thin Air*, Greg wrote, "My mental effort to give an element of order to this circle of life, death and mountains, came to nothing." Yet the observations about cultural perceptions of wealth, religion, and mortality ring so powerfully in "In Another Tongue" that the reader feels Child *did* find order within the circle. After the K2 tragedy of 1986, he was trying to salve the climbing community's sense of loss by showing the austere Balti outlook on mountain climbing. With forty-two concise paragraphs, he transcended climbing fiction and created a durable work of literature.

In 1987, Greg won the American Alpine Club Literary Award. A year later, *Thin Air: Encounters in the Himalaya* was released by a British publisher, Patrick Stephens. Allen Steck reviewed it in the 1989 issue of *The American Alpine Journal*: "Humor, irony, pathos, and, of course the beauty of the Baltoro landscape, all find their way into the narrative." Unfortunately, the scantily marketed book (reprinted in the United States by Gibbs Smith in 1990) sold only a few thousand copies.

Greg drew his own conclusions. "Mediocrity rules in every aspect of our lives," he says. "If someone who doesn't climb writes a climbing book, that book will sell well, but if a climber writes a heartfelt and honest account about climbing, the book might as well be thrown into a dust bin."

In his work for climbing magazines, Greg felt that he was writing more to promote the ethos of climbing literature than he was for money. Nonetheless, his talent landed him contracts to write an *Encyclopedia of Climbing* for Facts on File Inc, a collection of reprinted and several newly written mountaineering stories entitled *Mixed Emotions* for The Mountaineers Books, and in the summer of 1993, Laurel Books Expedition Series will reprint and mass market *Thin Air* in shopping malls and chain bookstores. He also has assignments for publications ranging from *Outside* to *Australian Geographic* to *Backpacker*. These jobs would represent a lot of work to most writers, but Child is nonchalant.

Getting up Nameless Tower was one more similar piece of unfinished business for Child. When attempting this climb in 1989, he and Mark Wilford were trapped for seven days in their portaledge. Child nearly succumbed to hypothermia, Wilford came unclipped from his rappel device and saved himself from a 2,000-foot plunge by catching the rappel rope, and their portaledge collapsed twice before they got inside laughing with adrenaline. Child's judgment about retreating immediately, instead of waiting another day as Wilford preferred, saved their lives. Undoubtably, Thexton really had influenced Child to be more analytical about risk taking. Child and Wilford were so weak they barely rappelled to the bottom.

Wilford has happily soloed desperates such as the north faces of Alberta and the Eiger, yet he relishes his partnership with Child. "You would think that someone who'd done as many good routes as him would be a hard guy," Wilford says, "but he's not. He's really sensitive. . . . [But] he can be blunt if someone isn't doing their share on a climb."

The spire began to obsess Greg. He figured that Nameless Tower would leave him alone only when he reached the summit. Even his success on K2 in 1990 was only a temporary reprieve. For two years he released himself from expeditions by lecturing around the world; the fees made his writing income seem trivial. But Nameless Tower followed him everywhere.

Greg often told his audiences that neither Everest nor K2 are the ultimate climbs, and that the future of climbing is on peaks people haven't heard of, such as Nameless Tower. "I'm just astounded by the dominancy of Everest in America; Europeans are much more sophisticated. And Australians tend to be interested in whatever you do."

In Australia, Child and Mortimer were given the coveted Explorer Award by the Australian Geographic Society. His mother, uncle, and brother sat in the front row of that particular lecture; 500 others sat transfixed in the audience. Afterward, his mother confronted him. "K2," she said, "that must be enough, right?" Greg just smiled.

"This year [1991] was the first he didn't go to the Himalaya," Salley said, "and there's been a lot less stress."

So her husband substituted international lecturing boondoggles for far flung-climbing expeditions. During one evening's bus ride after a lecture in Italy, Child dumped Chianti on his nearest drunken companions. When the Austrian alpinist Kurt Diemberger joked that "Greg should write his next book, *Thick* Air," about the weekend's debauchery, Child shouted, "No, Kurt, I'll call it Thin *Hair*." The balding Diemberger smiled gamely.

At various speaking events, amid the press of sport coats and ties, Child habitually dresses in a black leather jacket. Nonetheless, with his round, wire-rimmed glasses perched on his precisely carved face, as he articulates some broad-minded concept from the latest *Granta*, he could just as easily pass as a university academic.

While his behavior portends youthfulness, lines are beginning to etch his face. He is courting his thirty-sixth birthday.

* * *

In July 1992, he and Wilford and Rob Slater started up an unclimbed line on the South Face of Nameless Tower. In the middle of the climb, Slater decided to quit alpine climbing. (With characteristic loyalty, Greg refuses to divulge any less-than-flattering details about any of his partners.) Slater went home; Wilford and Child kept climbing.

After three weeks of effort, they began jumaring their frozen ropes before dawn on August 23. Child could almost taste the summit. When a refrigerator-size boulder came booming down the wall beside them, Child thought, "Good lord, here's another reason why we're not going to climb Nameless Tower." Every two or three seconds, rubble roared out from the hollow created by the boulder. Finally, 100 feet away, on a route option they had considered, a 600-foot slab of granite broke loose and thundered into space. "It's been there for millions of years," Greg says, "and it waits to fall not only the day we go for the top, but the hour that we get above it. Talk about luck."

To many climbers, reaching the summit after so long would have at least equalled completion. But Child has little to say about the summit or finishing the climb; if anything, he acts curiously diminished by their accomplishment. Perhaps because he and Wilford had originally tried to do the route alpine style, they considered the later siege ascent a consolation prize. He is more interested in describing the near miss of the rockfall, or how desperately cold the gearless bivouac below the summit was.

Once they reached the bottom, cleaning the fixed ropes took another day. Then Child, Wilford, and a group of friends contributed enough money so that the pregnant wife of Rasool — their Sirdar and Child's friend from many trips to Pakistan — could afford prenatal care at a hospital. During the grinding trek and bus journey homeward, the proverbial worm of success turned within Greg. Once back with Salley in Seattle, he began to wonder why. Seven years and thousands of dollars for what? More gray hairs? Another gripping story?

He is haunted by the anticlimax. Moreover, if climbing Nameless Tower formerly defined Greg, he has now plumbed some undefined, obsessional part of his personality that he is ready to discard.

Sitting in his basement office, with sheafs of paper and random files from his *Encyclopedia*-in-progress surrounding him like the cataclysm on the Tower, Greg wrestles with the burden of inglorious completion. "Succeeding isn't the main part," he says. Although it is antithetical for Child to pen any abstractions, during an interview he allows that "Somewhere between the bottom of the climb and the summit is the answer to the mystery of why we climb." More typically, in his K2 story he had written: "Maybe Himalayan climbing is just a bad habit, like smoking, of which one says with cavalier abandon, 'must give this up some day, before it kills me.'"

Mark Wilford. *Photo by Greg Child*

The Wilford Case

MARK WILFORD

By John Sherman

[From CLIMBING, October 1991]

A friend of Mark Wilford once remarked, "If God exists, then He must spend a disproportionately large amount of time on The Wilford Case." Indeed, Wilford's record of bold ascents and life-threatening near-misses is equaled by few. Ken Duncan, a hotshot 1970s Colorado climber, compares him to one of America's great all-rounders, who died young while climbing. Duncan calls Wilford "another Tobin Sorenson, but with better luck so far."

Consider the record: surviving four rollovers (Wilford is quick to note that he was driving in only three of these). Or pulling the car-door-size flake off the Salvation Roof in Eldorado and, in the subsequent fall, ripping out all of his gear except for a single one-quarter-inch bolt hanging halfway out of its hole in the roof.

Then there's the first time he tried a winter solo of the 1,500-foot East Face of Longs Peak — the time a whiteout moved in and Wilford started down, faster than planned. Wilford had slipped placing an anchor and had been pulled backward by his heavy pack. He couldn't grasp the rappel lines. His only hope was the tiny overhand knots he'd tied in the ends of his eight- and nine-millimeter raplines. Given the force his fall would put on these knots, the small diameter of his ropes, and the large gaps in his carabiner brake system, it seemed a futile safety measure; when he hit the end of his ropes the knots would cinch into knuckle-size balls and squirt through his brakes. There would be a slight jerk on his harness, then a 200-foot freefall to the deck.

As fate would have it, this wasn't Wilford's day to die. An instant before the knots reached his brake system, a piton dangling from his rack got sucked into his brake biners. The pin filled enough of the gap to stop the knots from squeezing through. Wilford rode out the rope stretch and ended suspended in the middle of the blank granite face. Two A3 anchors later, he was on the ground.

In a climbing world increasingly obsessed with big numbers and risk-free ascents, Wilford stands apart as a climber whose motivation is derived from the sense of adventure, the thrill of danger, and the satisfaction of pushing one's limits. Wilford is best known for his alpine achievements, in particular the first American solo of the North Face of the Eiger; however, to call Wilford just an alpinist would be akin to calling Bo Jackson just a football player. Randy Joseph, a Colorado climbing guide and frequent partner of Wilford since high school, puts it this way: "It doesn't really matter what Mark's climbing on, boulders, rock, ice, or mixed ground, he's state of the art."

Wilford is modest about his achievements. Talk to his friends and partners and you're sure to hear many Wilford stories he wouldn't have told himself. When pressed for the details surrounding these tales, Wilford recounts the facts in a straightforward and simple manner. Annoyed by braggarts, Wilford prefers understatement to exaggeration.

In climbing, he is outspoken about his traditionalist beliefs. He's determined to protect certain crags for traditionalist climbing and has backed up his words with a bolt-hungry crowbar. He believes that the means are just as important as the end; hence, he declines to master the common practice of hangdogging. "I consider it cheating," he says flatly. Some people view traditional climbers as "conservative," but nobody who has met Wilford would give him that tag. His wildness, on and off the rock, is the stuff of legends.

* * *

Wilford grew up in Fort Collins, Colorado. His engineer father located the family at a safe distance from his workplace — the nuclear weapons plant at Rocky Flats. Mark's first snow climb was at age eleven, his first foray onto rock at thirteen. People who met Wilford later, in his twenties, are astonished to learn that he had been a clean-living kid ("pure as the driven snow," declared one early partner). As a teen, Wilford's penchant for risk earned him the nickname "the Wacko Kid," bestowed by his fellow Horsetooth Hardcores, a group of local boulderers bonded by a ritual January 23 plunge through a hole cut in the ice of Horsetooth Reservoir.

During high school, he often bouldered with Hardcore and Front Range bouldering legend Steve Mammen. Not satisfied with Horsetooth's treacherous landings, Wilford and Mammen discovered a way to add extra fear to each spring day's session. They called it ice walking. The goal was simple. Walk across the ice to the opposite bank of the reservoir, half a mile away.

At first it was easy. There were few cracks in the ice and the surface felt solid. As spring wore on, the ice thinned. Soon the surface was laced with cracks; the chunks of ice were held together like a jigsaw puzzle. With each step, the surface would flex and creak. Should a section come loose, it would be curtains. When it finally became a matter of leaping from floe to floe, and when to get to solid ice the pair broke through on their first three steps from the shore, Wilford and Mammen mutually decided to call it quits. In retrospect, Mammen calls it "the most dangerous thing I've ever done."

In the fall of 1977, Wilford enrolled at the University of Colorado in Boulder. College did nothing to quiet Wilford down. To the contrary, it introduced him to the joys of partying. One night about 11 P.M., Wilford returned to his dorm room from partying downstairs and started packing his climbing gear. It was winter (Wilford's week-old beer chunks were still frozen to the windowsill), and Wilford was inspired to climb the First Flatiron. It would have to be solo, because his intended partner, Blake, bailed out. Blake declined Wilford's offer to join the ascent when he learned that Wilford didn't want to climb it the next day, but rather that night. His aggressive driving having resulted in the suspension of his license some time before, Wilford was forced to hike to the First Flatiron from the dorm.

The extended approach warmed Wilford up. At the base, he stripped off his warmer layers of clothing and stuffed them in his pack. He tied the pack to one end of a haul line, clipped the other end of the line to his harness, then started up the snow-plastered slabs. Climbing in the dark, without a headlamp, he worked his way up until the haul line came taut. He stopped to haul his pack, which became stuck partway up. Unable to free the pack, Wilford cast the haul line off and continued up, convinced that the exertion of climbing would make his spare clothes unnecessary.

Things went well for several pitches until Wilford found himself atop a four-by-eighteen-inch flake, unable to crack the moves above and too gripped to reverse the moves below. It was 1 A.M. and the winter sun would be a long time in rising. Unanchored, he stood atop the flake all night long, fighting off sleep and hypothermia. Morning dawned, but the light gave no clues about how to free climb off the flake. In desperation, Wilford cut off the shoulder sling of his alpine hammer by hammering the webbing against the rock. He then removed his belt, made of one-inch webbing, and tied it to the shoulder sling. Looping these over his bivy flake, he then had just enough webbing to allow himself to tension traverse over to a nearby crack and escape from the face. He was late to class that day.

Engineering studies were eating into Wilford's climbing time. A decision had to be made. Would it be a life of button-down geek shirts, Pencil-Pals, and calculator holsters? No. Wilford opted for a career as a full-time climber. For the next decade he would work as little as possible, and only to support his habit.

For starters, he dropped out halfway through his second semester and went to Yosemite, where he traded Valley honemaster Jim Bridwell "something illicit" for a pair of wall boots. He then started up the Salathé Wall with Colorado's Charlie Fowler. Conditions were abominable, but while other parties bailed, Wilford and Fowler persevered. By the time they reached the top, Wilford looked like a tertiary syphilitic — his leg was bruised and swollen from a wrecking ball swing into Hollow Flake, his hands were twice their normal size and were oozing pus from numerous infections, the constant soakings in frigid meltwater cascades had whitened, wrinkled, and softened his skin to a pasty mush reminiscent of cauliflower gone bad, and to top it all off, he was enveloped in a rash of itching, weeping blisters courtesy of the poison oak bushes on Mammoth Terraces. Things could have been worse, though — he could have been in midterms.

Wilford seems not to *want* to climb, but to *need* to climb. He devours rock in huge quantities and is particularly drawn to the extra challenge of first ascents. One project was to free the Diagonal Direct on the Lower East Face of Longs Peak, a grade V. When Wilford was in high school, he and Ken Duncan had done its first winter ascent. Now out of college, but still in his late teens, Wilford teamed up with Pat Adams. The crux pitch is a dicey proposition — 5.11 tips jams and thin face moves protected by a nickel-thick stopper backed up by poor gear below. Wilford delicately worked through the crux and seemed to have the first free ascent in the bag, when a hummock of grass he was grasping tore out of the crack. Wilford went whistling off, stripping the puny #2 stopper from the crack. The next nut pulled. At the belay, Adams watched Wilford whip by. After Wilford had gone fifty feet, the rope pulled taut around Adam's waist, jerking him upward against the anchor nuts. They pulled. A few seconds later, both climbers came to a swinging stop, dangling on opposite ends of the rope and suspended by a single nut thinner than a pack of matches. After reestablishing the anchor, Wilford went up again and passed the crux but was forced to climb back down when his haul line became stuck. The pair retreated.

Experiences like the one Wilford had on the Diagonal Direct gave him the confidence to push himself farther in the realm of high-stakes, high-difficulty climbing. He would, in fact, attack risky climbs throughout his career, not just for a limited period.

One of Wilford's most fearsome creations was Spinal Tap, a first free ascent he bagged in 1986. The route lies alongside the Big Thompson River in Colorado's Front Range on a granite crag of indistinct character save for one perfectly cleaved face that is eighty feet tall and twenty-five feet wide. From the opposite bank of the river, the face appears as flawless as a sheet of plate glass. Only with binoculars can a hairline seam be seen slicing up the center of the nearly vertical face. Apart from a couple of tiny notches in the seam, there appears to be nothing to hold onto besides a thin coating of lichen. When Wilford first tried leading it free, there was a bolt left from the first aid ascent. Aghast at Wilford's audaciousness in trying to free their route, the first ascent party tried to scare Wilford off by chopping their own bolt.

To Wilford, the loss of the only good piece of protection on the pitch only upped the stakes and therefore the rewards of success. Now Wilford's best piece was a .5 Lowe Tricam that he filed down to .3 size to fit a horizontal slot fifteen feet below the crux. Above the modified Tricam, the protection consisted of exclusively #1 and #2 RPs and Crack-N-Ups, all equipped with Yates Screamer fall-arresting devices.

After dicing past the microscopic B1+ crux edging section, Wilford was without footholds. He tossed one dyno, then a second, his feet paddling against the burnished wall. One more lunge and he'd gain the key horizontal groove marking the end of the crux section. He missed. All the stitches on the first Screamer tore apart, as did the cable on the RP to which it was attached. The next piece was plucked from the crack. After falling thirty feet, the third Screamer blew apart, stitch by stitch, slowing Wilford down until, with only a few stitches left, he came to a stop dangling from a Crack-N-Up.

It took Wilford five attempts spread over two years to finally succeed on this test piece. Graded 5.13 — R or X — Spinal Tap has yet to see a second lead. Steve Mammen, who seconded the first ascents of both Spinal Tap and Colorado's most famous mind-control challenge, Perilous Journey, says, "If someone pointed a gun at my head and said, 'you have a choice, I'm going to shoot you; you can climb Spinal Tap, or you can climb Perilous Journey, what's your choice?' I would take Perilous Journey by far."

Wilford has based his 5.13 rating of Spinal Tap on the amount of effort it required, both physical and mental, to lead from the ground up. He feels that the Yosemite Decimal System (YDS) "has been bastardized" because "you can't equate traditional climbing and Eurostyle climbing." Wilford has proposed that Eurostyle ascents be given European (French) grades, and that traditional ascents be given YDS grades.

Asked why he sticks to traditional climbing even though it lacks the glitter and glory of sport climbing, Mark says, "I haven't compromised my style to be competitive." Several years ago he was tempted, when every climber and his grandmother were out cranking 5.13 — everyone except him. His self-confidence sagged but returned in even larger measure when he realized that it was just numbers increasing, not standards. Sure, people were ticking bigger numbers than he, but in what style? When it came to an accurate measure of a climber's ability — on-sight ascents — most of the overnight sensations he met had nothing on him.

Wilford believes that the dividends gained from traditional ascents are worth the extra effort. He credits traditional climbing with teaching him self-preservation, respect for the rock, and the value of trying hard and not giving up. He says:

Traditional climbing doesn't hold you back. It actually
makes you a better climber because instead of hanging
on bolts you've got to learn how to downclimb to a rest,
and how to rest. You have to be more of an on-sight
climber — you're not going to have so many opportunities at a crux section.

The ability to downclimb, a skill Wilford feels is being lost, is
essential in high bouldering, mountaineering, soloing, and necky
leads.

"Climbing has given me the best times of my life," says Mark.
"I owe the sport something." He intends to repay the debt by pre-
serving certain areas for the evolution of traditional climbing. In
the past, he has spoken out in anger over the bashing of traditional ethics. One published letter to the editor, prompted by the
demise of traditional ethics in Eldorado Canyon, was signed Mark
"The Chisel" Wilford. This was back in the days when climbers
used chisels to chop bolts, not holds. Penned in haste, his antago-
nistic words were ill taken.

Then came the period when numbers rose and his confidence
waned. It was the mid 1980s. Hype was king, and the trend to be
hyped was sport climbing. Wilford remained quiet. At the time,
very few voices were speaking up for traditionalism. Now he's not
afraid to raise his voice, but he does so in a more diplomatic way
than before. He tries to relate the positive aspects of traditional-
style climbing more than the negative effects of sport climbing,
such as overcrowding, closure of areas, and environmental insensi-
tivity. He cites Czechoslovakia as an area that has stuck to traditional ethics since the late 1800s and therefore still has potential
for new routes 100 years later. He'd like to see certain areas such as
Yosemite, Joshua Tree, Estes Park, and Rocky Mountain National
Park granted that kind of respect.

"My biggest problem is with bolts next to cracks and rap-
bolting in traditional areas," Mark says. He's removed many bolts
he's found offensive, but only after he has led the climb on clean
gear. If he hasn't led the route before it was bolted, he has his part-

ner tape off the hangers so that he can't chicken out and clip them. Not all aspects of sport climbing offend Wilford. He has been in several competitions, the on-sight nature of which he appreciates, and he currently makes his living as a climbing-gear sales rep, a job that depends on the popularity of climbing.

* * *

Whether Wilford seeks adventure or vice versa is unclear. At Cabo San Lucas he was on the beach when a girl from an Atlanta ad agency naively chased an errant football into the knee-deep water. Although it was a pleasant sunny day at the beach, an off-shore storm was pushing enormous waves up on the shore. She struggled as the first wave pounded her into the sand, then dragged her out to sea. When she came back in on the second wave, her body was limp as a rag doll's. A bevy of onlookers watched horrified as the downshore current swept her toward the rocks bordering the beach.

A rescue attempt appeared suicidal. Randy Joseph, who was with Wilford on the beach, thought about rushing in on the next wave, "but Mark beat me to it," Joseph recalls. A Canadian cyclist joined Wilford. They grabbed the woman and were all swept out together. Randy remembers how all three bodies could be seen inside the translucent wave, being lifted twenty-five feet up, then slammed into the sand. The force of the impact was enough to rip Wilford's earring out. The woman's jewelry had long since been stripped. A human chain from the beach finally pulled them in, one wave short of dashing into the rocks.

The woman was in bad shape. She was coughing up sand and seawater. When she came to, the first person she saw was Wilford — the strong chin, the high cheekbones, the dark eyes and hair. "She fell in love with Wilford immediately," says Joseph. When Wilford got back to Fort Collins, a billboard downtown greeted him, proclaiming in three-foot letters, "Mark Wilford, my life-saver. I love you. Deb."

Women have been a distraction for Wilford ever since he lost his virginity in the Fort Collins cemetery (she was alive). "I like girls. I've just had some unfortunate luck with them. They've led me astray," says Mark, then adds, "I've led some of them astray also." The constant traveling involved with climbing and repping causes problems with maintaining long-term relationships with women. Wilford is single at the time of this writing but expects that his heart will be broken several times before this goes to print. "I have an easier time dealing with loose rock," he admits. "It's more predictable."

Wilford, confused about women? Didn't he have it all figured out at age twenty-five, when he starred with Jeff Lowe in the movie *Cloudwalker?* In it Wilford offers this observation: "Climbing gives me something that a female can give me. I feel a great comfort, a completeness there that's almost orgasmic." Says Mark today, "I was just reading a script. The filmmaker put those words in my mouth."

Many people have wanted to put words in Wilford's mouth or make him out to be someone he isn't. For instance, they ask him for his ideology on death, believing that someone who regularly solos dangerous alpine routes must brood constantly about the subject. Wilford, however, is a nuts-and-bolts guy, not a philosopher. He presents himself simply, explaining the obvious, remarking on the usual, getting a kick out of honking at cows or, when they don't flinch, facing down the bulls with his car. When it comes to death, he just says he hopes to die of old age, although he, not to mention his passengers, suspects his end will come in a car crash.

In 1983, it almost did — on another trip to Baja California when Wilford was in his mid-twenties at the height of a wild streak. Mike McCarron, South Side Chicago's best climber, describes the trip as a "three-week binge." Adventure came in the form of a black Trans Am. Wilford personally prefers compact European sports cars. Nevertheless, he was awed by the power of the Trans Am's 6.6-liter engine. He had already made the speedometer read zero the hard way but had yet to drop the needle back into double digits when he failed to comprehend a traffic sign. For all he knew, *Curva Peligrosa* was Spanish for Burma Shave, not dangerous curve ahead. The ebony muscle car hurtled off the road at eighty miles per hour. After one and a half rolls, it came to rest in a dry riverbed.

Wilford was knocked out briefly, the guy in the back was unscathed, and Glen, the kid that "owned" the car, wasn't moving. "At that point," Mark recalls, "I was really bummed because I thought I'd killed Glen." Fortuitously, the next car by contained two paramedics who checked Glen out, then assured Mark that Glen was just unconscious and would recover. Just as that worry was assuaged, the cops arrived and the real bummer began. (Traffic offenses are felonies in Mexico.)

The cops hauled Wilford off to a hospital. Despite his lacerations and grotesque hematomas about the skull and elsewhere, the doctor insisted Wilford was faking his injuries. He jabbed him in the butt with a huge syringe anyway. Next, the cops took him to jail.

The cell was square, twenty-five-by-twenty-five feet. One wall was bars, the others solid and windowless. A hole in the corner and one lightbulb in the ceiling completed the interior decoration. Half a dozen drunks and two blood-caked fighters shared the cell with Wilford. Barely able to move due to his injuries, Wilford was desperately hoping that none of his cellmates would mess with him. Only one person got close, a drunk pushed into the cell who, for a second, remained upright, spinning like a barely nicked bowling pin before falling toward the concrete floor. His cranium impacted ten feet from Wilford, the sharp crack heard by all. The cop gave the drunk's head a quick check, then left the cell before blood started trickling out the prisoner's ears.

The next day McCarron showed up to bail Wilford out. "I've smelled better zoos," Mike says, "but Mark looked right at home in there with his amigos." Indeed, Wilford's clothes were plastered to him with blood — not that changing them was an option. McCarron explains, "He couldn't take his shirt off because his head was so swollen."

The Federales came to take him from jail to the judge in the capital, La Paz. It was Wilford's chance to strike a deal. The Federales wanted the Trans Am engine for a patrol car. As it had become obvious that the car really didn't belong to Glen, Mark and Mike happily turned it over along with, of course, every penny that they had. The Federales then released Wilford.

The next week was spent waiting for escape money to be wired, obtaining all the painkillers that Wilford and his uninjured friends would need, and dodging the local and state police who, jealous that the feds had received all the bribes, wanted to shake Wilford down for their cut.

As far as Wilford is concerned, money is a necessary evil, whether it's for bribing Federales or funding expeditions to far-flung locales. In the tradition of dedicated climbers, Wilford has worked off-season manual-labor jobs to support himself — roughnecking in Wyoming and working high steel in the winter. The physicality and risk of such jobs appeal to Wilford. He says:

> High steel work was just like alpine climbing. I had to wear four layers of pants and seven layers of shirts. My hands were constantly numb. The best part was walking unroped across snow-covered beams fifty feet off the deck. I loved the exposure.

* * *

In 1987, Wilford moved back to Fort Collins in an effort to distance himself from the wild life and bad influences of his former home in Boulder. The move has been effective. What would have been partying time he now spends on restoring his Triumph TR3 from the frame up, or collecting rocks, fossils, and old coins. Wilford is calmer now and shows little emotion other than happy nonchalance or mild exuberance. (The raucous boys in the neighboring frat house might disagree. Shy one window courtesy of

Wilford's pitching arm, they would argue that Wilford can still display considerable anger.)

A year after his homecoming, Wilford gave up manual labor in favor of a career as a sales rep in the climbing industry. This job would seem boring compared to his former occupations. Nevertheless, even repping has its risks. On a sales trip last winter in Canada, Wilford managed his fourth vehicle rollover.

Wilford's reputation as one of the world's best all-around climbers helps him in his job. When he tells a client that a tool works, that client knows Wilford is speaking from experience. To get this experience means doing a lot of climbing. At the ISPO show in 1988, Wilford was given some new ice gear to test. What better testing ground than the North Face of the Eiger?

Wilford's first American solo of the Eiger Nordwand is a well-publicized story — how he got off-route early, then corrected himself and picked up the pace, only to run into a group of eight Spaniards, the lowest of which was dangling from the end of a rope, taking a crap. "That was the first thing they tried to drop on me," recalls Mark. Fortunately, Wilford dodged the falling debris, caught up with the Spaniards, and managed to climb by some and stem over the rest without losing too much time. Two hundred feet higher, he dislodged a two-foot-thick icicle that crashed amongst the Spaniards, shaking them up a bit and providing good footage for the documentary they were filming.

The tensest moment of the climb was on The Rotten Crack pitch. At this point, Wilford almost backed off the wall. The holds were all loose, like a pile of unmortared bricks, and were held together only by their own weight and by the thin wedges of ice between them. Partway up he was confronted with a dreadfully exposed bulge. The only pro was a shaky fixed pin and a sorry-sounding piton Wilford tapped in as a backup. He clipped in to these with a six-millimeter daisy chain and started bouldering the moves. After trying three different sequences, Wilford reached the lip of the bulge and cleared off a ledge smaller than a magazine.

"I was freaking," says Mark. Why? Because his daisy chain had come taut. It wasn't long enough for him to press out the mantle on the tiny ledge. Wilford uncocked his arms and was left dangling from the lip by numb hands that were pumping out fast. Already he had lost enough strength that he would be unable to reverse the moves. There were only two choices — fall on the suspect pins to his death or cut the daisy chain and free solo the mantle.

If you had viewed the scene from above, it would have looked like this: Two hands visible at the lip, nothing else. Then just one hand at the lip, clamped on for dear life, fingers turning purple. Vital seconds pass and the knuckles bleach white. Just when it appears that the hand will give out and slide off, the other hand slaps the lip. There's a mighty heave and a face appears, eyes ablaze with fear, jaws clenched so tight the teeth threaten to bite through the open pocketknife. Wilford presses the mantle and struggles to lift his foot the extra inch to get the crampons over the lip. He stands up on the ledge, hugging the wall. Backing off is no longer an option.

When the next party up came across the severed daisy chain, they assumed the worst — that Wilford was halfway down to Grindelwald, or at least parts of him were. As it turned out, the next worst thing happened — Wilford was at the summit quaffing the beer left for them by a thoughtful compadre.

While soloing the Eiger Nordwand is a sure way to make the history books, many of Mark's accomplishments have been lost in obscurity, especially his bouldering accomplishments. He has been one of the foremost developers of bouldering around Fort Collins, where the list of developers is impressive: Gill, Mammen, Borgman, and Holloway to name a few. Mark is particularly known for his high bouldering exploits and his willingness to push standards on loose rock. One of his favorite areas is the Vast Wastelands, the miles upon miles of Dakota Sandstone hogbacks north of Fort Collins. The problems are tall, the rock quality variable, the landings bad, and the property owners feisty when they catch you — all factors that appeal to Wilford. To quote Mammen, "You're in for trouble if try to go up there and follow Mark.

You'll probably end up in Poudre Valley Hospital." Wilford's skill at loose rock climbing has kept him alive in the mountains. Nevertheless, he's paid the price to obtain this skill. Numerous dumps into rocky landings have left Wilford's ankles in shambles. The ligaments are so stretched now that instead of his ankles spraining, they just fold over.

Wilford's latest bouldering accident occurred in Pakistan. He was there to climb Nameless Tower but was lured by a twenty-foot boulder 5,000 feet beneath the summit. Every climber who had reached the final micro-edging move on this problem had backed off. Wilford was determined to do the move. As it turned out the others had chosen wisely. Wilford slipped, shishkabobbing his knee on a granite spike at the base. Wilford was feeling bad. The huge gap beneath his kneecap exposed the bone beneath. Severed nerves let their complaints be known. So did his partner, alpine ace Greg Child. Child had failed on an earlier attempt on this peak and was in no mood to fail again, especially due to a partner jerking around at the base.

Luck prevailed, and it stormed for the next ten days. Child's anger subsided, as did Wilford's guilt. Wilford became obsessed with hygiene, douching the wound with hydrogen peroxide, not bending his knee, and doing anything he could to avoid infection and speed healing. By the time the weather cleared, Wilford was able to go up on the wall.

Mark describes the epic he and Greg then had as "one of the closest times I've come to buying it." He says this softly, pensively, the memory obviously still fresh and disturbing. Things went relatively well for nine days. Greg did the brunt of the leading, encountering much hard aid on the way. A thousand feet above them loomed huge icicles which, if they fell, would turn the climbers into sloppy joe filling. The icicles were hanging in; the weather wasn't. The idea of retreat was discussed, then discarded.

The crack they had been climbing was exquisite, of Butter-balls quality for a pitch and a half. Unfortunately, it ended in the middle of a blank face, not the ledge they had hoped for. Wilford pendulumed right to a blunt arête he could hook, then nailed up a rising traverse to the right. The light began to wane as sleet lashed the face. It was one of Wilford's hardest aid leads, taking four hours to reach the end. He knocked away a thin sheet of verglas to expose a vertical crack, then hammered in the anchor — five knifeblades.

Meanwhile, at the other end of the rope, Child had been stuck at a hanging belay, completely exposed to the storm and unable to move to keep warm. The beautiful crack he was anchored to had turned into a drain spout, drenching him with ice water. The sleet froze on contact with his body, armoring him in ice. By the time Child cut the haul bags loose, he was dangerously hypothermic. After screaming around the corner, the haul bags came to rest eighty feet below Wilford. (Because of the zigzag line the pitch took, the haul line traveled a much shorter distance between belays than the lead line.) Wilford leaned back on the hauling system, but the bags wouldn't budge. He jumped. They still wouldn't budge.

Child tried to follow the pitch. He got nowhere, because his jumars refused to grip the rope that had become, in Child's words, "a wire of ice." He screamed to Wilford to throw him another rope. The only dry rope, however, was in the haul bag. Wilford redoubled his efforts to pull the bags up. He jumped so hard on the hauling system, he pulled out one of the anchor pins. His only choice was to rap down the free looped end of the haul line to get to the bags. When he reached the bottom of the loop and could descend no further, his feet were just above the bag. Child was screaming, "I can't feel my hands. Can't you hurry?"

To reach the bags, Wilford had to flip upside down. In this position he could just reach the bags and extract a rope. It was getting darker and colder as Wilford raced up the eight-millimeter haul line. The rope got icier every second. The closer he got to the anchor, the more the jumars would slip. If he didn't reach the anchor soon, he'd freeze to death jugging in place.

Back at the belay, Wilford quickly anchored the dry rope,

then started rappelling sideways across the face, holding on to the lead line to get to the arête. Wilford clipped the rope into his last good piece on the arête, then was unable to cross the section he'd pendulumed past on the lead. "From the arête I could see Greg," Wilford recalls, "and he's just fucked — sitting there on his way out."

Wilford tried throwing the rope to Child. It missed. He tried again. Another miss. After many attempts he finally got the cord to Child. Child then had no choice but to cut loose from the anchor and take the terrifying swing across the face, around the arête, and into the unseen beyond. As he put it to Wilford before committing, "If this cold doesn't kill me, the jumar will."

They both made it to the anchor, where they managed to get a bolt in and pull up the haul bags. By now it was dark, and their first attempt to erect the portaledge ended tragically when the frame collapsed while they pulled the fly on. Wilford was doing most of the work at the belay because Child was so frozen and, to worsen matters, had lost a glove.

"I was getting panicky," Child admits. Reassembling the ledge became, he says, "a bloody long ordeal." Child has praise for Wilford's handling of the situation. "He was very strong up there. He's very calm. He doesn't get flustered or scared." When they finally got in the assembled portaledge it was after midnight. Child produced some pills that can help prevent frostbite by increasing circulation in the body's extremities. These pills, however, move blood away from the body's core and can induce shock if one doesn't get warm right away. They took the pills. Child shoved his hands in Wilford's armpits, while Wilford's feet warmed in Child's crotch.

Meanwhile, back in the sport-climbing world, dozens of would-be champions were ingesting performance-enhancing chemicals and stuffing their fingers in training boards — all in the hopes of qualifying at Snowbird. While they had to shun the refrigerator to slim down, Wilford was in a refrigerator, burning all the fat he could to survive the harrowing retreat off Nameless

Tower. A month later, he joined the lycra-clad hordes at Snowbird.

The results were a surprise to some, but not to those who know Mark. By dint of his style of climbing, his on-sight ability is exceedingly well developed. The difference between him and the rest of the pack at Snowbird is that when Wilford climbs, a lot more is at stake than money and pride. At an organized competition, the worst scenario is having a bad day. In Wilford's league, you can't have a bad day, because when you do, it could be your last.

Kitty Calhoun. *Photo by Jonathan Waterman*

The Education of an Alpinist

KITTY CALHOUN

by Jonathan Waterman

[From CLIMBING, April 1988]

I n Kathmandu in the fall of 1987, the leader of a large German expedition to Manaslu wondered about the young-looking American. She was petite, alluring, with none of the hardness that most alpinists wear like a badge on their sleeves. Moreover, she had a self-effacing manner and a distinctive Carolina drawl as she helped her three male companions sort gear for Dhaulagiri. The burly German approached one of the American men and gestured toward Kitty Calhoun. "Is *that* your basecamp manager?" Colin Grissom smiled. "No, she's the leader of our climb."

In 1987, there was much ballyhoo about several Himalayan expeditions. *Outside* magazine touted "The Women of Everest," all members of lavishly outfitted and heavily sponsored expeditions. Neither of these two teams summitted. Then the keynote presentation at the AAC annual meeting was on the American conquest of Makalu, replete with an army of porters, high-altitude Sherpas, oxygen, and fixed ropes. Meanwhile, scarcely anyone had heard of Calhoun and her friends on Dhaulagiri. Beating the media drums is not her style.

The foursome went to the mountain on a shoestring budget of $14,000 round-trip from Seattle and shared twenty porters with a Spanish team. These tactics were partly due to the inherent frugality of most full-time climbing nomads, but a prized philosophical thread of simplicity — which eludes many Himalayan expeditions — was deliberately woven into the Dhaulagiri climb. Calhoun had vetoed basecamp lawnchairs, fixed ropes, and oxygen. A friend had given her a high-altitude suit, but otherwise, she had sewn her own clothing.

Catherine Howell Calhoun, age twenty-seven, is an enigma. At first meeting, she appears to be shy, but this is only a veneer. She rides a tight rein over her emotions and is an intensely private yet gracious soul. She is also decidedly reticent, and if she has done any good climbs, or suffered an epic, she would be the last one to spin the traditional climbing yarn. In fact, she would much sooner listen to someone else's story than tell her own.

Her climbing style is to return again and again to the fray. Jim Gilchrist described one of her early leads in the Gunks. "She fell off the crux and knocked me from my hanging stance, then insisted on going right back up, saying, 'I'm gonna do this climb!', then pendulumed back into me again. If I didn't take the lead, she would've continued bashing me off."

When pressed, she will concede to knockouts: snow blindness and mountain sickness, a partner with frostbite in the Tetons, bivouacs with no gear (one partner dubbed her the "bivi queen"), and a ride in an avalanche, which she described as "delightful, like falling into a bed of feathers."

Since she started climbing, Calhoun wanted to guide, so she worked for the Colorado Outward Bound School for several years. She told Dunham Gooding of the American Alpine Institute that she wanted to guide in South America. Gooding replied that her Spanish-speaking ability was weak. Calhoun immediately found a tutor and spent every available moment of the next few weeks learning the language. Gooding hired her.

Her fellow guides and past partners agree that drive and

determination are the Calhoun trademark. Perhaps lacking the natural gifts of some climbers, she has always climbed by narrowing her focus, gritting her teeth, and sweating out the object of her desire until it was done. Over the past several years, in spring, summer, and fall, she has guided more than two dozen big peaks in South America and Nepal. Because of this, and her penchant for snow and ice, the bulk of Calhoun's personal climbing is performed in winter.

Despite Calhoun's motivation, she claims to have no idols. She is also innocently oblivious to many big-name peaks and routes and has read only a few mountaineering books. However, she often carries *The New Testament* in her pack, which she has read several times, seeking the answers to what kind of existence might lay beyond that of arctic winds, cold stone, and sweeping ice faces. After numerous scrapes in the mountains with mentors like Lyle Dean, Alan Kearney, Bobby Knight, Andy Selters, and Peter Athans, she has become a formidable alpinist. But it was a long apprenticeship.

So Calhoun has logged time in storms and high bivouacs, times when your life story comes tumbling out and there are no longer any secrets. Regardless of these epics, her various partners still feel that they really don't know her; the talk has never flowed. While guiding in the Himalaya, according to one of her clients, Calhoun spends as much time with the yak herders as she does with anyone else. The yak herders don't speak English, but apparently, her broad smile and outgoing manner are all the communication they need.

When asked why she loves the mountains so much, she replies, "Because they're *purty.*" And as you wait for further elaboration, she abruptly concludes with her patented full smile and piercing eyes, as if the rest of the answer is either none of your business, or so obvious that you shouldn't have asked in the first place. Those who haven't climbed with her might interpret such long smiles and short conversations as vacuous behavior. But this misses the target. Calhoun is impassioned about mountaineering to the exclusion of almost anything else in her life, including relationships and a "normal" career. Such passion and focus resonate with brilliance.

Her first ice-climbing lead was up New Hampshire's serious Black Dike, on Cannon Cliffs. On a winter climbing trip with Bobby Knight that ranged from Colorado, to the Tetons, to Canada, Knight said if one day went by without climbing, Calhoun was happy, as long as they were skiing. But if two days went by without climbing, she would act devastated. Indeed, one winter, while walking up Aspen Mountain (she couldn't afford the lift tickets) on beat-up skis and mountaineering bindings, her long baleful looks indicated she wanted to be elsewhere, maybe ice climbing, or perhaps she was weighing an invitation to Everest against a possible Makalu trip. At the end of a long day of chasing strong skiers, Calhoun insisted we finish on the steepest bump run. "Otherwise," she said, "how will I ever get any better?" And at Glenwood Icefall, after leading the second pitch without protection, she took over the final lead of a rotten pillar, which I gladly relinquished. She swung up onto it, left leg bridged out on a tenuous icicle, and began knocking off huge dinner plates, finally calling it quits after three tries. Predictably, Calhoun went back the next day but failed again.

Of course, Calhoun is not the only North American woman active in the mountains. Sharon Wood's accomplishments on Everest and Huascarán Sur speak for themselves, and before Catherine Freer's death, she was on the cutting edge of alpine climbing. Vera Komarkova and Arlene Blum also inspired a large following of expedition-style protégés. And one could easily count off another dozen experienced alpine climbers. Nonetheless, the United States does not have a Wanda Rutkiewicz knocking off 8,000-meter peaks, and there are few women who climb big and technically difficult peaks alpine style. So why is there such a dearth of *las alpinistas* in this country? Calhoun speculates that women have bought the premise that the typically male attributes of strength and size are essential to mountaineering. She feels that good judgment fills out her 115 pounds and five-foot-three-inch frame.

There are countless women rock climbers; a few excel by exceptional strength, most others through grace and delicacy. Calhoun believes this could explain many women's disinterest in alpine climbing — because it is hard to find grace in a cold arena where anything goes, where you curse and smash in your tools and scrape your knees onto holds. Calhoun explains:

> There's a lot more to mountaineering than rock climbing. You not only have to climb rock, but you have to route find, climb quickly on lousy pro, know the weather, understand how to stay warm, coordinate logistics, and deal with foreign cultures. It's sustained, too, like you can't just go back down to the bar at the end of the day.

* * *

On Dhaulagiri, the nearest bar was many days away, and the climb would be Calhoun's most extended effort. Initially, she wanted to muster a team of women. At one point, she opened up the women's issue of *Climbing* magazine, hoping to discover some alpine partners, but was disappointed that many of the women in those pages climbed only rock. As the countdown for Dhaulagiri ticked closer, Calhoun decided she wouldn't be able to find female partners for the East Face.

In the final analysis, the climbing alone is paramount to Calhoun, and it makes little difference whom she climbs with. When she finds other women partners, she sees it simply as "opening up more opportunities." Accordingly, just before the trip, she recruited Matt and John Culberson and Colin Grissom. Grissom said: "There's no pride involved when I turn around and say, 'Kitty will you break trail now because I can't do it for a while.' I can't do that with a guy." Her strengths on Dhaulagiri, he commented, were tremendous patience and an ability to hang in there until the job was done.

When they arrived at the talus-strewn, 15,000-foot basecamp, Calhoun discovered that the East Face had become a nightmare. While guiding in the area a year before, Calhoun had seen ice arcing 5,000 feet to the summit; now there was only sodden, rotten rock. Her dream faded, but only momentarily.

* * *

Calhoun had already learned how to adapt to the ever-evolving agendas of big climbs. To objectively gauge the potential of a high-altitude climber, it is one thing to count successful climbs blessed with luck, blue skies, and good conditions. However, those who are uncommitted to mountaincraft will falter once the plans change or the epics begin. So the real assessment of an alpinist can only begin after he or she has confronted injury, storm, failure, and finally, the possibility of death. Such is the fabric of Kitty Calhoun's career.

The year before Dhaulagiri, she had set off with Andy Selters up the awe-inspiring North Face of Thelay Sagar in the Garwhal Himalaya. Pondering their broken portaledge, Selters asked, "Where are we going to sleep?" Calhoun was unfazed and replied, "We'll fix it."

At 20,000 feet, a storm moved in and pummeled them with avalanches for eight days. They retreated, adding their names to this route's scorecard of broken, would-be suitors. It was the hardest climb that she'd ever kicked her frontpoints into. "We were *scairt.* There was an awful lot of time to think about things during that storm. It was just like when I was on the Cassin. I thought, why is this happening, it doesn't seem fair."

In 1985, Calhoun had learned the meaning of commitment at 18,000 feet on Denali's Cassin Ridge. Having run out of food, she and Grissom worried about their position as the storm ripped the tent. When the gale ended five days later, they finished the route, but Calhoun was fatigued from lack of food and had to count steps to keep her concentration. She nearly blacked out.

And during the summer of 1983 in Peru, Calhoun started up the Bouchard Route on the South Face of Chacaraju but turned around at 18,000 feet with a bad stomach ache. She tasted this bile-raising defeat until she came back three years later and stepped into the ring for another round. At the crux, she was tired, so her partner started up, then confessed he had never led ice. Calhoun took over and ended up leading most of the steep, 3,000-foot face.

The descent took twenty-one rappels. During a bivouac on the way down, they were knocked off their ledge by spindrift avalanches. The next day, Calhoun reached the end of the ropes and dangled on a vertical cliff with no rock protection for a rappel anchor. She cammed a snowfluke into a horizontal crack and prepared for the next rappel.

Two mornings later in Huaraz, the *arriero* for Calhoun's next trip knocked on her hotel room door. She woke up, then went back into her dreamworld — back up into the mountains, where she guided her clients up Huascarán and Pisco.

* * *

At the Dhaulagiri basecamp, Calhoun pushed her latest project into focus, abandoning the East Face and lying out a strategy for the Northeast Ridge. The Japanese agreed to let the Americans on their route, provided they help fix ropes through the icefall and onto the ridge. Calhoun and company moved quickly to a 19,500-foot col and watched the Japanese trigger an avalanche above. Fortunately, no one was hurt.

The following day, Calhoun, Grissom, and the Culbersons were climbing above 22,000 feet while clipped into some Japanese fixed line. Suddenly, a slab of wind-deposited snow released under their weight, and they began plunging down the North

Face. The pickets zippered out, one by one. Grissom's harness carabiner unclipped from the fixed line and hooked into John Culberson's harness just as the last picket held, checking a 3,000-foot ride to the glacier.

They traversed off the North Face and back down to the col. Grissom had hurt his knee, while John had a black eye and a sore ankle. Calhoun suggested a rest day. Then, her arm felt wet, so she took a look. The rope had burned through three layers of clothing and down into the muscle tissue. They descended to basecamp and licked their wounds, reading magazine articles about rock climbing in the sun. Resolve weakened.

The Spaniards made an alpine-style attempt, then the Japanese collapsed a crevasse bridge and declared the mountain unsafe. But Calhoun had tasted this sort of thing before on Thelay Sagar, on Chacaraju, and on numerous other peaks. Retreat meant unequivocal failure, a knockdown punch that would follow her everywhere. She had to duck back under the ropes.

Calhoun pulled on her gloves, had the cook fire up 100 more chapattis, then she and Grissom and John started back up. For ten days, their universe consisted of fighting back nausea, breaking trail, sucking thin air into hungry lungs, sliding frozen poles into tent sleeves, and melting snow into water. Finally, on October 16, 1987, they reached the top. They descended in the teeth of a storm that punished climbers throughout Nepal. It had snowed several feet at basecamp, and they trudged out through the unrecognizable lowlands, losing their way several times in cul-de-sacs. Matt poked in a collapsed tent for food and uncovered the body of a trekker.

In Marpha, they drank sweet tea and filled their bellies with real food. They had every reason to be happy, for they had climbed Dhaulagiri as a small team, completely self-sufficient, and they had come away from the mountain as closer friends. But, with her intrinsic focus — which some might label obsession — Calhoun began considering another project.

"When I finished Dhaulagiri, I was thinking I wouldn't do any more 8,000-meter peaks because of the avalanche danger,"

Calhoun said. "But as time goes by, I start forgetting how awful it was. Even rock climbers trying hard climbs say, 'I'm not going to put myself in this situation again,' then the next day they're back on the same climb."

* * *

When asked what's next, Calhoun says her fantasy route would involve just one partner, preferably Grissom, for they have established a rapport — the indelible and unspoken communication that is the nucleus of an accomplished rope team. "It would have to be something big with a lot of varied climbing, at altitude. Something that would take a lot of days," she drawled, "so that *Ah* can concentrate and forget about everything else." It might be the French Pillar on Makalu. Or it wouldn't be surprising to see her back trading blows with the North Face of Thelay Sagar.

To begin to understand Kitty Calhoun, you have to see these mountains. But who is *she*? She climbs giant peaks, yet she is barely over five feet tall. She learned to speak fluent Spanish in three weeks, although she has forgotten her partner's name from Chacaraju. She is an inspired and self-directed climber, but she chose Dhaulagiri after asking Selters to suggest a peak. She wants to settle down and have a family, yet says she gets too much out of alpine climbing to quit. She doesn't pay rent and roams the far-flung corners of the earth with a fiercely independent style, then she spends more than a month at home with her parents and sisters. She was nervous to the point of distraction about being photographed at Glenwood Icefall, but several weeks later, she went back and nonchalantly soloed the climb. She is a rare bird, soaring on her dreams like the chough, which is sometimes seen above 7,000 meters in the Himalaya, balanced on an updraft, where there is no nest or food or logical words to explain its presence in such high places.

* * *

In Seattle during the fall of 1987, Calhoun flew back from Dhaulagiri on the same plane with Mimi Stone, one of the women who had attempted Everest. After they passed through customs, Stone was stopped by reporters. They didn't ask about the diminutive woman with the shy smile, for she didn't look like a Himalayan hardwoman, nor would anything but Everest catch the news. Calhoun sidestepped the gathering throng, happy to avoid what she calls "the fashion show," and went off to find some ice cream.

About the Writers

Jeremy Bernstein, a staff writer for *The New Yorker* for thirty-one years, is a professor of Physics at the Stevens Institute of Technology. He has actively followed climbing as both a writer and a client since the 1940s. In addition to more than a dozen books he has written on science, he has authored three mountaineering books: *Mountain Passages, Ascent,* and *In the Himalaya.* He makes his home in both New York City and Aspen.

Tim Cahill helped conceive *Outside* magazine in the early 1970s. His forays out into the steep corners of the world are usually bold and then hilarious in the retelling. He has become one of North America's most beloved adventurer journalists because of his self-deprecating prose and his love for sticking his neck out on the metaphorical chopping block of adventure. His popular books include: *A Wolverine is Eating my Leg, Jaguars Ripped My Flesh, Buried Dreams,* and *Road Fever.* He makes his home in Livingston, Montana. At presstime he is writing a book about an unexploited piece of Africa.

Michael Kennedy is the editor and publisher of the world-respected *Climbing* magazine. After beating the sun to work and confronting demands of magazine acquistion, production, and fulfillment, Michael can often be found in the Elk Mountains: endurance running, mountain biking, alpine skiing, or rock climbing. Every few years, he returns to the big ranges, where he has left indelible marks as a proponent of light and fast alpine climbing. In summer of 1993, for instance, he climbed the West Face of Huntington in two days.

Jon Krakauer lives in Seattle and makes his living as a freelance writer. Krakauer-credited photographs also appear beside his stories in *Outside, Mens Journal,* and *Smithsonian.* Although he is univerally considered a master at climbing portraiture, he is himself a climber of no small stature, having specialized in granite, ice-shrouded spires throughout the Americas, including the Devils Thumb (solo), The Mooses Tooth, and Cerro Torre in Alaska. His book *Eiger Dreams* was first published in 1990.

Alison Osius has been climbing for 15 years. She was on the U.S. Climbing Team (for sport climbing competitions) as a member or alternate from 1988 through 1992, when she was ranked third in the nation, and has won several national titles. She received her M.A. degree in journalism from Columbia University, and in between gobbling up steep and difficult rock around the country, she worked as an editor at the Salt Lake City *Tribune, Ultra Sport* magazine in Boston, and *Climbing,* in Carbondale, Colorado, where she is now a senior editor. Her artful biography of Hugh Herr, *Second Ascent,* was released in 1990.

David Roberts, from Cambridge, Massachusetts, aside from holding a Ph.D in literature, has earned his place as the bard of North American mountaineering. His first book, *Mountain of My Fear,* describing his first ascent on Alaska's Mount Huntington, was acclaimed by the poet W.H. Auden. His book, *Once They Moved Like the Wind: Cochise, Geronimo, and the Apache Wars,* was recently published by Simon and Shuster. Roberts created such routes as the unrepeated Harvard Route on Denali's Wickersham Wall, throughout Alaska.

John Sherman can be found wherever the rock is dry and it is convenient to park his truck—often in El Paso, Texas. He is renowned for his wicked humor visa vi stories and artful photographs that appear in *Climbing* magazine. He is also considered one of the country's top boulderers. He has coauthored *Hueco Tanks: A Climber's and Boulderer's Guide,* published by Chockstone Press. His book, *A Guide to Bouldering in North America,* is due to be published in 1994 by the American Alpine Club Press.

314

ABOUT THE WRITERS

Geoffrey Tabin started climbing at Devils Lake WI in 1972. In his years working through medical school, Tabin sought out the highest summit on each continent, and in 1989, he became the fourth person to climb each of the "Seven Summits." His book of stories, *Blind Corners; Adventures on the Peaks of Seven Continents,* is due out in August. He graduated from Harvard Medical School and at press time he is in his last year of residency in opthamology at Brown University.

In addition to her occasional work as a writer, *Beth Wald* is perhaps best known for her photography. Her action climbing photographs and portraits of indigenous peoples have been published internationally in numerous magazines. She speaks Russian, has wandered the globe and is known by her friends as fountain of creative enthusiasm for her many projects. At press time, she is exploring the cultures of Tibet and Nepal with Annie Whitehouse.

Jonathan Waterman lives in Crested Butte, Colorado, in a cottage close to the high peaks. His first book, *Surviving Denali,* an overview of casualties on Mount McKinley, published in 1983 (and republished with new material in 1991). *High Alaska* followed in 1988. Waterman's latest work, *In the Shadow of Denali; Life and Death on Mount McKinley,* shall be published by Dell's "Laurel Expedition Series" in April 1994. He makes his living as a freelance writer, developing and writing adventure films for PBS and ESPN, and managing the AAC Press.

Ed Webster began climbing at age 11 in a highway quarry near his home in Lexington, Massachusetts. In 1990, he reached the South Summit of Everest via the unclimbed Kangshung Face. After losing parts of his fingers, he has gracefully returned to both rock and Himalayan climbing. Webster's articles and photographs have appeared in *Sports Illustrated, Readers Digest, Ascent, Climbing, Rock and Ice,* and *Iwa To Yuki.* He is also the author of *Rock Climbs in the White Mountains.*